Computational Approaches to the Network Science of Teams

Business operations in large organizations today involve massive, interactive, and layered networks of teams and personnel collaborating across hierarchies and countries on complex tasks. To optimize productivity, businesses need to know: What communication patterns do high-performing teams have in common? Is it possible to predict a team's performance before it starts work on a project? How can productive team behavior be fostered? This comprehensive review for researchers and practitioners in data mining and social networks surveys recent progress in the emerging field of network science of teams. Focusing on the underlying social network structure, the authors present models and algorithms characterizing, predicting, optimizing, and explaining team performance, along with key applications, open challenges, and future trends.

LIANGYUE LI is an applied scientist at Amazon. He received his Ph.D. in computer science from Arizona State University. He has served as a program committee member in top data-mining and artificial intelligence venues such as SIGKDD, ICML, AAAI, and CIKM. He has given a tutorial at Web Search and Data Mining (WSDM) 2018, Knowledge Discovery in Databases (KDD) 2018, and a keynote talk at the Conference on Information and Knowledge Management (CIKM) 2016 Workshop on Big Network Analytics (BigNet 2016).

HANGHANG TONG is an associate professor at University of Illinois at Urbana–Champaign since August 2019. Before that, he was an associate professor at Arizona State University; an assistant professor at City College, City University of New York; a research staff member at IBM T. J. Watson Research Center; and a postdoctoral fellow at Carnegie Mellon University. He received his M.Sc. and Ph.D. degrees, both in machine learning, from Carnegie Mellon University in 2008 and 2009. His research interest is in large-scale data mining for graphs and multimedia. He received several awards, including the National Science Foundation (NSF) CAREER award (2017); the Industrial Conference on Data Mining (ICDM) 10-Year Highest Impact Paper Award (2015); four best paper awards (TUP'14, CIKM'12, SDM'08, and ICDM'06); six "best of conference" (ICDM'18, KDD'16, SDM'15, ICDM'15, SDM'11, and ICDM'10); one best demo, honorable mention (SIGMOD'17); and one best demo candidate, second place (CIKM'17). He has published over 100 referred articles. He is the editor-in-chief of SIGKDD Explorations, an action editor of *Data Mining and Knowledge Discovery*, and an associate editor of *Neurocomputing Journal*. He has served as a program committee member in multiple data-mining, database, and artificial intelligence venues such as SIGKDD, SIGMOD, AAAI, WWW, and CIKM.

Computational Approaches to the Network Science of Teams

Amazon

University of Illinois, Urbana–Champaign

CAMBRIDGE
UNIVERSITY PRESS

CAMBRIDGE
UNIVERSITY PRESS

University Printing House, Cambridge CB2 8BS, United Kingdom

One Liberty Plaza, 20th Floor, New York, NY 10006, USA

477 Williamstown Road, Port Melbourne, VIC 3207, Australia

314–321, 3rd Floor, Plot 3, Splendor Forum, Jasola District Centre, New Delhi – 110025, India

79 Anson Road, #06–04/06, Singapore 079906

Cambridge University Press is part of the University of Cambridge.

It furthers the University's mission by disseminating knowledge in the pursuit of
education, learning, and research at the highest international levels of excellence.

www.cambridge.org
Information on this title: www.cambridge.org/9781108498548
DOI: 10.1017/9781108683173

First published 2021

Printed in the United Kingdom by TJ Books Limited, Padstow Cornwall

A catalogue record for this publication is available from the British Library.

Library of Congress Cataloging-in-Publication Data
Names: Li, Liangyue, 1989– author. | Tong, Hanghang, author.
Title: Computational approaches to the network science of teams /
Liangyue Li, Hanghang Tong.
Description: Cambridge ; New York, NY : Cambridge University Press, 2021. |
Includes bibliographical references and index.
Identifiers: LCCN 2020021921 (print) | LCCN 2020021922 (ebook) |
ISBN 9781108498548 (hardback) | ISBN 9781108683173 (ebook)
Subjects: LCSH: Teams in the workplace–Evaluation. |
Performance–Measurement. | Business networks–Mathematical models. |
Social sciences–Network analysis. | Network analysis
(Planning)–Data processing. | Algorithms.
Classification: LCC HD66 .L54 2021 (print) | LCC HD66 (ebook) |
DDC 658.4/022072–dc23
LC record available at https://lccn.loc.gov/2020021921
LC ebook record available at https://lccn.loc.gov/2020021922

ISBN 978-1-108-49854-8 Hardback

To my parents, Meifang Xu and Qing Li.

L. L.

To my parents, Xiazhen He and Yingen Tong, for their selfless love.

H. T.

Contents

1

Introduction

1.1 Motivations

In defining the essence of professional teamwork, Hackman and Katz [41] stated that teams function as "purposive social systems," defined as people who are readily identifiable to each other by role and position and who work interdependently to accomplish one or more collective objectives. Teams are increasingly indispensable to achievement in any organization. This is perhaps most evident in multinational organizations where communication technology has transformed the geographically dispersed teams and networks. Business operations in large organizations now involve large, interactive, and layered networks of teams and personnel communicating across hierarchies and countries during the execution of complex and multifaceted international businesses. Despite the organizations' substantial dependency on teams, fundamental knowledge about the conduct of team-enabled operations is lacking, especially at the *social, cognitive,* and *information* level in relation to team performance and network dynamics. What do high-performing engineering/design/sale teams share in common with respect to their communication patterns? How can we predict a team's performance before it starts to work on the assigned project? How can we foster productive behavioral changes of team members and leaders in order to optimize performance?

1.2 Research Objectives and Key Challenges

Generally speaking, the **team performance** can be viewed as the **composite** of the following three aspects, including (1) its **users**, (2) **tasks** that the team performs, and (3) the **networks** that the team is embedded in or operates on, i.e.,

1

$$\text{team performance} = f(\text{users, tasks, networks}) \tag{1.1}$$

The goal of this book is to create new instruments to *predict*, *optimize*, and *explain* teams' performance in the context of composite networks (i.e., social-cognitive-information networks). This research objective involves a number of key challenges, many of which can be attributed to **the complexity of teams**. Specifically, the complexity of the teams comes from all the following five components of Eq. (1.1).

- *Challenge 1: the complexity of the users.* There are three basic types of users, including the individuals (e.g., team members), team leaders (e.g., project managers), and the "owners" of human resource (e.g., HR in an organization). While, in general, different types of users are collaborative in nature, their goals are not always consistent with each other. For certain tasks, the team members or its leader might have to make a decision within a short time period, with incomplete and partial knowledge of its embedded environment/networks, and possibly under great stress.
- *Challenge 2: the complexity of tasks.* Within an organization, there are often multiple teams for a variety of different types of tasks, such as engineering teams, support teams, business teams, planning teams, etc. Each type of team might have its own "secret recipe" for success. For example, a successful engineering team might heavily rely on its execution of plan, while a planning team might need more innovation. Some tasks might be collaborative, while others might be competitive with each other. How can an organization optimize the performance of a target team in the presence of an adversarial team? From an organization perspective, how can it strengthen an existing team (e.g., by expanding the team size) without hurting others?
- *Challenge 3: the complexity of networks.* The challenges come from the environment that the team is embedded in or operates on, i.e., the fact that such networks are often *big*, meaning that they are large in size (*volume*), highly volatile in dynamics (*velocity*), spreading over multiple channels/layers/platforms (*variety*), and noisy and incomplete (*veracity*). In the book, we assume the networks are undirected, but the methods presented can be easily extended to handle the directionality of networks.
- *Challenge 4: the complexity of performance.* There is no single performance measure of the team, but rather a set of intercorrelated metrics. For example, the impact metrics for research teams include citation-based number of citations, h-index, online usage based view counts, download counts, and network-based centrality, all of which might be correlated with each other [13].

- *Challenge 5: the complexity of composite (e.g., $f()$).* The composite itself, which composes different aspects/metrics into the performance measure(s), is far beyond a many-to-one linear process. Instead, it is likely to be a many (aspect) to many (performance measures) nonlinear process.

1.3 Research Tasks Overview

In this book, we take a multidisciplinary approach, consisting of machine learning, visualization, and optimization, to tackle three complementary research tasks.

Task 1: Team Performance Prediction. Understanding the dynamic mechanisms that drive the success of high-performing teams can provide the key insights into building the best teams and hence lift the productivity and profitability of the organizations. From the algorithmic perspective, the interesting problems are to forecast the long-term performance of teams (*point prediction*) as well as the pathway to impact (*trajectory prediction*). For research teams, early prediction of their performance has many important implications, ranging from personal career development and recruitment search, to the jurisdiction of research resources. The impact pathway often provides a good indicator of the shift of the research frontier and can also help trigger an early intervention should the impact trajectory step down in the near future. On the other hand, as the ancient Greek philosopher Aristotle articulated more than 2,000 years ago that "*the whole is more than the sum of its parts*," it is worthwhile to quantitatively examine the relationship between the team-level and individual-level performances and leverage that to build a joint predictive model.

Task 2: Team Performance Optimization. In this task, we focus on the problem of optimizing/enhancing an existing team. For example, if the team leader perceives the need to enhance certain expertise of the entire team, who shall we bring into the team (i.e., *team expansion*)? If we need to reduce the size of an existing team (e.g., for the purpose of cost reduction), who shall leave the team (i.e., *team shrinkage*) so that the remaining team is least impacted? If the team leader sees a conflict between certain team members, how shall we resolve it (i.e., *team conflict resolution*)? In case the desired team configuration changes over time, how can we reflect such dynamics in the team enhancement process (i.e., *team evolution*)? We solve all these enhancement scenarios based on a team member replacement algorithm we developed recently [58]. On the other hand, teams can be often viewed as a dynamic system. We present the solution to plan the sequential optimization actions to maximize the cumulative performance using reinforcement learning.

Task 3: Team Performance Explanation. The basics of team effectiveness were identified by J. Richard Hackman, who uncovered a groundbreaking insight: what matter most to collaboration are certain enabling conditions. Recent studies found that three of Hackman's conditions – a compelling direction, a strong structure, and a supportive context – continue to be particularly critical to team success [40]. In this task, we aim to reveal the "secret recipe" for success by developing an explanation model for the aforementioned team performance prediction models as well as the performance optimization models. Such explanations can provide insights to *why* some teams are predicted to be successful and *why* we should bring a certain member to the team. Understanding the reasons behind predictions and recommendations is critical in assessing *trust*, which is especially fundamental if decisions (e.g., funding allocations) need to be made based on a prediction.

As an emerging form of teams, human–agent teams promises a superior performance that would significantly surpass the best of both human-only teams as well as agent-only teams by having human and agent members focus on their best, often complementary, strength. At the end of the book, we have discussed the research tasks and open challenges in the recent trend of human agent teaming.

1.4 Impacts and Benefits

In the context of composite networks, this book will establish effective algorithms and tools for the performance prediction and optimization of teams along with explanations. The research presented in the book will help organizations make a better decision to perform certain tasks that need collaborative effort within a team. Based on our work in this book, we will build a system of team enhancement (i.e., prediction, optimization, explanation). The visualization component of this system can be used to track individual and team performance over time, and provide feedback to individuals to foster productive behavior change. To the best of our knowledge, this is the first comprehensive effort that integrates interactive visualization mechanisms, machine learning models, and advanced network analysis algorithms for optimizing teams. The preliminary results (e.g., publications, presentations, and prototype systems) are available at team-net-work.org.

2

Team Performance Characterization

2.1 Collective Intelligence

The notion of individual intelligence was first proposed by Charles Spearman when he noticed that school kids who did well in one school subject tend to do well in many other school subjects [84]. The observations that the average correlation among individuals' performance on a variety of cognitive tasks is positive and the first factor extracted using a factor analysis accounts for about 30–50% of the variance indicate the existence of general intelligence. The first factor is usually referred to as general intelligence. We can give people a relatively limited set of items, and the scores of these items can predict how they perform across a variety of domains and over a long period of time. Such an intelligence test can predict not only how kids do in school in multiple subjects, but also the probability that they would be successful in their future career. These are perhaps the most empirically replicated facts in most of the psychology.

A group of researchers at Carnegie Mellon University (CMU) set out to test whether a similar notion of collective intelligence exists in a team of people, i.e., whether a single factor exists from the team's performance on a variety of tasks [97]. They enlisted 40 and 152 teams of size two to five members for their two studies. They assigned a diverse set of group tasks to these teams. The tasks can be categorized into four types, namely, "generate," "choose," "negotiate," and "execute." The results support their initial hypothesis that the average correlation among the teams' scores on the diverse set of tasks is positive, and the factor analysis reveals that one single factor can account for more than 43% of the variance. Additionally, the collective intelligence score calculated using the first factor can strongly predict the team's performance on a future criterion tasks (e.g., video game and architectural design). Surprisingly, the average team member intelligence and the maximum team

5

member intelligence are not that predictive of the future performance, which tells us that simply assigning a team of smart people does not promise a smart team. But what are the ingredients that are important to an intelligent team? Surprisingly, the team processes, e.g., group cohesion, motivation, and satisfacation, traditionally regarded as important to team performance, are not predictive of collective intelligence. The collective intelligence is found to be positively correlated with the average social perceptiveness of the team members and negatively correlated with the variance in the number of speaking turns by team embers.

2.2 Virtual Teams in Online Games

The aforementioned research about collective intelligence (CI) is mainly on traditional teams where team members have face-to-face interactions. It would be interesting to examine whether the collective intelligence also exists in virtual teams. Virtual teams are diverse, dispersed, digital, and dynamic, e.g., the Multiplayer Online Battle Arena (MOBA) teams. Considering that such teams perform tasks at a fast pace without explicit face-to-face or verbal communitication, other means of coordination might play a more critical role here, e.g., tacit coordiation, or coordinations that happen without explicit verbal communication [48]. Studying how collective intelligence works in such MOBA teams could also inform the operations of other virtual teams commonly seen in business world, where teams are dipsersed across geographical boundaries and making decisions at a fast pace.

One recent study [48] examines collective intelligence in *League of Legends (League)* teams, a popular game with a worldwide monthly active user base of 67 million. In *League*, a match is between two teams of five members, and teams can be formed either through the game's matchmaking algorithms or by recruiting other players in the game community. One team's goal is to destroy the opponent team's base. The authors hypothesized that (1) CI will predict team performance in *League*, (2) social perceptiveness and proportion of women will be positively associated with CI in *League*, and (3) CI will not be associated with equality of contribution to conversation or decision making in *League* teams. In order to know the CI, game performance, and team characteristics, the authors collected data from three sources: (1) all team members completed a questionnaire on their own about information on their demographics, psychological variables, cognition, affect, etc; (2) the teams took the Test of Collective Intelligence (TCI), an online test battery, as a group to measure the collective intelligence of each team; and (3) the play statistics including the team performances are provided by Riot Games. There were 248 teams that completed all components of the study, and 85% of the teams are all males. The authors find that CI also exists in *League* teams from factor analysis, and it is positively correlated with the performance measure of the teams controlling for individual and team play time. Besides, CI is positively correlated with the number of women on the team and is positively correlated with social perceptiveness, but the proportion of women and social perceptiveness are not correlated. What's interesting is that the equality of communication measured by standard deviation of chat lines and chat word count is not significantly correlated with CI. In addition, CI is negatively correlated with some group processes, e.g., perceived equality in decision making and frequency of game-specific communication. These suggest that highly dispersed and dynamic virtual teams tend to adopt a tacit coordination method.

2.3 Networks in Sports Teams

Recently, a number of works started to examine the network structure in sports teams in relation to their performances [35, 39]. Using Euro Cup 2008 tournament data, researchers constructed a directed network of "ball flow" among players in the team [35], where nodes represent players and edge weights indicate the number of successful passes between two players. They used the betweenness centrality of the player with regard to the opponent's goal as the performance measure of a player and defined the team-level performance as the average performance of the top-k players. They found that the difference between two teams' defined performance measure is indicative of their winning probability. In a similar study, researchers used English Premier League soccer team data to find that increased network density among team members leads to increased team performance, and increased centralization of team play decreases the performance [39].

2.4 Networks in GitHub Teams

Social coding platforms such as GitHub offer a unique experience to developers as they can subscribe to activities of other developers. Using GitHub data, researchers constructed two types of networks [87]: a project–project network, where nodes represent projects and two nodes are connected if they share at least one common developer; and developer–developer network, where nodes represent developers and two nodes are connected if they have collaborated in the same project. They found that in the project–project network, the diameter of the largest connected component is 9 with the average shortet path 3.7, which is more interconnected than human networks; and in the developer–developer network, the average shortest path is 2.47. Compared with the average shortest path of Facebook 4.7, we see social coding enables substantially more collaborations among developers.

3

Team Performance Prediction

In this chapter, we introduce our work on team performance prediction, including long-term performance prediction and performance trajectory forecasting [62]. We also explore the relationship between the team-level and individual-level performances and design a joint prediction model for the prediction of both. We describe their problem definitions and the key ideas behind our solutions. We focus on research teams for the performance prediction purpose.

3.1 Long-Term Performance Forecasting

Understanding the dynamic mechanisms that drive the high-impact scientific work (e.g., research papers, patents) is a long-debated research topic and has many important implications, ranging from personal career development and recruitment search, to the jurisdiction of research resources. Scholars, especially junior scholars, who could master the key to producing high-impact work would attract more attention as well as research resources and thus put themselves in a better position in their career development. High-impact work remains one of the most important criteria for various organizations (e.g., companies, universities, and governments) to identify the best talent, especially at their early stages. It is highly desirable for researchers to judiciously search the right literature that can best benefit their research.

Recent advances in characterizing and modeling scientific success have made it possible to forecast the long-term impact of scientific work. Wuchty et al. [98] observe that papers with multiple authors receive more citations than solo-authored ones. Uzzi et al. [91] find that the highest-impact science work is primarily grounded in atypical combinations of prior ideas while embedding them in conventional knowledge frames. Recently, Wang et al. [93] developed a mechanistic model for the citation dynamics of individual papers. In the data mining community, efforts have also been made to predict the long-term success. Castillo et al. [19] estimate the number of citations of a paper based on the information of past articles written by the same author(s). Yan et al. [99] design effective content (e.g., topic diversity) and contextual (e.g., author's h-index) features for the prediction of future citation counts. Despite much progress, the following four key algorithmic challenges in relation to predicting long-term scientific impact have largely remained open.

C1 *Scholarly feature design:* many factors could affect scientific work's long-term impact, e.g., research topic, author reputation, venue rank, citation networks' topological features, etc. Among them, which bears the most predictive power?

C2 *Nonlinearity:* the effect of the preceding scholarly features on long-term scientific impact might be way beyond a linear relationship.

C3 *Domain heterogeneity:* the impact of scientific work in different fields or domains might behave differently; yet some closely related fields could still share certain commonalities. Thus, a one-size-fits-all or one-size-fits-one solution might be suboptimal.

C4 *Dynamics:* with the rapid development of science and engineering, a significant number of new research papers are published each year, even on a daily basis, with the advent of arXiv.[1] The predictive model needs to handle such streamlike data efficiently, to reflect the recency of the scientific work.

In this study, we design a joint predictive model – Impact Crystal Ball (iBall in short) – to forecast the long-term scientific impact at an early stage by collectively addressing the preceding four challenges. First (for C1), we found that the citation history of a scholarly entity (e.g., paper, researcher, venue) in the first three years (e.g., since its publication date) is a strong indicator of its long-term impact (e.g., the accumulated citation count in ten years); and adding additional contextual or content features brings few marginal benefits in terms of prediction performance. This not only largely simplifies the feature design, but also enables us to forecast the long-term scientific impact at its early stage. Second (for C2), our joint predictive model is flexible, being able to characterize both the linear and nonlinear relationship between the features and the impact score. Third (for C3), we set out to jointly learn a predictive model to differentiate distinctive domains, while taking into consideration the

---

[1] arxiv.org.

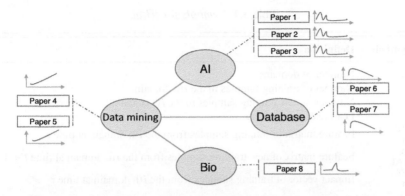

Figure 3.1 An illustrative example of our joint predictive model. Papers from the same domain (e.g., AI, databases, data mining, and bio) share similar patterns in terms of attracting citations over time. Certain domains (e.g., AI and data mining) are more related to each other than other domains (e.g., AI and bio). We want to jointly learn four predictive models (one for each domain), with the goal of encouraging the predictive models from more related domains (e.g., AI and data mining) to be "similar" to each other.

commonalities among these similar domains (see an illustration in Figure 3.1). Fourth (for C4), we further devise a fast online update algorithm to adapt our joint predictive model efficiently over time to accommodate newly arrived training examples (e.g., newly published papers).

Our main contributions can be summarized as follows:

- **Algorithms:** we design a joint predictive model – iBall – for the long-term scientific impact prediction problem, together with its efficient solvers.
- **Proofs and analysis:** we analyze the correctness, the approximation quality, and the complexity of our algorithms.
- **Empirical evaluations:** we conduct extensive experiments to demonstrate the effectiveness and efficiency of our algorithms.

3.1.1 Problem Statement

In this section, we first present the notations and then formally define the long-term scientific impact prediction for scholarly entities (e.g., research papers, researchers, conferences).

Table 3.1 lists the main symbols used. We use bold capital letters (e.g., $\mathbf{A}$) for matrices, bold lowercase letters (e.g., $\mathbf{w}$) for vectors, and lowercase letters (e.g., λ) for scalars. For matrix indexing, we use a convention similar to Matlab as follows, e.g., we use $\mathbf{A}(i, j)$ to denote the entry at the ith row and jth column

Table 3.1 *Symbols for iBall.*

Symbols	Definition
n_d	Number of domains
n_i	Number of training samples in the ith domain
m_i	Number of new training samples in the ith domain
d	Feature dimensionality
$\mathbf{X}_t^{(i)}$	Feature matrix of training samples from the ith domain at time t
$\mathbf{x}_{t+1}^{(i)}$	Feature matrix of new training samples from the ith domain at time $t+1$
$\mathbf{Y}_t^{(i)}$	Impact vector of training samples from the ith domain at time t
$\mathbf{y}_{t+1}^{(i)}$	Impact vector of new training samples from the ith domain at time $t+1$
$\mathbf{A}$	Adjacency matrix of the domain relation graph
$\mathbf{w}^{(i)}$	Model parameter for the ith domain
$\mathbf{K}^{(i)}$	Kernel matrix of training samples in the ith domain
$\mathbf{K}^{(ij)}$	Cross-domain kernel matrix of training samples in the ith and jth domains

of a matrix $\mathbf{A}$, $\mathbf{A}(i, :)$ to denote the ith row of $\mathbf{A}$ and $\mathbf{A}(: , j)$ to denote the jth column of $\mathbf{A}$. Besides, we use prime for matrix transpose, e.g., $\mathbf{A}'$ is the transpose of $\mathbf{A}$.

To differentiate samples from different domains at different time steps, we use superscript to index the domain and subscript to indicate timestamp. For instance, $\mathbf{X}_t^{(i)}$ denotes the feature matrix of all the scholarly entities in the ith domain at time t and $\mathbf{x}_{t+1}^{(i)}$ denotes the feature matrix of new scholarly entities in the ith domain at time $t+1$. Hence, $\mathbf{X}_{t+1}^{(i)} = [\mathbf{X}_t^{(i)}; \mathbf{x}_{t+1}^{(i)}]$. Similarly, $\mathbf{Y}_t^{(i)}$ denotes the impact vector of scholarly entities in the ith domain at time t and $\mathbf{y}_{t+1}^{(i)}$ denotes the impact vector of new scholarly entities in the ith domain at time $t+1$. Hence, $\mathbf{Y}_{t+1}^{(i)} = [\mathbf{Y}_t^{(i)}; \mathbf{y}_{t+1}^{(i)}]$. We will omit the superscript and/or subscript when the meaning of the matrix is clear from the context.

With the preceding notations, we are ready to define the long-term impact prediction problem in both static and dynamic settings as follows:

Problem 3.1   Static Long-Term Scientific Impact Prediction

Given: feature matrix $\mathbf{X}$ and impact $\mathbf{Y}$ of scholarly entities
Predict: the long-term impact of new scholarly entities

We further define the dynamic impact prediction problem as:

Problem 3.2   Dynamic Long-Term Scientific Impact Prediction

Given: feature matrix $\mathbf{X_t}$ and new training feature matrix $\mathbf{x_{t+1}}$ of scholarly entities, the impact vector $\mathbf{Y_t}$, and the impact vector of new training samples $\mathbf{y_{t+1}}$

Predict: the long-term impact of new scholarly entities

3.1.2 Empirical Observations

In this subsection, we perform an empirical analysis to highlight some of the key challenges on the *AMiner* citation network [86]. This is a rich, real dataset for bibliography network analysis and mining. The dataset contains 2,243,976 papers, 1,274,360 authors, and 8,882 computer science venues. For each paper, the dataset provides its titles, authors, references, publication venue, and publication year. The papers date from year 1936 to 2013. In total, the dataset has 1,912,780 citation relationships extracted from ACM library.

Feature design. Prior work [19, 99] has proposed some effective features for citation count prediction, e.g., topic features (topic rank, diversity), author features (h-index, productivity), and venue features (venue rank, venue centrality). Other work [93] makes predictions only on the basis of the early years' citation data and finds that the future impact of majority papers fall within the predicted citation range. We conducted an experiment to compare performance of different features. Figure 3.2 shows the root mean squared error using different features with a regression model for the prediction of ten years' citation count. For example, "three years" means using the first three years' citation as feature, and "three years + content" means using the first three years' citation along with content features (e.g., topic, author features). The result shows that adding content features (the right three bars in the figure) brings little improvement for citation prediction.

Nonlinearity. To see if the feature has linear relationship with the citation, we compare the performance of different methods using only the first three years' citation history. In Figure 3.3, the nonlinear models (iBall-fast, iBall-kernel, Kernel-combine) all outperform the linear models (iBall-linear, Linear-separate, Linear-combine). See Sections 3.1.3 and 3.1.4 for details of these models. It is clear that complex relationship between the features and the impact cannot be well characterized by a simple linear model – the prediction performance for all the linear models is even worse than for the baseline method (using the summation of the first three years' citation counts).

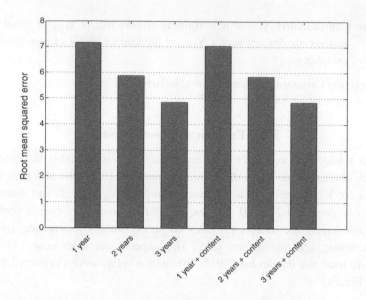

Figure 3.2 Prediction error comparison with different features.

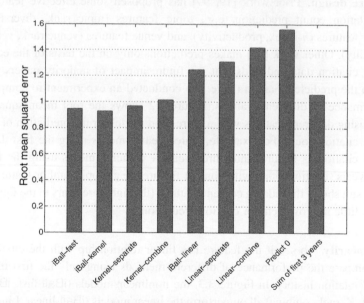

Figure 3.3 Root mean squared error comparisons using different methods. The citation count is normalized in this figure. See Section 3.1.4 for normalization details.

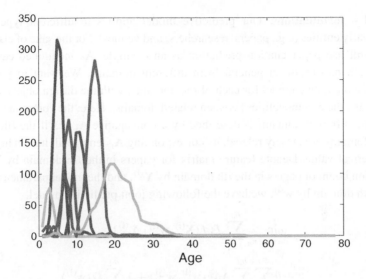

Figure 3.4 Visualization of papers' citation behavior. Different shades encodes different citation behaviors.

Domain Heterogeneity. To get a sense of the dynamic patterns of the citation count, we construct a paper-age citation matrix $\mathbf{M}$, where $\mathbf{M}_{ij}$ indicates the number of citations the ith paper receives in the jth year after it gets published. The matrix $\mathbf{M}$ is then factorized as $\mathbf{M} \approx \mathbf{WH}$ using nonnegative matrix factorization (NMF) [55]. We visualize the first six rows of $\mathbf{H}$ in Figure 3.4, which can give us different clustering citation dynamic patterns. As can be seen from the figure, the solid gray line has a very small peak in the first three years and then fades out very quickly; the solid black line picks up very fast in the early years and then fades out; and the gray dashed line indicates a delayed pattern where the scientific work only receives some amount of attentions decades after it gets published. This highlights that impact of scientific work from different domains behaves differently.

3.1.3 Our Algorithms

In this subsection, we present our joint predictive model to forecast the long-term scientific impact at an early stage. We first formulate it as a regularized optimization problem; then present effective, scalable and adaptive algorithms; and follow up with theoretical analysis in terms of the optimality, the approximation quality, as well as the computational complexity.

iBall – formulations. Our predictive model applies to different types of scholarly entities (e.g., papers, researchers, and venues). For the sake of clarity, we will use paper citation prediction as an example. As mentioned earlier, research papers are in general from different domains. We want to jointly learn a predictive model for each of the domains, with the design objective to leverage the commonalities between related domains. Here, the commonalities among different domains is described by a nonnegative $\mathbf{A}$, i.e., if the ith and jth domains are closely related, its corresponding $\mathbf{A}_{ij}$ entry will have a higher numerical value. Denote feature matrix for papers in the ith domain by $\mathbf{X}^{(i)}$, citation count of papers in the ith domain by $\mathbf{Y}^{(i)}$, and the model parameter for the ith domain by $\mathbf{w}^{(i)}$, we have the following joint predictive model:

$$
\min_{\mathbf{w}^{(i)}, i=1,\dots,n_d} \sum_{i=1}^{n_d} \mathcal{L}[f(\mathbf{X}^{(i)}, \mathbf{w}^{(i)}), \mathbf{Y}^{(i)}]
$$

$$
+ \theta \sum_{i=1}^{n_d} \sum_{j=1}^{n_d} \mathbf{A}_{ij} g(\mathbf{w}^{(i)}, \mathbf{w}^{(j)}) + \lambda \sum_{i=1}^{n_d} \Omega(\mathbf{w}^{(i)}), \tag{3.1}
$$

where $f(\mathbf{X}^{(i)}, \mathbf{w}^{(i)})$ is the prediction function for the ith domain, $\mathcal{L}(.)$ is a loss function, $g(\mathbf{w}^{(i)}, \mathbf{w}^{(j)})$ characterizes the relationship between the model parameters of the ith and jth domains, $\Omega(\mathbf{w}^{(i)})$ is the regularization term for model parameters and θ, λ are regularization parameters to balance the relative importance of each aspect.

As can be seen, this formulation is quite flexible and general. Depending on the loss function we use, our predictive model can be formulated as a regression or classification task. Depending on the prediction function we use, we can have either linear or nonlinear models. The core of our joint model is the second term that relates parameters of different models. If $\mathbf{A}_{ij}$ is large, meaning the ith and jth domains are closely related to each other, we want the function value $g(.)$ that characterizes the relationship between the parameters to be small.

iBall – linear formulation: if the feature and the output can be characterized by a linear relationship, we can use a linear function as the prediction function and the Euclidean distance for the distance between model parameters. The linear model can be formulated as follows:

$$
\min_{\mathbf{w}^{(i)}, i=1,\dots,n_d} \sum_{i=1}^{n_d} \|\mathbf{X}^{(i)} \mathbf{w}^{(i)} - \mathbf{Y}^{(i)}\|_2^2
$$

$$
+ \theta \sum_{i=1}^{n_d} \sum_{j=1}^{n_d} \mathbf{A}_{ij} \|\mathbf{w}^{(i)} - \mathbf{w}^{(j)}\|_2^2 + \lambda \sum_{i=1}^{n_d} \|\mathbf{w}^{(i)}\|_2^2, \tag{3.2}
$$

where θ is a balance parameter to control the importance of domain relations, and λ is a regularization parameter. From the preceding objective function, we can see that, if the ith domain and jth domain are closely related, i.e., $\mathbf{A}_{ij}$ is a large positive number, it encourages a smaller Euclidean distance between $\mathbf{w}^{(i)}$ and $\mathbf{w}^{(j)}$. The intuition is that for a given feature, it would have a similar effect in predicting the papers from two similar/closely related domains.

iBall – nonlinear formulation: As indicated in our empirical studies (Figure 3.3), the relationship between the features and the output (citation counts in ten years) is far beyond linear. Thus, we further develop the kernelized counterpart of the preceding linear model. Let us denote the kernel matrix of papers in the ith domain by $\mathbf{K}^{(i)}$, which can be computed as $\mathbf{K}^{(i)}(a,b) = k(\mathbf{X}^{(i)}(a,:), \mathbf{X}^{(i)}(b,:))$, where $k(\cdot,\cdot)$ is a kernel function that implicitly computes the inner product in a high-dimensional reproducing kernel Hilbert space (RKHS) [6]. Similarly, we define the cross-domain kernel matrix by $\mathbf{K}^{(ij)}$, which can be computed as $\mathbf{K}^{(ij)}(a,b) = k(\mathbf{X}^{(i)}(a,:), \mathbf{X}^{(j)}(b,:))$, reflecting the similarity between papers in the ith domain and jth domain. Different from the linear model where the model parameters in different domains share the same dimensionality (i.e., the dimensionality of the raw feature), in the nonlinear case, the dimensionality of the model parameters are the same as the number of training samples in each domain, which is very likely to be different across different domains. Thus, we cannot use the same distance function for $g(.)$. To address this issue, the key is to realize that the predicted value of a test sample using kernel methods is a linear combination of the similarities between the test sample and all the training samples. Therefore, instead of restricting the model parameters to be similar, we impose the constraint that the predicted value of a test sample using the training samples in its own domain and using training samples in a closely related domain be similar. The resulting nonlinear model can be formulated as follows:

$$
\min_{\mathbf{w}^{(i)}, i=1,\dots,n_d} \sum_{i=1}^{n_d} \| \mathbf{K}^{(i)} \mathbf{w}^{(i)} - \mathbf{Y}^{(i)} \|_2^2
$$

$$
+ \theta \sum_{i=1}^{n_d} \sum_{j=1}^{n_d} \mathbf{A}_{ij} \| \mathbf{K}^{(i)} \mathbf{w}^{(i)} - \mathbf{K}^{(ij)} \mathbf{w}^{(j)} \|_2^2 + \lambda \sum_{i=1}^{n_d} \mathbf{w}^{(i)'} \mathbf{K}^{(i)} \mathbf{w}^{(i)} \tag{3.3}
$$

where θ is a balance parameter to control the importance of domain relations, and λ is a regularization parameter. From the preceding objective function, we can see that, if the ith domain and jth domain are closely related, i.e., $\mathbf{A}_{ij}$ is a large positive number, the predicted value of papers in the ith domain computed using training samples from the ith domain ($\mathbf{K}^{(i)}\mathbf{w}^{(i)}$) should be similar to that using training samples from the jth domain ($\mathbf{K}^{(ij)}\mathbf{w}^{(j)}$).

iBall – Closed-Form Solutions. It turns out that both iBall linear and nonlinear formulations have the following closed-form solutions:

$$\mathbf{w} = \mathbf{S}^{-1}\mathbf{Y}. \tag{3.4}$$

iBall linear formulation. In the linear case, we have that $\mathbf{w} = [\mathbf{w}^{(1)}; \dots ; \mathbf{w}^{(n_d)}]$, $\mathbf{Y} = [\mathbf{X}^{(1)'}\mathbf{Y}^{(1)}; \dots ; \mathbf{X}^{(n_d)'}\mathbf{Y}^{(n_d)}]$, and $\mathbf{S}$ is a block matrix composed of $n_d \times n_d$ blocks, each of size $d \times d$, where d is the feature dimensionality. $\mathbf{S}$ can be computed as follows:

$$\begin{array}{cc} {\scriptstyle i\text{th block column}} & {\scriptstyle j\text{th block column}} \end{array}$$

$$\left[\begin{array}{ccc} \cdots & \cdots & \cdots \\ \cdots & \mathbf{X}^{(i)'}\mathbf{X}^{(i)} + \left(\theta \sum_{j=1}^{n_d} \mathbf{A}_{ij} + \lambda \right)\mathbf{I} & -\theta\mathbf{A}_{ij}\mathbf{I} \\ \cdots & \cdots & \cdots \end{array} \right] \begin{array}{c} \\ {\scriptstyle i\text{th block}} \\ {\scriptstyle \text{row}} \\ \\ \end{array} \tag{3.5}$$

iBall nonlinear formulation. In the nonlinear case, we have that $\mathbf{w} = [\mathbf{w}^{(1)}; \dots ; \mathbf{w}^{(n_d)}]$, $\mathbf{Y} = [\mathbf{Y}^{(1)}; \dots ; \mathbf{Y}^{(n_d)}]$, and $\mathbf{S}$ is a block matrix composed of $n_d \times n_d$ blocks with the (i, j)th block of size $n_i \times n_j$, where n_i is the number of training samples in the ith domain. $\mathbf{S}$ can be computed as follows:

$$\begin{array}{cc} {\scriptstyle i\text{th block column}} & {\scriptstyle j\text{th block column}} \end{array}$$

$$\left[\begin{array}{ccc} \cdots & \cdots & \cdots \\ \cdots & \left(1 + \theta \sum_{j=1}^{n_d} \mathbf{A}_{ij}\right)\mathbf{K}^{(i)} + \lambda\mathbf{I} & -\theta\mathbf{A}_{ij}\mathbf{K}^{(ij)} \\ \cdots & \cdots & \cdots \end{array} \right] \begin{array}{c} \\ {\scriptstyle i\text{th block}} \\ {\scriptstyle \text{row}} \\ \\ \end{array} \tag{3.6}$$

iBall – Scale-Up with Dynamic Update. The major computation cost for the closed-form solutions lies in the matrix inverse $\mathbf{S}^{-1}$. In the linear case, the size of $\mathbf{S}$ is $(dn_d) \times (dn_d)$, and so its computational cost is manageable. However, this is not the case for a nonlinear closed-form solution since the matrix $\mathbf{S}$ in Eq. (3.6) is of size $n \times n$, where $n = \sum_{i=1}^{n_d} n_i$, which is the number of all the training samples. It would be very expensive to store this dense matrix ($O(n^2)$ space) and to compute its inverse ($O(n^3)$ time), especially when the number of training samples is very large, and the model receives new training examples constantly over time (dynamic update). In this subsection, we devise an efficient algorithm to scale up the nonlinear closed-form solution and efficiently update the model to accommodate the new training samples over time. The key of the iBall algorithm is to use the low-rank approximation of the $\mathbf{S}$ matrix to approximate the original $\mathbf{S}$ matrix to *avoid* the matrix inversion, and at each time step efficiently update the low-rank approximation itself.

After new papers in all the domains are seen at time step $t+1$, the new $\mathbf{S}_{t+1}$ computed by Eq. (3.6) becomes

$$
\begin{bmatrix}
\cdots & \overset{i\text{th block column}}{\cdots} & \cdots & \overset{j\text{th block column}}{\cdots} & \cdots \\
\cdots & \left(1+\theta \sum_{j=1}^{n_d} \mathbf{A}_{ij}\right)\mathbf{K}_{t+1}^{(i)} + \lambda\mathbf{I} & & -\theta\mathbf{A}_{ij}\mathbf{K}_{t+1}^{(ij)} & \begin{matrix} i\text{th block} \\ \text{row}\end{matrix} \\
\cdots & & \cdots & &
\end{bmatrix}
\tag{3.7}
$$

where $\mathbf{K}_{t+1}^{(i)}$ is the new within-domain kernel matrix for the ith domain and $\mathbf{K}_{t+1}^{(ij)}$ is the new cross-domain kernel matrix for the ith and jth domains. The two new kernel matrix can be computed as follows:

$$
\mathbf{K}_{t+1}^{(i)} = \begin{bmatrix} \mathbf{K}_t^{(i)} & (\mathbf{k}_{t+1}^{(i)})' \\ \mathbf{k}_{t+1}^{(i)} & \mathbf{h}_{t+1}^{(i)} \end{bmatrix} \quad
\mathbf{K}_{t+1}^{(ij)} = \begin{bmatrix} \mathbf{K}_t^{(ij)} & \mathbf{k}_{t+1}^{(ij*)} \\ \mathbf{k}_{t+1}^{(i*j)} & \mathbf{h}_{t+1}^{(i*j*)} \end{bmatrix}
\tag{3.8}
$$

where $\mathbf{k}_{t+1}^{(i)}$ is the matrix characterizing the similarity between new training samples and old training samples and can be computed as $\mathbf{k}_{t+1}^{(i)}(a,b) = k(\mathbf{x}_{t+1}^{(i)}(a,:),\mathbf{X}_t^{(i)}(b,:))$; $\mathbf{h}_{t+1}^{(i)}$ is the similarity matrix among new training samples and can be computed as $\mathbf{h}_{t+1}^{(i)}(a,b) = k(\mathbf{x}_{t+1}^{(i)}(a,:),\mathbf{x}_{t+1}^{(i)}(b,:))$. $\mathbf{k}_{t+1}^{(i*j)}$ is the matrix characterizing the similarity between new training samples in the ith domain and old training samples in the jth domain and can be computed as $\mathbf{k}_{t+1}^{(i*j)}(a,b) = k(\mathbf{x}_{t+1}^{(i)}(a,:)),\mathbf{X}_t^{(j)}(b,:)$. Similarly, $\mathbf{k}_{t+1}^{(ij*)}$ measures the similarity between old training samples in the ith domain and new training samples in the jth domain and can be computed as $\mathbf{k}_{t+1}^{(ij*)} = k(\mathbf{X}_t^{(i)}(a,:),\mathbf{x}_{t+1}^{(j)}(b,:))$; $\mathbf{h}_{t+1}^{(i*j*)}$ is the similarity matrix between new training samples from both ith and jth domains and is computed as $\mathbf{h}_{t+1}^{(i*j*)} = k(\mathbf{x}_{t+1}^{(i)}(a,:),\mathbf{x}_{t+1}^{(j)}(b,.))$.

Given that $\mathbf{S}_t$ is a symmetric matrix, we can approximate it using top-r eigen-decomposition as $\mathbf{S}_t \approx \mathbf{U}_t\Lambda_t\mathbf{U}_t'$, where $\mathbf{U}_t$ is an $n \times r$ orthogonal matrix and Λ_t is an $r \times r$ diagonal matrix with the largest r eigenvalues of $\mathbf{S}_t$ on the diagonal. If we can directly update the eigen-decomposition of $\mathbf{S}_{t+1}$

after seeing the new training samples from all the domains, we can efficiently compute the new model parameters as follows:

$$\mathbf{w}_{t+1} = \mathbf{S}_{t+1}^{-1}\mathbf{Y}_{t+1} = \mathbf{U}_{t+1}\Lambda_{t+1}^{-1}\mathbf{U}_{t+1}'\mathbf{Y}_{t+1}, \qquad (3.9)$$

where $\mathbf{Y}_{t+1} = [\mathbf{Y}_t^{(1)}; \mathbf{y}_{t+1}^{(1)}; \ldots; \mathbf{Y}_t^{(n_d)}; \mathbf{y}_{t+1}^{(n_d)}]$. Here, Λ_{t+1}^{-1} an $r \times r$ diagonal matrix, whose diagonal entries are the reciprocals of the corresponding eigenvalues of Λ_{t+1}. In this way, we avoid the computationally costly matrix inverse in the closed-form solution.

Comparing $\mathbf{S}_{t+1}$ with $\mathbf{S}_t$, we find that $\mathbf{S}_{t+1}$ can be obtained by inserting into $\mathbf{S}_t$ at the right positions with some rows and columns of the kernel matrices involving new training samples, i.e., $\mathbf{k}_{t+1}^{(i)}$, $\mathbf{h}_{t+1}^{(i)}$, $\mathbf{k}_{t+1}^{(i*j)}$, $\mathbf{k}_{t+1}^{(ij*)}$, $\mathbf{k}_{t+1}^{(i*j*)}$. From this perspective, $\mathbf{S}_{t+1}$ can be seen as the sum of the following two matrices:

$$
\underbrace{
\begin{bmatrix}
\ddots & & & & \\
\cdots & \begin{bmatrix} \alpha_i \mathbf{K}_t^{(i)} & 0 \\ 0 & 0 \end{bmatrix} & & \begin{bmatrix} -\theta \mathbf{A}_{ij}\mathbf{K}_t^{(ij)} & 0 \\ 0 & 0 \end{bmatrix} & \\
\cdots & & & & \\
& & \ddots & &
\end{bmatrix}
}_{\tilde{\mathbf{S}}_t}
\qquad (3.10)
$$

*i*th block column   *j*th block column

*i*th block row

$$
+ \underbrace{
\begin{bmatrix}
\ddots & & & & \\
\cdots & \begin{bmatrix} 0 & \alpha_i(\mathbf{k}_{t+1}^{(i)})' \\ \alpha_i\mathbf{k}_{t+1}^{(i)} & \alpha_i\mathbf{h}_{t+1}^{(i)} + \lambda\mathbf{I} \end{bmatrix} & & \begin{bmatrix} 0 & -\theta\mathbf{A}_{ij}\mathbf{k}_{t+1}^{(ij*)} \\ -\theta\mathbf{A}_{ij}\mathbf{k}_{t+1}^{(i*j)} & -\theta\mathbf{A}_{ij}\mathbf{h}_{t+1}^{(i*j*)} \end{bmatrix} & \\
\cdots & & & & \\
& & \ddots & &
\end{bmatrix}
}_{\Delta\mathbf{S}}
$$

*i*th block column   *j*th block column

*i*th block row

$$\qquad (3.11)$$

$$\stackrel{\text{def}}{=} \tilde{\mathbf{S}}_t + \Delta\mathbf{S} \qquad (3.12)$$

where we denote $1 + \theta\sum_{j=1}^{n_d}\mathbf{A}_{ij}$ by α_i. The top-r eigen-decomposition of $\tilde{\mathbf{S}}_t$ can be directly written out from that of $\mathbf{S}_t$ as $\tilde{\mathbf{S}}_t \approx \tilde{\mathbf{U}}_t\Lambda_t\tilde{\mathbf{U}}_t'$, where $\tilde{\mathbf{U}}_t$ can be obtained by inserting into $\mathbf{U}_t$ corresponding rows of 0, the same row positions as we insert into $\mathbf{S}_t$ the new kernel matrices. We present Algorithm 1 to update the eigen-decomposition of $\mathbf{S}_{t+1}$, based on the observation that $\mathbf{S}_{t+1}$ can be viewed as $\tilde{\mathbf{S}}_t$ perturbed by a low-rank matrix $\Delta\mathbf{S}$. In line 5 of Algorithm 1, the only difference between the partial QR decomposition and the standard one, is that since $\tilde{\mathbf{U}}_t$ is already orthogonal, we only need to perform the Gram–Schmidt procedure starting from the first column of $\mathbf{P}$.

Algorithm 1: Eigen update of S_{t+1}

Input: (1)eigen pair of S_t: U_t, Λ_t;

(2)feature matrices of new papers in each domain: $\mathbf{x}_{t+1}^{(i)}, i = 1, \ldots, n_d$;

(3)adjacency matrix of domain relation graph $\mathbf{A}$;

(4)balance parameters θ, λ

Output: eigen pair of S_{t+1}: U_{t+1}, Λ_{t+1}

---

1 Obtain $\tilde{U}_t$ by inserting into U_t rows of 0 at the right positions;

2 Compute $\mathbf{k}_{t+1}^{(i)}, \mathbf{h}_{t+1}^{(i)}, \mathbf{k}_{t+1}^{(i,j)}, \mathbf{k}_{t+1}^{(ij*)}, \mathbf{k}_{t+1}^{(i*j*)}$ for $i = 1, \ldots, n_d, j = 1, \ldots, n_d$;

3 Construct sparse matrix ΔS;

4 Perform eigen-decomposition of ΔS: $\Delta S = \mathbf{P} \Sigma \mathbf{P}'$;

5 Perform partial QR decomposition of $[\tilde{U}_t, \mathbf{P}]$:$[\tilde{U}_t, \Delta \mathbf{Q}]\mathbf{R} \leftarrow QR(\tilde{U}_t, \mathbf{P})$;

6 Set $\mathbf{Z} = \mathbf{R}[\Lambda_t \ \mathbf{0}; \mathbf{0} \ \Sigma]\mathbf{R}'$;

7 Perform full eigen-decomposition of $\mathbf{Z}$: $\mathbf{Z} = \mathbf{V}\mathbf{L}\mathbf{V}'$;

8 Set $U_{t+1} = [\tilde{U}_t, \Delta \mathbf{Q}]\mathbf{V}$ and $\Lambda_{t+1} = \mathbf{L}$;

9 **Return**: U_{t+1}, Λ_{t+1}.

Algorithm 2: iBall – scale-up with dynamic update

Input: (1)eigen pair of S_t: U_t, Λ_t;

(2)feature matrices of new papers in each domain: $\mathbf{x}_{t+1}^{(i)}, i = 1, \ldots, n_d$;

(3)citation count vectors of new papers in each domain:

$\mathbf{y}_{t+1}^{(i)}, i = 1, \ldots, n_d$;

(4)adjacency matrix of domain relation graph $\mathbf{A}$;

(5)balance parameters θ, λ

Output: (1) updated model parameters $\mathbf{w}_{t+1}$, (2) eigen pair of S_{t+1}:

$\quad U_{t+1}$, Λ_{t+1}

---

1 Update the eigen-decomposition of S_{t+1} using Algorithm 1 as:

$\quad S_{t+1} \approx U_{t+1} \Lambda_{t+1} U_{t+1}'$;

2 Compute the new model parameters: $\mathbf{w}_{t+1} = U_{t+1} \Lambda_{t+1}^{-1} U_{t+1}' \mathbf{Y}_{t+1}$;

3 **Return**: $\mathbf{w}_{t+1}$, U_{t+1} and Λ_{t+1}.

Building upon Algorithm 1, we have the fast iBall algorithm (Algorithm 2) for scaling up the nonlinear solution with a dynamic model update.

iBall – Proofs and Analysis. In this subsection, we will provide some analysis regarding the optimality, the approximation quality as well as the computational complexity of our algorithms.

A. Correctness of the closed-form solutions of the iBall linear and non-linear formulations: In Lemma 3.3, we prove that the closed-form solution given in Eq. (3.4) with **S** computed by Eq. (3.5) is the fixed-point solution to the linear formulation in Eq. (3.2) and the closed-form solution given in Eq. (3.4) with **S** computed by Eq. (3.6) is the fixed-point solution to the non-linear formulation in Eq. (3.3).

Lemma 3.3. *(Correctness of closed-form solution of the iBall linear and non-linear formulations.) For the closed-form solution given in Eq. (3.4), if **S** is computed by Eq. (3.5), it is the fixed-point solution to the objective function in Eq. (3.2); and if **S** is computed by Eq. (3.6), it is the fixed-point solution to the objective function in Eq. (3.3).*

Proof   Omitted for brevity. See [57] for detail.   □

B. Correctness of the Eigen Update of S_{t+1}: The critical part of Algorithm 2 is the subroutine Algorithm 1 for updating the eigen-decomposition of S_{t+1}. According to Lemma 3.4, the only place that approximation error occurs is the initial eigen-decomposition of S_0. The eigen updating procedure won't introduce additional error.

Lemma 3.4. *(Correctness of Algorithm 1.) If $S_t = U_t \Lambda_t U_t'$ holds, Algorithm 1 gives the exact eigen-decomposition of S_{t+1}.*

Proof   Omitted for brevity. See [64] for details.   □

C. Approximation Quality: We analyze the approximation quality of Algorithm 2 to see how much the learned model parameters deviate from the parameters learned using the exact iBall nonlinear formulation. The result is summarized in Theorem 3.5.

Theorem 3.5. *(Error bound of Algorithm 2.) In Algorithm 2, if $\frac{\sum_{i \notin \mathcal{H}} \lambda_t^{(i)}}{\sum_i \lambda_{t+1}^{(i)}} < 1$, the error of the learned model parameters is bounded by:*

$$\|\mathbf{w}_{t+1} - \hat{\mathbf{w}}_{t+1}\|_2 \leq \frac{\sum_{i \notin \mathcal{H}} \lambda_t^{(i)}}{\left(\sum_i \lambda_{t+1}^{(i)}\right)^2 (1 - \delta)} \|\mathbf{Y}_{t+1}\|_2, \qquad (3.13)$$

where $\mathbf{w}_{t+1}$ is the model parameter learned by the exact iBall nonlinear formulation at time $t + 1$, $\hat{\mathbf{w}}_{t+1}$ is the updated model parameter output by Algorithm 2 from time t to $t + 1$; $\lambda_t^{(i)}$ and $\lambda_{t+1}^{(i)}$ are the largest ith eigenvalues of S_t and S_{t+1} respectively; and $\delta = \|(\tilde{U}_t \Lambda_t \tilde{U}_t' + \Delta S)^{-1}(\tilde{S}_t - \tilde{U}_t \Lambda_t \tilde{U}_t')\|_F$, $\mathcal{H}$ is the set of integers between 1 and r, i.e., $\mathcal{H} = \{a|a \in [1, r]\}$.

Proof Suppose we know the exact $\mathbf{S}_t$ at time t and its top-r approximation: $\hat{\mathbf{S}}_t = \mathbf{U}_t \Lambda_t \mathbf{U}_t'$. After one time step, we can construct $\Delta \mathbf{S}$, and the exact $\mathbf{S}_{t+1}$ can be computed as $\mathbf{S}_{t+1} = \tilde{\mathbf{S}}_t + \Delta \mathbf{S}$. The model parameters learned by the exact nonlinear model is

$$\mathbf{w}_{t+1} = \mathbf{S}_{t+1}^{-1} \mathbf{Y}_{t+1} = (\tilde{\mathbf{S}}_t + \Delta \mathbf{S})^{-1} \mathbf{Y}_{t+1}. \tag{3.14}$$

If we allow approximation as in Algorithm 2, the approximated model parameter is

$$\hat{\mathbf{w}}_{t+1} = \hat{\mathbf{S}}_{t+1}^{-1} \mathbf{Y}_{t+1} = (\tilde{\mathbf{U}}_t \Lambda_t \tilde{\mathbf{U}}_t' + \Delta \mathbf{S})^{-1} \mathbf{Y}_{t+1}. \tag{3.15}$$

If we denote $\tilde{\mathbf{S}}_t + \Delta \mathbf{S}$ by $\mathbf{B}$ and $\tilde{\mathbf{U}}_t \Lambda_t \tilde{\mathbf{U}}_t' + \Delta \mathbf{S}$ by $\mathbf{C}$, we have the following:

$$\|\mathbf{B} - \mathbf{C}\|_F = \|\tilde{\mathbf{S}}_t - \tilde{\mathbf{U}}_t \Lambda_t \tilde{\mathbf{U}}_t'\|_F \le \sum_{i \notin \mathcal{H}} \lambda_t^{(i)}, \tag{3.16}$$

where the last inequality is due to the following fact:

$$
\begin{aligned}
\| \sum_i a_i \mathbf{u}_i \mathbf{u}_i' \|_F &= \sqrt{\operatorname{tr}\left(\sum_i a_i^2 \mathbf{u}_i \mathbf{u}_i'\right)} = \sqrt{\sum_i a_i^2 \operatorname{tr}(\mathbf{u}_i \mathbf{u}_i')} \\
&= \sqrt{\sum_i a_i^2} \le \sum_i |a_i|.
\end{aligned} \tag{3.17}
$$

If we denote $\|\mathbf{C}^{-1}(\mathbf{B} - \mathbf{C})\|_F$ by δ, we know that

$$\delta \le \|\mathbf{C}^{-1}\|_F \|\mathbf{B} - \mathbf{C}\|_F \le \frac{\sum_{i \notin \mathcal{H}} \lambda_t^{(i)}}{\sum_i \lambda_{t+1}^{(i)}} < 1. \tag{3.18}$$

From matrix perturbation theory [38], we will reach the following:

$$
\begin{aligned}
\|\mathbf{w}_{t+1} - \hat{\mathbf{w}}_{t+1}\|_2 &= \|\mathbf{B}^{-1} \mathbf{Y}_{t+1} - \mathbf{C}^{-1} \mathbf{Y}_{t+1}\|_2 \\
&\le \|\mathbf{B}^{-1} - \mathbf{C}^{-1}\|_F \|\mathbf{Y}_{t+1}\|_2 \\
&\le \frac{\|\mathbf{C}^{-1}\|_F^2 \|\mathbf{B} - \mathbf{C}\|_F}{1 - \delta} \|\mathbf{Y}_{t+1}\|_2 \\
&\le \frac{\sum_{i \notin \mathcal{H}} \lambda_t^{(i)}}{\left(\sum_i \lambda_{t+1}^{(i)}\right)^2 (1 - \delta)} \|\mathbf{Y}_{t+1}\|_2.
\end{aligned} \tag{3.19}
$$

$\square$

D. Complexities: Finally, we analyze the complexities of Algorithm 1 and Algorithm 2. In terms of time complexity, the savings are twofold: (1) we only need to compute the kernel matrices involving new training samples; and (2) we avoid the time-consuming large matrix inverse operation. In terms of space complexity, we don't need to maintain the huge $\mathbf{S}_t$ matrix, but instead store its top-r eigen pairs, which is only of $O(nr)$ space.

Theorem 3.6. *(Complexities of Algorithm 1 and Algorithm 2.) Algorithm 1 takes $O((n + m)(r^2 + r'^2))$ time and $O((n + m)(r + r'))$ space. Algorithm 2* *also takes* $O((n + m)(r^2 + r'^2))$ *time and* $O((n + m)(r + r'))$ *space, where m is the total number of new training samples.*

Proof   Time complexity of Algorithm 1: Steps 1 through 3 take $O(nm)$ time, where n is total number of training samples from the previous step, and m is the total number of new training samples. Eigen-decomposition of ΔS in step 4 takes $O(nmr')$, where r' is the rank of ΔS, since ΔS is a sparse matrix with $O(nm)$ nonzero entries. QR decomposition in step 5 takes $O((n + m)r'^2)$ since we only need to start from the columns in **P**. Steps 6 and 7 both take $O((r + r')^3)$ time. The last line takes at most $O((n+m)(r + r')^2)$. The overall time complexity is $O((n + m)(r^2 + r'^2))$.

Space complexity of Algorithm 1: The storage of eigen pairs requires $O((n+ m)r)$ space. Steps 1 through 3 take $O(mn)$ space. Eigen-decomposition of ΔS in step 4 takes $O((n + m)r')$ space. QR decomposition in step 5 needs $O((n + m)(r + r'))$ space. Steps 6 and 7 take $O((r + r')^2)$ space, and line 8 needs $O((n+m)(r +r'))$. The overall space complexity is $O((n+m)(r+r'))$.

Time complexity of Algorithm 2: Updating eigen-decomposition of S_{t+1} in step 1 takes $O((n + m)(r^2 + r'^2))$ time, and computing the new learning parameter in step 2 takes $O(n + m)r$ time. The overall time complexity is $O((n + m)(r^2 + r'^2))$.

Space complexity of Algorithm 2: Updating eigen-decomposition of S_{t+1} in step 1 takes $O((n + m)(r + r'))$, and computing the new learning parameter in step 2 takes $O((n + m)r)$ space. The overall space complexity is $O((n + m)(r + r'))$.   □

3.1.4 Experiments

In this subsection, we design and conduct experiments mainly to inspect the following aspects:

- *Effectiveness:* How accurate are our algorithms for predicting scholarly entities' long-term impact?
- *Efficiency:* How fast are our algorithms?

Experiment Setup. We use the real-world citation network dataset AMiner[2] to evaluate our algorithms. The statistics and empirical observations are

---

[2] http://arnetminer.org/billboard/citation.

described in Section 3.1.1. Our primary task is to predict a paper's citations after 10 years given its citation history in the first three years. Thus, we only keep papers published between year 1936 and 2000 to make sure they are at least 10 years old. This leaves us 508,773 papers. Given that the citation distribution is skewed, the 10-year citation counts are normalized to the range of $[0, 7]$. Our algorithm is also able to predict citation counts for other scholarly entities including researchers and venues. We keep authors whose research career (when they publish the first paper) began between years 1960 and 2000 and venues that were founded before year 2002. This leaves us 315,340 authors and 3,783 venues.

For each scholarly entity, we represent it as a three-dimensional feature vector, where the ith dimension is the number of citations the entity receives in the ith year after its life cycle begins (e.g., paper gets published, researchers publish the first paper). We build a k-nn graph ($k = 5$) among different scholarly entities, use METIS [46] to partition the graph into balanced clusters, and treat each cluster as a domain. We set the domain number (n_d) to be 10 for both papers and researchers; and 5 for venues. The Gaussian kernel matrix of the cluster centroids is used to construct the domain–domain adjacency matrix $\mathbf{A}$.

To simulate the dynamic scenario where training samples come in stream, we start with a small initial training set and at each time step add new training samples to it. The training samples in each domain are sorted by starting year (e.g., publication year). In the experiment, for papers, we start with 0.1% initial training data and at each update add another 0.1% training samples. The last 10% samples are reserved as test samples, i.e., we always use information from older publications for the prediction of the latest ones. For authors, we start with 0.2% initial training data and at each update add another 0.2% training data and use the last 10% for testing. For venues, we start with 20%, add 10% at each update and use last 10% for testing.

The root mean squared error (RMSE) between the the actual citation and the predicted one is adopted for accuracy evaluation. All the experiments were performed on a Windows machine with four 3.5GHz Intel Cores and 256GB RAM.

Repeatability of Experimenal Results: The AMiner citation dataset is publicly available. We have released the code of the algorithms through the authors' website. For all the results reported in this section, we set $\theta = \lambda = 0.01$ in our joint predictive model. Gaussian kernel with $\sigma = 5.1$ is used in the nonlinear formulations.

Effectiveness Results. We perform the effectiveness comparisons of the following nine methods:

1 *Predict 0:* directly predict 0 for test samples since majority of the papers have 0 citations.
2 *Sum of the first three years:* assume the total number of citations doesn't change after three years.
3 *Linear-combine:* combine training samples of all the domains for training using linear regression model.
4 *Linear-separate:* train a linear regression model for each domain separately.
5 *iBall-linear:* jointly learn the linear regression models as in our linear formulation.
6 *Kernel-combine:* combine training samples of all the domains for training using kernel ridge regression model [80].
7 *Kernel-separate:* train a kernel ridge regression model for each domain separately.
8 *iBall-kernel:* jointly learn the kernel regression models as in our nonlinear formulation.
9 *iBall-fast:* our algorithm for speeding up the joint nonlinear model.

A. Overall paper citation prediction performance. The RMSE result of different methods for test samples from all the domains is shown in Figure 3.5.

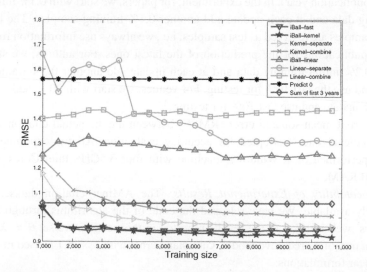

Figure 3.5 Overall paper citation prediction performance comparisons. Lower is better.

Table 3.2 *p-value of statistical significance.*

Predict 0	Linear-combine	Linear-separate	iBall-linear	Sum of first 3 years	Kernel-combine	Kernel-separate	iBall-fast
iBall-kernel 0	5.53e-16	6.12e-17	1.16e-13	1.56e-219	1.60e-72	8.22e-30	3.39e-14

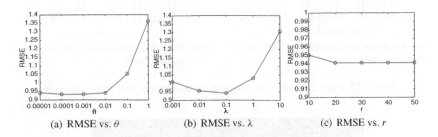

(a) RMSE vs. θ　　　　(b) RMSE vs. λ　　　　(c) RMSE vs. r

Figure 3.6 Sensitivity study on iBall-fast: study the effect of the parameters θ, λ and r in terms of RMSE.

We have the following observations: (1) The nonlinear methods (iBall-fast, iBall-kernel, Kernel-separate, Kernel-combine) outperform the linear methods (iBall-linear, Linear-separate, Linear-combine) and the straightforward "Sum of first three years" is much better than the linear methods, which reflects the complex nonlinear relationship between the features and the impact. (2) The performance of iBall-fast is very close to iBall-kernel and sometimes even better, which confirms the good approximation quality of the model update and the possible denoising effect offered by the low-rank approximation. (3) The iBall family of joint models is better than their separate versions (Kernel-separate, Linear-separate). To evaluate the statistical significance, we perform a t-test using 1.4% of the training samples and show the p-values in Table 3.2. From the result, we see that the improvement of our method is significant. To investigate parameter sensitivity, we perform parametric studies with three parameters in iBall-fast, namely, θ, λ, and r. Figure 3.6 shows that our method is stable in a large range of the parameter space.

B. Domain-by-domain paper citation prediction performance. In Figure 3.7, we show the RMSE comparison results for two domains with different total training sizes. iBall-kernel and its fast version iBall-fast consistently outperform other methods in both of the domains. In the first domain, some linear methods (Linear-separate and Linear-combine) perform even worse than the baseline ("Predict 0").

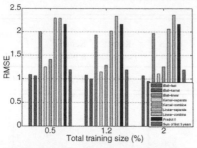
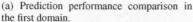

(a) Prediction performance comparison in the first domain.

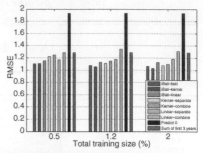

(b) Prediction performance comparison in the second domain.

Figure 3.7 Paper citation prediction performance comparison in two domains.

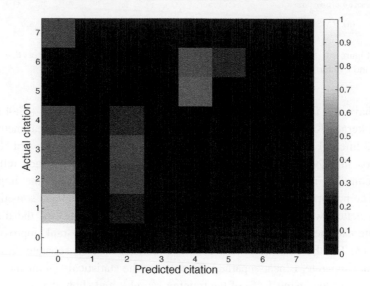

Figure 3.8 Prediction error analysis: actual citation vs. predicted citation.

C. Prediction error analysis. We visualize the actual citation versus the predicted citation using iBall as a heat map in Figure 3.8. The (x, y) square means among all the test samples with actual citation y, the percentage that have predicted citation x. We observe a very bright region near the $x = y$ diagonal. The prediction error mainly occurs in a bright strip at $x = 1, y \geq 1$. This is probably due to the delayed high impact of some scientific work, as

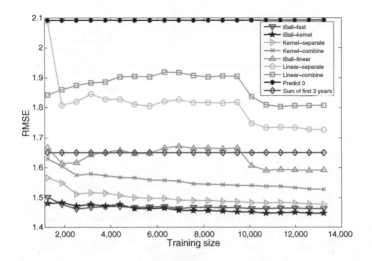

Figure 3.9 Author citation prediction performance comparison. Lower is better.

suggested by the solid black and black dashed lines in Figure 3.4, i.e., some papers only pick up attention many years after they were published.

D. Author and venue citation prediction performance. We also show the RMSE comparison results for the impact prediction of authors and venues in Figures 3.9 and 3.10 respectively. Similar observations can be made as the paper impact prediction, except that for the venue citation prediction, iBall-linear can achieve the similar performance as iBall-fast and iBall-kernel. This is probably due to the effect that venue citation (which involves the aggregation of the citations of all of its authors and papers) prediction is at a much coarser granularity, and thus a relatively simple linear model is sufficient to characterize the correlation between features and outputs (citation counts).

Efficiency Results.
A. Running time comparison. We compare the running time of different methods with different training sizes and show the result in Figure 3.11 with time in log scale. All the linear methods are very fast ($< 0.01s$) as the feature dimensionality is only 3. Our iBall-fast outperforms all other nonlinear methods and scales linearly.

B. Quality vs. speed. Finally, we evaluate how our methods balance between the prediction quality and speed. In Figure 3.12, we show the RMSE

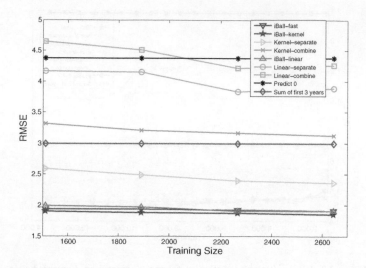

Figure 3.10 Venue citation prediction performance comparison. Lower is better.

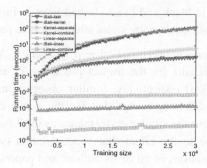

Figure 3.11 Comparison of running time of different methods. The time axis is of log scale.

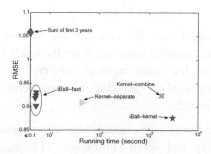

Figure 3.12 Quality vs. speed with 88,905 training samples.

versus running time of different methods with 88,905 total training samples. For iBall-fast, we show its results using different rank r for the low-rank approximation. Clearly, iBall-fast achieves the best trade-off between quality and speed as its results all lie in the bottom-left corner.

3.2 Performance Trajectory Forecasting

The emerging research area on the "science of science" (e.g., understanding the intrinsic mechanism that drives high-impact scientific work, foreseeing the success of scientific work at an early stage) has been attracting extensive research attention in the recent years, most of which is centered around the citation counts of the scholarly entities (e.g., researchers, venues, papers, institutes) [91, 93]. From the prediction perspective, more often than not, it is of key importance to forecast the pathway to impact for scholarly entities (e.g., how many citations a research paper will attract in each of several consecutive years in the future). The impact pathway often provides a good indicator of the shift of the research frontier. For instance, the rapid citation count increase of the deep learning papers reveals an emerging surge of this topic. The impact pathway can also help trigger an early intervention should the impact trajectory step down in the near future. Research resources could be more judiciously allocated if the impact pathway can be forecast at an early stage. For example, the research management agency could proactively allocate more resources to those rising fields.

The state of the art has mainly focused on modeling the long-term scientific impact for the early prediction. For example, Wang et al. [93] integrate preferential attachment, a temporal citation trend, and the underlying "fitness" of the paper into designing a generative model for the citation dynamics of individual papers. Yan et al. [99] focus on designing effective scholarly features (e.g., content features, author features, venue features) for the future citation count prediction. Li et al. propose a joint predictive model to encourage similar research domains to share similar model parameters.

Despite their own success, all the existing work on impact forecasting is essentially for *point prediction*, to predict the number of cumulative citations of a paper in the future. They are not directly applicable to forecasting the impact pathway, e.g., citation counts in each of the next 10 years. One baseline solution is to treat the impacts across different years independently and to train a separate model for each of the impacts. This treatment might ignore the inherent relationship among different impacts across different years, and thus might lead to suboptimal performance. Having this in mind, a better way could be to apply the existing multilabel learning [115] or multitask learning [23] methods to exploit the relation among impacts across different years. Nonetheless, these general-purpose multilabel/multitask learning approaches might overlook some unique characteristics of the impact pathway prediction, which is exactly the focus of this work.

In this work, we aim to develop a new predictive model tailored for scholarly entity impact pathway prediction. To be specific, our model will focus on the following two design objectives:

- **D1. Prediction Consistency.** Intuitively, the scholarly impacts at certain years might be correlated with each other, which, if vetted carefully, could boost the prediction performance (i.e., multilabel or multitask learning). Here, one difficulty for impact pathway prediction is that such a relation structure is often not accurately known a priori. Thus a good predictive model should be capable of simultaneously inferring the impact relation structure from the training data and leveraging such (inferred) relation to improve the prediction performance.
- **D2. Parameter Smoothness.** For a given feature of the predictive model, we do not expect its effect on the impacts of adjacent years would change dramatically. For instance, the effect of "fitness" defined in [93], capturing a scientific work's perceived novelty and importance, is unlikely to change greatly but rather gradually fade away over years. A good predictive model should be able to capture such temporal smoothness.

We present a new predictive model (*iPath*) to simultaneously fulfill these two design objectives. First, we exploit the prediction consistency (i.e., D1) in the *output* space. Second, to encode the parameter smoothness (i.e., D2) between adjacent time steps, we impose a linear transition process in the *parameter space* from one time step to the next. We formulate it as a regularized optimization problem and design an effective alternating strategy to solve it. Our method is flexible, being able to handle both linear and nonlinear models.

The main contributions can be summarized as follows:

- **Problem Definitions.** We define a novel scholarly impact pathway prediction problem, to predict the impact of a scholarly entity at several consecutive time steps in the future.
- **Algorithm and Analysis.** We present and analyze a new predictive model (*iPath*) for the impact pathway forecasting problem.
- **Empirical Evaluations.** We conduct extensive experiments to validate the effectiveness of our algorithm.

Table 3.3 *Symbols for* iPath.

Symbols	Definition
n	Number of scholarly entities
d	Feature dimension, i.e., number of time steps observed
l	Length of the forecasting horizon into the future
$\mathbf{w}_i$	Model parameter for predicting the ith impact
$\mathbf{X}$	Feature matrix
$\mathbf{Y}$	Impact matrix
$\mathbf{A}$	Adjacency matrix of the impact graph
$\mathbf{A}_0$	Prior knowledge of the impact graph structure
$\mathbf{B}$	Transition matrix
$\mathbf{K}$	Kernel matrix
E	Energy function
$\Phi_c(\cdot)$	Potential defined on a maximal clique c

3.2.1 Problem Definition

In this subsection, we first present the notations used (summarized in Table 3.3) and then formally define the pathway to impact forecasting problem.

We use bold uppercase letters for matrices (e.g., $\mathbf{A}$), bold lowercase letters for vectors (e.g., $\mathbf{v}$), and lowercase letters (e.g., α) for scalars. For matrix indexing, we use a convention similar to Matlab's syntax as follows. We use $\mathbf{A}(i, j)$ to denote the entry at the intersection of the ith row and jth column of matrix $\mathbf{A}$, $\mathbf{A}(i, :)$ to denote the i-th row of $\mathbf{A}$ and $\mathbf{A}(: , j)$ to denote the j-th column of $\mathbf{A}$. Besides, we use prime for matrix transpose (e.g., $\mathbf{A}'$ is the transpose of $\mathbf{A}$).

For a given scholarly entity (e.g., research papers, researchers, conferences), after observing the impacts in the first few years, we want to forecast its impacts in the next several years (e.g., 10 or 20 years) into the future. Formally, we denote $\mathbf{x} \in \mathbb{R}^d$ as the impacts observed in the first d time steps, and want to predict the impact pathway $\mathbf{y} = (y_1, y_2, \ldots, y_l)'$ afterward, where y_i is the citation count in the ith future time step, and l is the length of the horizon we want to look into the future. Mathematically, the task is to learn a predictive function $f : \mathbf{x} \rightarrow \mathbf{y}$ from the training set $\mathcal{D} = \{(\mathbf{x}_i, \mathbf{y}_i)|i = 1, 2, \ldots, n\}$, where n is the number of training samples. For convenience, let $\mathbf{X}$ be the feature matrix by stacking all the features (i.e., impact values of the first d time steps) of the n scholarly entities as its rows, that is, $\mathbf{X} = [\mathbf{x}_1, \mathbf{x}_2, \ldots, \mathbf{x}_n]'$. Similarly, let $\mathbf{Y}$ be the impact matrix by stacking all the impacts (i.e., values of all the l future time steps) of the n scholarly entities as its rows, that is, $\mathbf{Y} = [\mathbf{y}_1, \mathbf{y}_2, \ldots, \mathbf{y}_n]'$.

With the preceding notations, we formally define the pathway to impact forecasting problem as follows:

Problem 3.7   Pathway to Impact Forecasting

Given: feature matrix $\mathbf{X}$ and impact matrix $\mathbf{Y}$ of n scholarly entities.

Predict: the impacts in each of the continuous future time steps of a new
            scholarly entity.

Remarks: At the high level, this problem setting bears some similarities to the classic multilabel learning [115] or multitask learning [23] (i.e., predicting each impact is treated as a task). Nonetheless, the impact pathway of a scholarly entity brings several unique characteristics as outlined in the beginning of Section 3.2, which in turn calls for a new method to solve it.

3.2.2 Our Solutions

In this subsection, we present a predictive model to forecast the pathway to impact. We first formulate it as a regularized optimization problem, and then present an effective alternating optimization algorithm to solve it.

iPath **Formulations.** Let us first summarize the key ideas behind our formulation. First, we want to leverage the relation across the impacts at different time steps so that closely related impacts are likely to have consistent predicted outputs. The relation among the impacts at different time steps is encoded in a nonnegative matrix $\mathbf{A}$, where the entry $\mathbf{A}_{ij}$ is a large positive value if the ith impact and jth impact are closely related. The matrix $\mathbf{A}$ can be regarded as the weight matrix of the impact relationship graph, where vertices are impacts at different time steps and an edge exists between two similar impacts. Second, one difficulty is that the impact relation might not be accurately known a priori. We address this by inferring a good relation that can benefit the prediction performance, while not deviating too far from the (noisy) prior knowledge of the relation. Third, as we mentioned in the problem definition, we focus on the impact pathway forecasting, where the effect of features on the impacts at adjacent time steps is expected to transition smoothly. To realize such smoothness, we impose a linear transition process $\mathbf{B}$ between model parameters of adjacent time steps $\mathbf{w}_t$ and $\mathbf{w}_{t+1}$.

Putting all the preceding aspects together, our model can be formulated as follows:

$$
\min_{\mathbf{W},\mathbf{B},\mathbf{A}} \underbrace{\mathcal{L}[f(\mathbf{X},\mathbf{W}),\mathbf{Y}]}_{\text{Empirical loss}} + \alpha \underbrace{\sum_{i=1}^{l}\sum_{j=1}^{l}\mathbf{A}_{ij}g(\mathbf{w}_i,\mathbf{w}_j)}_{\text{Prediction consistency}} + \beta \underbrace{\sum_{t=2}^{l}\|\mathbf{w}_t - \mathbf{B}\mathbf{w}_{t-1}\|_2^2}_{\text{Parameter smoothness}}
$$

$$
\underbrace{+ \gamma \|\mathbf{B} - \mathbf{I}\|_F^2 + \delta \sum_{i=1}^{l}\Omega(\mathbf{w}_i) + \epsilon \|\mathbf{A} - \mathbf{A}_0\|_F^2}_{\text{Regularizations}}
$$

$$
(3.20)
$$

where $\mathbf{W}$ is the parameter matrix of the prediction parameters for all the impacts as $\mathbf{W} = [\mathbf{w}_1, \mathbf{w}_2, \ldots, \mathbf{w}_l]$; $f(\mathbf{X},\mathbf{W})$ is the prediction function, which could be linear or nonlinear; $\mathcal{L}(\cdot)$ is the empirical loss between the predicted impacts and actual impacts; $g(\mathbf{w}_i,\mathbf{w}_j)$ characterizes the prediction consistency between the ith impact and the jth impact; $\|\mathbf{w}_t - \mathbf{B}\mathbf{w}_{t-1}\|_2^2$ instantiates the parameter smoothness; the rest terms are regularizations on $\mathbf{B}$, $\mathbf{W}$, and $\mathbf{A}$ respectively; $\mathbf{A}_0$ is the noisy prior knowledge about the impact/label relation; and α, β, γ, δ, and ϵ are the trade-off parameters.

Remarks: The second term models the prediction consistency. If the ith impact and the jth impact are similar, i.e., $\mathbf{A}_{ij}$ is a large positive number, then the function value $g(\cdot)$ that measures the consistency between the predicted values for the ith and jth impacts should be small. In addition, to address the challenge of inferring a good relation, we are learning a relation $\mathbf{A}$ in the model by regularizing it not to deviate too far from our prior knowledge of the impact relation ($\mathbf{A}_0$). The third term models the parameter smoothness by assuming a linear transition process between model parameters at two adjacent time steps. More specifically, the model parameter for time step t, $\mathbf{w}_t$ is close (in the form of Euclidean distance) to the model parameter for the last time step with some linear transition, $\mathbf{B}\mathbf{w}_{t-1}$. When $\mathbf{B}$ is an identity matrix, such smoothness will be a small Euclidean distance between the two parameters themselves. Our model will learn the model parameters $\mathbf{W}$, linear transition process $\mathbf{B}$, and the impacts relation $\mathbf{A}$ jointly.

iPath – *linear formulation:* in the linear case, the predictions are made by a linear weighted combination of the features, where the offset is absorbed by adding a constant to the feature. The linear model can be formulated as follows:

$$\min_{\mathbf{W},\mathbf{B},\mathbf{A}} \quad \|\mathbf{X}\mathbf{W} - \mathbf{Y}\|_F^2 + \alpha \sum_{i=1}^{l} \sum_{j=1}^{l} \mathbf{A}_{ij} \|\mathbf{X}\mathbf{w}_i - \mathbf{X}\mathbf{w}_j\|_2^2$$

$$+ \beta \sum_{t=2}^{l} \|\mathbf{w}_t - \mathbf{B}\mathbf{w}_{t-1}\|_2^2 + \gamma \|\mathbf{B} - \mathbf{I}\|_F^2 + \delta \sum_{i=1}^{l} \|\mathbf{w}_i\|_2^2 + \epsilon \|\mathbf{A} - \mathbf{A}_0\|_F^2$$

$$(3.21)$$

In this linear formulation, if $\mathbf{A}_{ij}$ is a large positive number, meaning the ith impact and the jth impact are similar, then the predicted values for the ith impact $\mathbf{X}\mathbf{w}_i$ and that for the jth impact $\mathbf{X}\mathbf{w}_j$ are consistent.

iPath – *nonlinear formulation:* in the nonlinear case, the predicted impact is no longer a linear combination of the features, but the linear combination of the *similarities* between the test sample and all the training samples, where the similarities are expressed in the kernel matrix $\mathbf{K}$. The (i, j)th entry of $\mathbf{K}$ can be computed as $\mathbf{K}(i, j) = \kappa(\mathbf{X}(i, :), \mathbf{X}(j, :))$, where $\kappa(\cdot, \cdot)$ is a kernel function that implicitly computes the inner product in the reproducing kernel Hilbert space (RKHS) [6]. The nonlinear model can be formulated as follows:

$$\min_{\mathbf{W},\mathbf{B},\mathbf{A}} \quad \|\mathbf{K}\mathbf{W} - \mathbf{Y}\|_F^2 + \alpha \sum_{i=1}^{l} \sum_{j=1}^{l} \mathbf{A}_{ij} \|\mathbf{K}\mathbf{w}_i - \mathbf{K}\mathbf{w}_j\|_2^2$$

$$+ \beta \sum_{t=2}^{l} \|\mathbf{w}_t - \mathbf{B}\mathbf{w}_{t-1}\|_2^2 + \gamma \|\mathbf{B} - \mathbf{I}\|_F^2 + \delta \sum_{i=1}^{l} \mathbf{w}_i' \mathbf{K}\mathbf{w}_i + \epsilon \|\mathbf{A} - \mathbf{A}_0\|_F^2.$$

$$(3.22)$$

From the objective function, we can see that if $\mathbf{A}_{ij}$ is a large positive number, meaning the ith impact and the jth impact are similar, then the predicted values for the ith impact $\mathbf{K}\mathbf{w}_i$ and that for the jth impact $\mathbf{K}\mathbf{w}_j$ are consistent.

***iPath* Optimization Solutions.** In this subsection, we introduce an effective alternating optimization strategy to solve *iPath*. Since the optimization for linear and nonlinear formulations are very similar, we will focus on the nonlinear case and omit the linear case (referred to as *iPath*-lin) due to space limitations. In nonlinear case, we need to solve Eq. (3.22), which involves the optimization for $\mathbf{W}$, $\mathbf{B}$, and $\mathbf{A}$. We apply an alternating strategy and each time optimize for one group of variables while fixing the others. The details are as follows:

#1. Optimize for W while others are fixed: when others are fixed, the objective function becomes

$$\min_{\mathbf{W}} \quad \|\mathbf{KW} - \mathbf{Y}\|_F^2 + \alpha \sum_{i=1}^{l} \sum_{j=1}^{l} \mathbf{A}_{ij} \|\mathbf{Kw}_i - \mathbf{Kw}_j\|_2^2$$

$$+ \beta \sum_{t=2}^{l} \|\mathbf{w}_t - \mathbf{Bw}_{t-1}\|_2^2 + \delta \sum_{i=1}^{l} \mathbf{w}_i' \mathbf{Kw}_i.$$

As it turns out, it has the following fixed-point solution:

$$vec(\mathbf{W}) = \mathbf{S}^{-1} vec(\mathbf{K}'\mathbf{Y}), \tag{3.23}$$

where $vec(\cdot)$ is the vectorization operation on a matrix by stacking the columns of a matrix into one column vector, and $\mathbf{S}$ is a block matrix composed of $l \times l$ blocks. The (i, j)th block of $\mathbf{S}$, $\mathbf{S}_{ij}$ can be written as follows:

$$\mathbf{S}_{ii} = \begin{cases} \left(1 + \alpha \sum_{j=1}^{l} \mathbf{A}_{ij}\right) \mathbf{K}'\mathbf{K} + \beta \mathbf{B}'\mathbf{B} + \delta \mathbf{K}, & \text{if } i = 1 \\ \left(1 + \alpha \sum_{j=1}^{l} \mathbf{A}_{ij}\right) \mathbf{K}'\mathbf{K} + \delta \mathbf{K}, & \text{if } i = l \\ \left(1 + \alpha \sum_{j=1}^{l} \mathbf{A}_{ij}\right) \mathbf{K}'\mathbf{K} + \beta(\mathbf{I} + \mathbf{B}'\mathbf{B}) + \delta \mathbf{K}, & \text{otherwise} \end{cases} \tag{3.24}$$

$$\mathbf{S}_{ij} = \begin{cases} -\alpha \mathbf{A}_{ij} \mathbf{K}'\mathbf{K} - \beta \mathbf{B}', & \text{if } i = j - 1 \\ -\alpha \mathbf{A}_{ij} \mathbf{K}'\mathbf{K} - \beta \mathbf{B}, & \text{if } i = j + 1 \\ -\alpha \mathbf{A}_{ij} \mathbf{K}'\mathbf{K}, & \text{otherwise} \end{cases} \tag{3.25}$$

#2. Optimize for B while others are fixed: when others are fixed, the objective function becomes

$$\min_{\mathbf{B}} \quad \beta \sum_{t=2}^{l} \|\mathbf{w}_t - \mathbf{Bw}_{t-1}\|_2^2 + \gamma \|\mathbf{B} - \mathbf{I}\|_F^2.$$

It has the following fixed-point solution:

$$\mathbf{B} = \left(\beta \sum_{t=2}^{l} \mathbf{w}_t \mathbf{w}_{t-1}' + \gamma \mathbf{I}\right) \left(\beta \sum_{t=2}^{l} \mathbf{w}_{t-1} \mathbf{w}_{t-1}' + \gamma \mathbf{I}\right)^{-1}. \tag{3.26}$$

#3. Optimize for A while others are fixed: when others are fixed, the objective function becomes

$$\min_{\mathbf{A}} \quad \alpha \sum_{i=1}^{l} \sum_{j=1}^{l} \mathbf{A}_{ij} \|\mathbf{Kw}_i - \mathbf{Kw}_j\|_2^2 + \epsilon \|\mathbf{A} - \mathbf{A}_0\|_F^2.$$

It has the following fixed-point solution:

$$\mathbf{A} = \mathbf{A}_0 - \mathbf{D}, \text{ where } \mathbf{D}_{ij} = \|\mathbf{Kw}_j - \mathbf{Kw}_i\|_2^2. \tag{3.27}$$

The optimization solution for the nonlinear model can be summarized as in Algorithm 3.

Algorithm 3: *iPath*-ker – forecasting the pathway to impact

Input: (1)feature matrix $\mathbf{X}$;
(2)impact matrix $\mathbf{Y}$;
(3)prior knowledge of the relation $\mathbf{A}_0$;
(4)balance parameters α, β, γ, δ and ϵ;
Output: model parameters $\mathbf{w}_i, i = 1, \ldots, l$

1 Initialize $\mathbf{W}$, $\mathbf{B}$ and $\mathbf{A}$;
2 Construct kernel matrix $\mathbf{K}$ from $\mathbf{X}$;
3 **while** *not converged* **do**
4 $\quad$ Update model parameters $\mathbf{W}$ by Eq. (3.23);
5 $\quad$ Update linear transition matrix $\mathbf{B}$ by Eq. (3.26);
6 $\quad$ Update impact relation $\mathbf{A}$ by Eq. (3.27);
7 **end**
8 Output model parameters $\mathbf{W}$.

3.2.3 Analysis and Comparisons

In this subsection, we will first analyze the complexity of the *iPath*, present some variants of it, and then provide a probabilistic interpretation for it, followed up by comparisons with some existing work.

Complexity Analysis. We summarize the time complexity of *iPath*-lin and *iPath*-ker in Theorem 3.8.

Theorem 3.8. *(Time Complexity).* iPath-*lin takes* $O(N \cdot (ndl^2 + d^3l^3))$ *time, and* iPath-*ker (Algorithm 3) takes* $O(N \cdot (n^3l^3 + n^2l^2))$ *time, where N is the number of iterations.*

Proof Omitted for brevity.   □

Remarks: In both *iPath*-lin and *iPath*-ker, the number of iterations is small in practice (typically in 5 to 10 iterations; see Section 3.2.4 for details). In *iPath*-lin, each iteration only takes linear time with respect to n. In *iPath*-ker, the major computational cost in each iteration is the inverse of a large matrix $\mathbf{S}$ in Eq. (3.23), which is of size nl by nl. One way to speed up is by low-rank approximation on such a large matrix. A top-r eigen-decomposition on $\mathbf{S}$ takes $O(n^2l^2r)$, where r is the rank. Then the inverse will become the multiplication of the eigenvector matrices and the inverse of the eigenvalue diagonal matrix, which is very easy to compute. Another way to speed up is to filter out those unpromising training samples. When new training samples arrive, we can first treat them as test samples and make predictions on them using the existing trained model. Those samples whose prediction error is smaller than a specified threshold will be discarded. In this way, the size of matrix $\mathbf{S}$ will also be reduced.

Variants. The *iPath* model is comprehensive in handling both the *prediction consistency* as well as the *parameter smoothness*. In the case when one or both aspects are not necessary for the prediction in some applications, our model can be naturally adapted to accommodate such special cases. In this subsection, we will discuss two of the variants.

Variant #1: known relation. If the relation among the impacts are accurately known a priori, we can fix the relation in the model instead of learning it. We can do this by setting ϵ to 0 and plug in the known relation matrix $\mathbf{A}$. In the optimization solution, we only need to optimize for $\mathbf{W}$ and $\mathbf{B}$ in this variant.

Variant #2: known relation without parameter smoothness. In some cases, the parameter smoothness might not hold and we do not need to consider the linear transition process between adjacent parameters. We can set β, γ, and ϵ to 0. This degenerates to the *iBall* model developed in Section 3.1. It is a special case of our *iPath* model without considering parameter smoothness and with known relation. Another difference is that *iPath* imposes the prediction consistency in the output space, instead of in the parameter space.

Probabilistic Interpretation. In this subsection, we will provide a probabilistic interpretation for *iPath*. Our algorithm can be represented by the graphical model shown in Figure 3.13. The shaded nodes $\mathbf{Y}_i$ are the impacts observed, and in the linear formulation they are linear combination of the features with a multivariate Gaussian noise:

$$\mathbf{Y}_i = \mathbf{X}\mathbf{w}_i + \mathbf{e}$$
$$\mathbf{e} \sim \mathcal{N}(\mathbf{0}, \sigma_y^2 \mathbf{I})$$
$$\mathbf{Y}_i | \mathbf{w}_i \sim \mathcal{N}(\mathbf{X}\mathbf{w}_i, \sigma_y^2 \mathbf{I}). \tag{3.28}$$

For the model parameters $\mathbf{w}_t$, we assume it is a linear transition of the parameter for the last time step $\mathbf{w}_{t-1}$, with a multivariate Gaussian noise:

$$\mathbf{w}_t = \mathbf{B}\mathbf{w}_{t-1} + \epsilon$$
$$\epsilon \sim \mathcal{N}(\mathbf{0}, \sigma_w^2 \mathbf{I})$$
$$\mathbf{w}_t | \mathbf{w}_{t-1} \sim \mathcal{N}(\mathbf{B}\mathbf{w}_{t-1}, \sigma_w^2 \mathbf{I}). \tag{3.29}$$

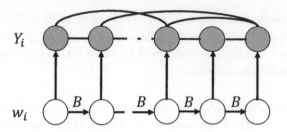

Figure 3.13 Graphical model representation of *iPath*.

The relation among the impacts is represented as an undirected graph of different impacts Y_i, with $\mathbf{A}$ as the weight matrix. If the ith impact $\mathbf{Y}_i$ and the jth impact $\mathbf{Y}_j$ are similar to each other, then the (i, j)th entry $\mathbf{A}_{ij}$ is a large positive number. To define the distribution over this undirected graph of impacts, we refer to Hammersley–Clifford theorem in Markov Random Field (MRF) [9] and express it in terms of an energy function E and clique potentials defined on maximal cliques of the undirected graph as

$$p(\mathbf{Y}) = \frac{1}{Z} \exp(-E(\mathbf{Y})), \text{where } E(\mathbf{Y}) = \sum_{c \in C} \Phi_c(\mathbf{Y}_c). \qquad (3.30)$$

Here C is the set of maximal cliques of the impact graph, Φ_c is a nonnegative function defined on the random variables in the clique, and Z is the partition function to ensure that the distribution sums to 1. If we only consider the potentials defined on the edge of the graph, as follows:

$$\Phi_{e=(\mathbf{Y}_i, \mathbf{Y}_j)} = \mathbf{A}_{ij} \|\mathbf{Y}_i - \mathbf{Y}_j\|_2^2 = \mathbf{A}_{ij} \|\mathbf{X}\mathbf{w}_i - \mathbf{X}\mathbf{w}_j\|_2^2 \qquad (3.31)$$

then, the distribution over the label graph is

$$p(\mathbf{Y}) = \frac{1}{Z} \exp\left(-\sum_{i=1}^{l} \sum_{j=1}^{l} \mathbf{A}_{ij} \|\mathbf{X}\mathbf{w}_i - \mathbf{X}\mathbf{w}_j\|_2^2\right). \qquad (3.32)$$

With these distributions defined, we aim to maximize the joint distribution described as follows:

$$\arg \max_{\mathbf{Y}, \mathbf{X}, \mathbf{W}} = p(\mathbf{w}_1) \prod_{t=2}^{l} p(\mathbf{w}_t | \mathbf{w}_{t-1}) \prod_{i=1}^{l} p(\mathbf{Y}_i | \mathbf{w}_i) p(\mathbf{Y}), \qquad (3.33)$$

where we assume $p(\mathbf{w}_1) \sim \mathcal{N}(\mathbf{0}, \sigma_1^2 \mathbf{I})$. If we maximize the preceding joint distribution, we can obtain the empirical loss, prediction consistency, and parameter smoothness terms in *iPath*.

Comparison with Existing Work. As we point out in Variants, *iBall* is a special case of our *iPath* model. The idea of *iBall* is to leverage the relation among impacts in the parameter space, i.e., if Y_i and Y_j are similar, then the parameters w_i for predicting Y_i and w_j for predicting Y_j are similar. The multi-label relationship learning *MLRL* method [115] also exploits such relation in the parameter space via maximum a posterior inference by assuming that W follows a matrix-variate normal distribution, but ignores the parameter smoothness. Our model *iPath* instead applies such relation in the output space and defines a linear transition process between two parameters at adjacent time steps.

3.2.4 Empirical Evaluations

In this subsection, we empirically evaluate the effectiveness of our algorithms for forecasting the pathway to impact.

Datasets To evaluate the performance of the *iPath* algorithms, we conduct experiments on the citation network dataset provided by AMiner [86],[3] which is a rich dataset for bibliography network analysis and mining. The dataset contains information of 2,243,976 papers, 1,274,360 authors, and 8,882 computer science venues. The information about a paper includes its title, authors, references, venue, and publication year. The papers date from the year 1936 to the year 2013. From these, we can extract the number of citations each paper/author obtains in each year ever since its publication year.

Experiment Setup. Our primary task is to forecast a paper's yearly citations from year six to year 15 after its publication, with the first five years' citation history observed. To ensure the papers are at least 15 years old, we only keep papers published between year 1960 and 1998. We process the author data in a similar way and keep those whose research career begins (when they publish the first paper) between year 1960 and 1990. For each scholarly entity (paper and author), we represent it as a five-dimensional feature vector, which is the yearly citation counts in the first five years. To evaluate our algorithm, we sort the scholarly entities by their starting year (e.g., publication year), train the model in the older entities, and always test on the latest ones. In the experiment, we incrementally add the training samples by this chronological order, and for the paper impact pathway prediction, we reserve the latest 10% samples as the

---

[3] https://aminer.org/billboard/citation.

test set; and for the author impact pathway prediction, we reserve the latest 6% samples as the test set.

RMSE between the actual citations and the predicted ones is used as our accuracy evaluation. All the parameters, including the Gaussian kernel's bandwidth, are chosen through a grid search. All the experiments are run on a Windows machine with four 3.5GHz Intel Cores and 256GB RAM.

Results and Analysis

1. Paper and author impact pathway prediction performance. We compare the prediction accuracy of the following methods:

- *ind-linear:* train a liner ridge regression model for the impact in each year separately.
- *ind-kernel:* train a kernel ridge regression model for the impact in each year separately.
- *MTL-robust:* treat predicting the impact in each year as a task and apply the robust multitask learning algorithm proposed in [23].
- *MLRL:* apply the multilabel learning method proposed in [115], where model parameters are assumed to conform matrix-variate normal distribution.
- *iBall-linear:* jointly learn the linear regression models as in.
- *iBall-kernel:* jointly learn the kernel ridge regression models as in.
- *iPath-lin:* our linear predictive model with prediction consistency and parameter smoothness.
- *iPath-ker:* our nonlinear predictive model with prediction consistency and parameter smoothness.

The RMSE results of the preceding methods for predicting the impact pathway of both research papers and authors are in Figures 3.14 and 3.15, respectively. We can make the following observations: (1) the nonlinear methods (ind-kernel, *iBall-kernel*, and *iPath*-ker) generally perform better than the linear methods (ind-linear, MTL-robust, MLRL, *iBall-linear*, and *iPath*-lin), which reflects that the impacts could be oversimplified by a linear combination of the features. (2) Among the linear methods, we find that MTL-robust does not help improve the prediction over ind-linear. The possible reason is that MTL-robust has the assumption that the model parameters admit a low-rank and sparse component, which might not be true in our case. The *iBall-linear* performs better than ind-linear, which shows that the impact relation exploitation can indeed help the forecasting. (3) Furthermore, learning a good relation can further boost the performance, as MLRL has lower RMSE than *iBall-linear*. Our *iPath*-lin performs the best among all the linear models,

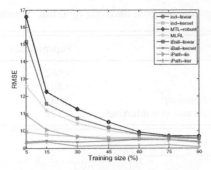

Figure 3.14 RMSE comparison of all the methods for paper impact pathway prediction.

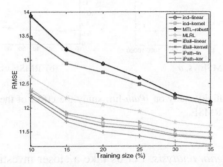

Figure 3.15 RMSE comparison of all the methods for author impact pathway prediction.

by integrating prediction consistency and parameter smoothness. It is even comparable with ind-kernel when training size is greater than 30% for the paper impact pathway prediction. (4) We can make the similar observation in the nonlinear case, as our *iPath*-ker performs better than *iBall*-ker, which itself is better than ind-kernel.

To evaluate the statistical significance, we perform a *t*-test between *iPath*-ker and the best competitor *iBall-kernel* with 30% of the training papers in the paper impact pathway prediction, and the *p*-value is 0.01, which suggests the significance of the improvement.

2. Sensitivity analysis. To investigate parameter sensitivity, we perform parametric studies with the two most important parameters in *iPath*, namely, α that controls the importance of prediction consistency, and β that controls the importance of parameter smoothness. Figure 3.16 shows that the model is stable in a large range of both parameter spaces.

Table 3.4 *Performance gain analysis of* iPath. *Smaller is better.*

RMSE	Paper impact	Author impact
Basic form	9.602	11.608
Basic form + relation	9.507	11.548
Basic form + relation + transition	9.335	11.489
Basic form + relation + transition + inferring	9.171	11.391

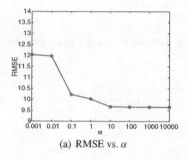

(a) RMSE vs. α

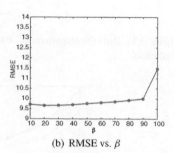

(b) RMSE vs. β

Figure 3.16 Sensitivity study on *iPath*-lin: study the effect of the parameters α and β in terms of RMSE.

3. Performance gain analysis. Let us take a closer investigation on where the performance gain of the *iPath* stems from. As we mentioned earlier, *iPath* integrates both *prediction consistency* and *parameter smoothness*. We analyze how they contribute to the performance gain. Table 3.4 shows the results of *iPath*-ker methods on both the paper (60% training) and author (25% training) impact pathway prediction. "Basic form" sets α, β, γ, and ϵ all to zero, essentially the ind-kernel method; "Basic form + relation" incorporates the relations among impacts; "Basic form + relation + transition" incorporates a known relation and the linear transition in the parameter space; "Basic form + relation + transition + inferring" considers them all with an inferred relation. From the table, we can see that as we incrementally incorporate the elements, the RMSE decreases gradually, which confirms that all these elements are beneficial in improving the prediction performance.

4. Robustness to noise in label graph. As *iPath* can learn a good relation for the prediction from our prior knowledge about the relation, we want to see how robust it is with regard to the noise level in our prior knowledge. To this end, we input the same relation matrix with noise to *iBall* (the matrix $\mathbf{A}$) and *iPath* (the matrix $\mathbf{A}_0$). The noise is added to each entry of the label matrix with value $0.1 \times$ NoiseLevel $\times$ rand, where rand is a random number from 0 to 1.

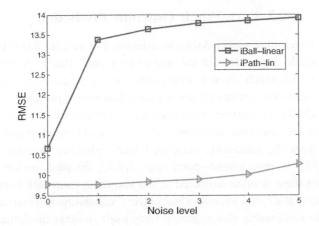

Figure 3.17 Robustness to noise on the label graph.

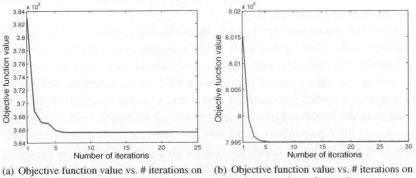

(a) Objective function value vs. # iterations on   (b) Objective function value vs. # iterations on
paper impact pathway forecasting.   author impact pathway forecasting.

Figure 3.18 Convergence analysis of *iPath*.

Figure 3.17 shows the RMSE results of both *iBall* and *iPath* under different noise levels for paper impact pathway prediction with 30% training samples. We observe a sharp performance drop of *iBall* when noise is added. In contrast, the *iPath* degenerates gradually with the noise level. This shows that *iPath* can learn a relatively good relation even if our prior knowledge is noisy.

5. Convergence analysis. To see how fast the *iPath* converges in practice, we plot the objective function value versus the number of iterations for both paper (15% training samples) and author (10% training samples) impact pathway forecasting as in Figure 3.18. We observe that *iPath* converges after five to 10 iterations.

3.3 Part–Whole Outcome Prediction

The great Greek philosopher Aristotle articulated more than 2,000 years ago that "the whole is greater than the sum of its parts." This is probably most evident in *teams*, which, through appropriate synergy, promise a collective outcome (i.e., team performance) that is superior than the simple addition of what each individual team member could achieve (i.e., individual productivity). For example, in the scientific community, the new breakthrough is increasingly resulting from the teamwork, compared with individual researcher's sole endevor [98]; in professional sports (e.g., NBA), the peak performance of a grass-root team is often attributed to the harmonic teamwork between the team players rather than the individual players' capability. Beyond teams, the *part–whole* relationship also routinely finds itself in other disciplines, ranging from crowdsourcing (e.g., community-based question answering [CQA] sites [103]), collective decision-making in an autonomous system (e.g., a self-orchestrated swarm of drones[4]), to reliability assessment of a networked system of components [22, 106].

From the algorithmic perspective, an interesting problem is to predict the outcome of the whole and/or parts [43]. In organizational teams, it is critical to appraise the individual performance, its contribution to the team outcome, as well as the team's overall performance [65]. In the emerging field of the "science of science," the dream of being able to predict breakthroughs, e.g., predicting the likelihood of a researcher making disruptive contributions and foreseeing the future impact of her research products (e.g., manuscripts, proposals, system prototypes), pervades almost all aspects of modern science [24]. In CQA sites, predicting the long-term impact of a question (*whole*) and its associated answers (*parts*) enables users to spot valuable questions and answers at an early stage. Despite much progress having been made, the existing work either develops separate models for predicting the outcome of whole and parts without explicitly utilizing the part–whole relationship [62], or implicitly assumes the outcome of the whole is a *linear* sum of the outcome of the parts [103], which might oversimplify the complicated part–whole relationships (e.g., nonlinearity).

The key to address these limitations largely lies in the answers to the following questions, i.e., to what extent are the outcome of parts (e.g., individual productivity) and that of the whole (e.g., team performance) correlated, beyond the existing linear, independency assumption? How can we leverage such potentially nonlinear and interdependent "coupling" effect to mutually improve the prediction of the outcome of the whole and parts collectively?

---

[4] CBS *60 Minutes* report: http://www.cbsnews.com/news/60-minutes-autonomous-drones-set-to-revolutionize-military-technology/.

This is exactly the focus of this work, which is highly challenging for the following reasons. First (*Modeling Challenge*), the relationship between the parts outcome and whole outcome might be complicated, beyond the simple addition or linear combination. For example, the authors in [100] empirically identified a nonlinear correlation between the impacts of questions and the associated answers, that is, the impact of a question is much more strongly correlated with that of the *best* answer it receives, compared to the *average* impact of its associated answers. However, the question of how to leverage such a nonlinear relationship between the parts and whole outcome has largely remained open. For teams, the team performance might be mainly dominated by a few top-performing team members, and/or be hindered by one or more struggling team members (i.e., the classic Wooden Bucket Theory, which says that "A bucket (whole) can only fill with the volume of water the shortest plank (parts) allows"). Moreover, the composing parts of the whole might not be independent with each other. In a networked system, the composing parts are connected with each other via an underlying network. Such part–part interdependency could have a profound impact on both the part outcome correlation as well as each part's contribution to the whole outcome. How can we mathematically encode the nonlinear part–whole relationship as well as part–part interdependency? Second (*Algorithmic Challenge*), the complicated part–whole relationship (i.e., nonlinearity and interdependency) also poses an algorithmic challenge, as it will inevitably increase the complexity of the corresponding optimization problem. How can we develop scalable algorithms whose theoretic properties are well understood (e.g., the convergence, the optimality, and the complexity)?

To address these challenges, in this book, we devise a joint predictive model named PAROLE to simultaneously and mutually predict the part and whole outcomes. First, *model generality*: our model is flexible in admitting a variety of linear as well as nonlinear relationships between the parts and whole outcomes, including *maximum aggregation, linear aggregation, sparse aggregation, ordered sparse aggregation*, and *robust aggregation*. Moreover, it is able to characterize part–part interdependency via a graph-based regularization, which encourages the tightly connected parts to share similar outcomes as well as have similar effect on the whole outcome. Second, *algorithm efficacy*: we present an effective and efficient block coordinate descent optimization algorithm, which converges to the coordinatewise optimum with a linear complexity. The main contributions of this section can be summarized as follows:

- **Models.** We devise a joint predictive model (PAROLE) that is able to admit a variety of linear as well as nonlinear part–whole relationships and encode the part–part interdependency.

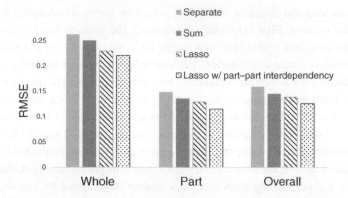

Figure 3.19 Prediction error comparison on *Movie* dataset. Lower is better. The right two bars are our methods, which encode the nonlinear part–whole relationship and the nonlinearity with part–part interdependency respectively.

- **Algorithms and analysis.** We present an effective and efficient block coordinate descent optimization algorithm that converges to the coordinatewise optimum with a linear complexity in both time and space.
- **Empirical evaluations.** We conduct extensive empirical studies on several real-world datasets and demonstrate that PAROLE achieves consistent prediction performance improvement and scales linearly. See Figure 3.19 for some sampling results.

3.3.1 Problem Definition

The main symbols are summarized in Table 3.5. We use bold capital letters (e.g., $\mathbf{A}$) for matrices and bold lowercase letters (e.g., $\mathbf{w}$) for vectors. We index the elements in a matrix using a convention similar to Matlab, e.g., $\mathbf{A}(:,j)$ is the jth column of $\mathbf{A}$, etc. The vector obtained by sorting the components in nonincreasing order of $\mathbf{x}$ is denoted by $\mathbf{x}_\downarrow$. Such sorting operation can be defined by a permutation matrix $\mathbf{P_x}$, i.e., $\mathbf{P_x}\mathbf{x} = \mathbf{x}_\downarrow$. We use $\mathcal{K}_{m+}$ to denote the *monotone nonnegative cone*, i.e., $\mathcal{K}_{m+} = \{\mathbf{x} \in \mathbb{R}^n : x_1 \geq x_2 \geq \ldots x_n \geq 0\} \subset \mathbb{R}^n_+$. Similarly, we use $\mathcal{K}_m$ for the monotone cone.

We consider predicting the outcome for both the whole and their composing parts. Figure 3.20 presents an illustrative example, which aims to predict the popularity (e.g., Facebook likes) of a particular movie (*whole*) and the popularity of the participating actors/actresses (*parts*). We denote the set of whole entities by $O = \{o_1, o_2, \ldots, o_{n_o}\}$, and denote the set of part entities

Table 3.5 *Symbols for PAROLE.*

Symbols	Definition
$\mathbf{F}^o, \mathbf{F}^p$	Feature matrices for whole and part entities
$\mathbf{y}^o, \mathbf{y}^p$	Impact vectors for whole and part entities
[3pt] $O = \{o_1, o_2, \ldots, o_{n_o}\}$	Set of whole entities
$\mathcal{P} = \{p_1, p_2, \ldots, p_{n_p}\}$	Set of part entities
$\phi(\cdot)$	Whole to parts mapping function
G^p	Network connectivity among part entities
a_j^i	Contribution of part p_j to whole o_i
n_o / n_p	Number of whole/part entities
[3pt]Agg$(\cdot)$	Function that aggregates parts outcome
e_i	Predicted whole outcome using whole feature vs. predicted whole outcome using aggregated parts outcome

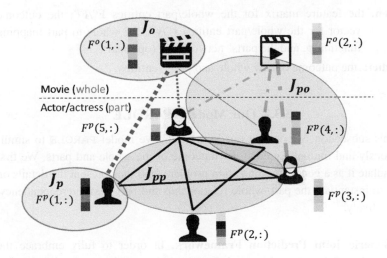

Figure 3.20 An illustrative example of part-whole outcome prediction where movies are the whole entities and the actors/actresses are the part entities. The four shadowed ellipses correspond to the key subobjectives in our PAROLE model (Eq. (3.34)).

hy $\mathcal{P} = \{p_1, p_2, \ldots, p_{n_p}\}$, where n_o and n_p are the number of the whole and parts, respectively. To specify the part–whole associations, we also define a mapping function ϕ that maps a whole entity to the set of its composing parts, e.g., $\phi(o_i) = \{p_{i_1}, p_{i_2}, \ldots, p_{i_{n_i}}\}$ (i.e., the edges between a movie and actors/actresses in Figure 3.20). Note that the two sets $\phi(o_i)$ and $\phi(o_j)$ might have overlap. In the example of movies as whole entities, one actor could participate in multiple movies. Let $\mathbf{F}^o$ be the feature matrix for the whole entities, where the ith row $\mathbf{F}^o(i, :)$ is the feature vector for the ith whole entity. Similarly, let $\mathbf{F}^p$ be the feature matrix for the part entities, where the jth row $\mathbf{F}^p(j, :)$ is the feature vector for the jth part entity. The outcome vector of the whole entities is denoted as $\mathbf{y}^o$, and the outcome vector of the part entities is denoted as $\mathbf{y}^p$. In addition, we might also observe a network connectivity among the part entities, denoted as G^p. In the movie example, the network G^p could be the collaboration network among the actors/actresses (the connections among the actors/actresses in Figure 3.20).

With the preceding notations, we formally define our PART–WHOLE OUT-COME PREDICTION problem as follows:

Problem 3.9   PART–WHOLE OUTCOME PREDICTION

Given: the feature matrix for the whole/part entities $\mathbf{F}^o/\mathbf{F}^p$, the outcome vector for the whole/part entities $\mathbf{y}^o/\mathbf{y}^p$, the whole to part mapping function ϕ, and the parts' network G^p (optional);

Predict: the outcome of new whole and parts' entities.

3.3.2 Our Model – PAROLE

In this subsection, we present our joint predictive model PAROLE to simultaneously and mutually predict the outcome of the whole and parts. We first formulate it as a generic optimization problem, and then present the details on how to instantiate the part–whole relationship and part–part interdependency, respectively.

A Generic Joint Prediction Framework. In order to fully embrace the complexity of the part–whole and part–part relationship, our joint predictive model should meet the following desiderata.

First (*part–whole relationship*), the outcome of the whole and that of the parts might be strongly correlated with each other. For example, the team outcome is usually a collective effort of the team members. Consequently, the team performance is likely to be correlated/coupled with each individual's productivity, which might be beyond a simple linear correlation. This is because a few top-performing team members might dominate the overall team performance, or conversely, a few struggling team members might drag down the performance of the entire team. Likewise, in the scientific community, a scientist's reputation is generally built by one or a few of her highest-impact work. Our joint predictive model should have the capability to encode such nonlinear part–whole relationships, so that the prediction of the parts outcome and that of the whole can mutually benefit from each other.

Second (*part–part interdependency*), the composing parts of a whole entity might be interdependent/interconnected via an underlying network, e.g., the collaboration network among the actors/actresses. The part–part interdependency could have a profound impact on the part–whole outcome prediction performance. That is, not only might the closely connected parts have similar effect on the whole outcome, but also these parts are very likely to share similar outcomes between themselves. Therefore, it is desirable to encode the part–part interdependency in the joint model to boost the prediction performance.

With these design objectives in mind, we present a generic framework for the joint predictive model as follows:

$$
\min_{\mathbf{w}^o, \mathbf{w}^p} \mathcal{J}
$$

$$
= \underbrace{\frac{1}{n_o} \sum_{i=1}^{n_o} \mathcal{L}[f(\mathbf{F}^o(i, :), \mathbf{w}^o), \mathbf{y}^o(i))]}_{\mathcal{J}_o:\ \text{predictive model for whole entities}} + \underbrace{\frac{1}{n_p} \sum_{i=1}^{n_p} \mathcal{L}[f(\mathbf{F}^p(i, :), \mathbf{w}^p), \mathbf{y}^p(i))]}_{\mathcal{J}_p:\ \text{predictive model for part entities}}
$$

$$
+ \underbrace{\frac{\alpha}{n_o} \sum_{i=1}^{n_o} h(f(\mathbf{F}^o(i, :), \mathbf{w}^o), \mathrm{Agg}(\phi(o_i)))}_{\mathcal{J}_{po}:\ \text{part–whole relationship}}
$$

$$
+ \underbrace{\frac{\beta}{n_p} \sum_{i=1}^{n_p} \sum_{j=1}^{n_p} G_{ij}^p g(f(\mathbf{F}^p(i, :), \mathbf{w}^p), f(\mathbf{F}^p(j, :), \mathbf{w}^p))}_{\mathcal{J}_{pp}:\ \text{part–part interdependency}} + \underbrace{\gamma(\Omega(\mathbf{w}^o) + \Omega(\mathbf{w}^p))}_{\mathcal{J}_r:\ \text{parameter regularizer}}
$$

$$
(3.34)
$$

where the objective function is a sum of five subobjective functions. The first two subobjectives $\mathcal{J}_o$ and $\mathcal{J}_p$ (the two most lightly shadowed ellipses in Figure 3.20) minimize the training loss for whole and parts outcome predictions, where $f(\cdot, \cdot)$ is the prediction function parameterized by $\mathbf{w}^o$ and $\mathbf{w}^p$. The prediction function could be either linear or nonlinear; and $\mathcal{L}(\cdot)$ is a loss function, e.g., squared loss for regression or logistic loss for classification. The core of the objective function is the third term $\mathcal{J}_{po}$ (the medium shadowed ellipse in Figure 3.20) and the fourth term $\mathcal{J}_{pp}$ (the darkest shadowed ellipse in Figure 3.20). $\mathcal{J}_{po}$ characterizes the part–whole relationship, where $\mathrm{Agg}(\cdot)$ is a function that aggregates the predicted outcomes of all the composing parts for the whole to a single outcome, e.g., maximum, summation/mean, or more complicated aggregations; and $h(\cdot)$ function measures the correlation between the predicted whole outcome and the aggregated predicted parts outcome. In $\mathcal{J}_{pp}$, the function $g(\cdot)$ characterizes the relationship of the predicted outcomes of parts i and j based on their connectivity G_{ij}^p, such that tightly connected parts would share similar outcomes. Lastly, $\mathcal{J}_r$ regularizes $\mathbf{w}^o$ and $\mathbf{w}^p$ to prevent overfitting. The regularization parameters α, β, and γ are used to balance the relative importance of each aspect.

Remarks: Depending on the specific choices of the aggregation function $\text{Agg}(\cdot)$ and the $h(\cdot)$ function, the model in Eq. (3.34) is able to admit a variety of part–whole relationships, which we elaborate in the following subsections.

Modeling Part–Whole Relationships.
Overview. In this subsection, we give the instantiations for a variety of part–whole relationships. For each whole entity o_i, define e_i as follows:

$$e_i = \mathbf{F}^o(i, :)\mathbf{w}^o - \text{Agg}(o_i) \tag{3.35}$$

which measures the difference between the predicted whole outcome using whole features (i.e., $\mathbf{F}^o(i, :)\mathbf{w}^o$) and predicted whole outcome using aggregated parts outcome (i.e., $\text{Agg}(o_i)$). Our model will be able to characterize a variety of part–whole relationships, by using (a) different aggregation functions $\text{Agg}(\cdot)$ with augmented regularizations; and (b) different loss functions on e_i (e.g., squared loss or robust estimator).

Maximum aggregation. Let us first consider using maximum as the aggregation function, which can model the correlation between the whole outcome and the maximum parts outcome. Given that the max function is not differentiable, we approximate it with a differentiable function that will largely facilitate the optimization process. In detail, we use the smooth "soft" maximum function, which was first used in economic literature for consumer choice [81]: $\max(x_1, x_2, \ldots, x_n) \approx \ln(\exp(x_1) + \exp(x_2) + \cdots + \exp(x_n))$, where the maximum is approximated by summing up the exponential of each item followed by a logarithm. With this, we define the maximum aggregation function as follows:

$$\text{Agg}(o_i) = \ln\left(\sum_{j \in \phi(o_i)} \exp(\mathbf{F}^p(j, :)\mathbf{w}^p)\right), \tag{3.36}$$

which approximates the maximum predicted parts outcome. The part–whole relationship with maximum aggregation can be formulated as follows:

$$\mathcal{J}_{po} = \frac{\alpha}{2n_o} \sum_{i=1}^{n_o} e_i^2 \tag{3.37}$$

where we use the squared loss to measure the difference between the predicted whole outcome and the predicted approximated maximum parts outcome.

For the remaining part–whole relationships, we instantiate $\text{Agg}(o_i)$ using a linear function as follows:

$$\text{Agg}(o_i) = \sum_{j \in \phi(o_i)} a_j^i \mathbf{F}^P(j, :) \mathbf{w}^P, \tag{3.38}$$

where each a_j^i is the weight of a particular part j's contribution to the whole o_i's outcome. Defining $\mathbf{a}_i$ as the vector whose components are a_j^i, $j \in \phi(o_i)$ and by imposing (i) different loss functions on e_i, and/or (ii) different norms on $\mathbf{a}_i$, we can model either linear or nonlinear part–whole relationships.

Linear aggregation. In this scenario, the whole outcome is a weighted linear combination of the parts outcome, where the weights determine each individual part's contribution to the whole outcome. The intuition of linear aggregation is that, in contributing to the final whole outcome, some parts play more important roles than the others. This part–whole relationship can be formulated as follows:

$$\mathcal{J}_{po} = \frac{\alpha}{2n_o} \sum_{i=1}^{n_o} e_i^2, \tag{3.39}$$

where we use the squared loss to measure the difference between the whole outcome and the aggregated parts outcome.

Remarks: this formulation generalizes several special part–whole relationships. The expression that "the whole is the sum of its parts" is a special case of Eq. (3.39) where various a_j^i is 1, which we refer to as *Sum* in the empirical study. The average coupling formulated in [103] is also its special case with $a_j^i = \frac{1}{|o_i|}$. Instead of fixing the weights, Eq. (3.39) allows the model to learn to what extent each part contributes to the prediction of the whole outcome. Nonetheless, in all these variants, we have assumed that the part outcomes always have a *linear* effect on the whole outcome.

Sparse aggregation. The previous linear aggregation assumes that each part would contribute to the whole outcome, which might not be the case as some parts have little or no effect on the whole outcome. This scenario can be seen in large teams, where the team performance could be primarily determined by a few members, who could either make or break the team performance. To encourage such a sparse selection among the composing parts of a whole entity, a natural choice is to introduce the l_1 norm on the vector $\mathbf{a}_i$ [88]:

$$\mathcal{J}_{po} = \frac{\alpha}{n_o} \sum_{i=1}^{n_o} \left(\frac{1}{2} e_i^2 + \lambda |\mathbf{a}_i|_1 \right), \tag{3.40}$$

where the l_1 norm can shrink some part contributions to exactly zero and the parameter λ controls the degree of sparsity.

Ordered sparse aggregation. In some cases, the team performance (i.e., the whole outcome) is determined by not only a few key members, but also the structural hierarchy between such key members within the organization. To model such parts performance ranking in addition to the sparse selection, we adopt the ordered weighted l_1 (OWL) norm [111] that is able to give more weight to those parts with bigger effect on the whole outcome. Such part–whole relationship can be formulated as follows:

$$\mathcal{J}_{po} = \frac{\alpha}{n_o} \sum_{i=1}^{n_o} \left(\frac{1}{2}e_i^2 + \lambda\Omega_{\mathbf{w}}(\mathbf{a}_i) \right), \tag{3.41}$$

where $\Omega_{\mathbf{w}}(\mathbf{x}) = \sum_{i=1}^{n} |x|_{[i]}w_i = \mathbf{w}^T |\mathbf{x}|_{\downarrow}$ is the ordered weighted l_1 norm, where $|x|_{[i]}$ is the ith largest component of the vector $|\mathbf{x}|$ and $\mathbf{w} \in \mathcal{K}_{m+}$ is a vector of nonincreasing nonnegative weights.

Robust aggregation. In all the preceding formulations, we model the difference between the whole outcome and the aggregated parts outcome using squared loss, which is prone to outlying parts/wholes. To address this issue, we employ robust regression models [53] to reduce the effect of outliers as follows:

$$\mathcal{J}_{po} = \frac{\alpha}{n_o} \sum_{i=1}^{n_o} \rho(e_i), \tag{3.42}$$

where $\rho(\cdot)$ is a nonnegative and symmetric function that gives the contribution of each residual e_i to the objective function. In this work, we consider two robust estimators, namely Huber and Bisquare estimators, as follows:

Method \ Case	$|e| \leq t$	$|e| > t$
Huber $\rho_H(e)$	$\frac{1}{2}e^2$	$t|e| - \frac{1}{2}t^2$
Bisquare $\rho_B(e)$	$\frac{t^2}{6}\left\{1 - [1 - (\frac{e}{t})^2]^3\right\}$	$\frac{t^2}{6}$

where the value t is a tuning constant. Smaller t values have more resistance to outliers.

Modeling Part–Part Interdependency. As mentioned in Section 3.3.2, the part–part interdependency, if it exists, can play two roles in the part–whole outcome predictions, i.e., closely connected parts would (a) have similar effect on the whole outcome and (b) share similar part outcomes between themselves.

A. The effect on the whole outcome: the closely connected parts might have similar impact on the whole outcome. It turns out we can use the same method to model such a part–part effect for various aggregation methods. Let us take *sparse aggregation* as an example and instantiate the term $\mathcal{J}_{po}$ in Eq. (3.34) as follows:

$$\mathcal{J}_{po} = \frac{\alpha}{n_o} \sum_{i=1}^{n_o} \left[\frac{1}{2} e_i^2 + \lambda |\mathbf{a}_i|_1 + \frac{1}{2} \sum_{k,l \in \phi(o_i)} G_{kl}^p (a_k^i - a_l^i)^2 \right], \tag{3.43}$$

where if the two parts k and l of o_i are tightly connected, i.e., $G_{k,l}^p$ is large, then the difference between their impacts on the whole outcome, a_k^i and a_l^i, is small.

B. The effect on the parts' outcomes: the tightly connected parts might share similar outcomes themselves. Such parts outcome similarity can be instantiated by a graph regularization as follows:

$$\mathcal{J}_{pp} = \frac{\beta}{2n_p} \sum_{i=1}^{n_p} \sum_{j=1}^{n_p} G_{ij}^p (\mathbf{F}^p(i, :) \mathbf{w}^p - \mathbf{F}^p(j, :) \mathbf{w}^p)^2, \tag{3.44}$$

where two tightly connected parts i and j with large $G_{k,l}^p$ are encouraged to be closer to each other in the output space, i.e., with similar predicted outcomes.

3.3.3 Optimization Algorithm

In this subsection, we present an effective and efficient block coordinate descent optimization algorithm to solve the joint prediction framework in Eq. (3.34), followed by the convergence and complexity analysis

Block Coordinate Descent Algorithm. The Eq. (3.34) is general, being able to admit a variety of different separate models ($\mathcal{J}_o$ and $\mathcal{J}_p$) as well as part–whole relationship ($\mathcal{J}_{po}$). Let us first present our algorithm to solve a specific instance of Eq. (3.34) by instantiating it using linear predictive functions, squared loss, and sparse aggregation as follows:

$$
\min_{\mathbf{w}^o, \mathbf{w}^p} \frac{1}{2n_o} \sum_{i=1}^{n_o} (\mathbf{F}^o(i,:)\mathbf{w}^o - \mathbf{y}^o(i))^2 + \frac{1}{2n_p} \sum_{i=1}^{n_p} ((\mathbf{F}^p(i,:)\mathbf{w}^p - \mathbf{y}^p(i))^2
$$

$$
+ \frac{\beta}{2n_p} \sum_{i=1}^{n_p} \sum_{j=1}^{n_p} G_{ij}^p (\mathbf{F}^p(i,:)\mathbf{w}^p - \mathbf{F}^p(j,:)\mathbf{w}^p)^2 + \frac{\gamma}{2}(\|\mathbf{w}^o\|_2^2 + \|\mathbf{w}^p\|_2^2)
$$

$$
+ \frac{\alpha}{n_o} \sum_{i=1}^{n_o} \left[\frac{1}{2} e_i^2 + \lambda |\mathbf{a}_i|_1 + \frac{1}{2} \sum_{k,l \in \phi(o_i)} G_{kl}^p (a_k^i - a_l^i)^2 \right].
$$

$$(3.45)$$

In the formulation, we identify three coordinate blocks, namely $\mathbf{w}^o$, $\mathbf{w}^p$, and various a_j^i. We employ a block coordinate descent (BCD) algorithm to optimize Eq. (3.45) by updating one coordinate block while fixing the other two.

1. Updating $\mathbf{w}^o$ while fixing others: Observing that only $\mathcal{J}_o$, $\mathcal{J}_{po}$, and $\mathcal{J}_r$ are functions of $\mathbf{w}^o$, we have

$$
\frac{\partial \mathcal{J}}{\partial \mathbf{w}^o} = \frac{\partial \mathcal{J}_o}{\partial \mathbf{w}^o} + \frac{\partial \mathcal{J}_{po}}{\partial \mathbf{w}^o} + \frac{\partial \mathcal{J}_r}{\partial \mathbf{w}^o}
$$
$$
= \frac{1}{n_o} (\mathbf{F}^o)'(\mathbf{F}^o \mathbf{w}^o - \mathbf{y}^o) + \gamma \mathbf{w}^o + \frac{\alpha}{n_o} (\mathbf{F}^o)'(\mathbf{F}^o \mathbf{w}^o - \mathbf{M}\mathbf{F}^p \mathbf{w}^p),
$$

$$(3.46)$$

where $\mathbf{M}$ is a n_o by n_p sparse matrix with $\mathbf{M}(i,j) = a_j^i$, for $j \in \phi(o_i)$. We then update $\mathbf{w}^o$ as $\mathbf{w}^o \leftarrow \mathbf{w}^o - \tau \frac{\partial \mathcal{J}}{\partial \mathbf{w}^o}$, where τ is the step size.

2. Updating $\mathbf{w}^p$ while fixing others: The subobjective functions that are related to $\mathbf{w}^p$ are $\mathcal{J}_p$, $\mathcal{J}_{pp}$, $\mathcal{J}_{po}$, and $\mathcal{J}_r$. Therefore,

$$
\frac{\partial \mathcal{J}}{\partial \mathbf{w}^p} = \frac{\partial \mathcal{J}_p}{\partial \mathbf{w}^p} + \frac{\partial \mathcal{J}_{pp}}{\partial \mathbf{w}^p} + \frac{\partial \mathcal{J}_{po}}{\partial \mathbf{w}^p} + \frac{\partial \mathcal{J}_r}{\partial \mathbf{w}^p}
$$
$$
= \frac{1}{n_p} (\mathbf{F}^p)'(\mathbf{F}^p \mathbf{w}^p - \mathbf{y}^p) + \frac{\beta}{n_p} (\mathbf{F}^p)' \mathcal{L}^p \mathbf{F}^p \mathbf{w}^p + \gamma \mathbf{w}^p
$$
$$
- \frac{\alpha}{n_o} (\mathbf{F}^p)' \mathbf{M}'(\mathbf{F}^o \mathbf{w}^o - \mathbf{M}\mathbf{F}^p \mathbf{w}^p),
$$

$$(3.47)$$

where $\mathcal{L}^p$ is the Laplacian of the graph G^p [4]. Similarly, $\mathbf{w}^p$ can be updated by $\mathbf{w}^p \leftarrow \mathbf{w}^p - \tau \frac{\partial \mathcal{J}}{\partial \mathbf{w}^p}$.

Algorithm 4: PAROLE – Part–Whole Outcome Predictions

Input: (1) the feature matrix for whole/part entities $\mathbf{F}^o/\mathbf{F}^p$, (2) outcome
vector for the whole/part entities $\mathbf{y}^o/\mathbf{y}^p$, (3) the whole to parts
mapping function ϕ, (4) the part–part network G^p (optional), (5)
parameters $\alpha, \beta, \gamma, \lambda, \tau$.

Output: Model parameters $\mathbf{w}^o$ and $\mathbf{w}^p$.

1 Initialize $\mathbf{w}^o$ and $\mathbf{w}^p$ and $a_j, j \in \phi(o_i), i = 1, \ldots, n_o$;

2 **while** *Not converged* **do**

3 $\quad$ Update $\mathbf{w}^o \leftarrow \mathbf{w}^o - \tau \frac{\partial \mathcal{J}}{\partial \mathbf{w}^o}$;

4 $\quad$ Update $\mathbf{w}^p \leftarrow \mathbf{w}^p - \tau \frac{\partial \mathcal{J}}{\partial \mathbf{w}^p}$;

5 $\quad$ Update $\mathbf{a}_i$ via proximal gradient descent for $i = 1, \ldots, n_o$;

6 **end**

---

3. Updating a_j^i while fixing others: Let us fix a whole o_i and the
subproblem with respect to $\mathbf{a}_i$ becomes

$$\min_{\mathbf{a}_i} \frac{1}{2} e_i^2 + \lambda |\mathbf{a}_i|_1 + \frac{1}{2} \sum_{k,l \in \phi(o_i)} G_{kl}^p (a_k^i - a_l^i)^2. \qquad (3.48)$$

Observing that the subproblem is a composite of a nonsmooth convex function
($\lambda |\mathbf{a}_i|_1$) and a differentiable convex function (the remaining terms), we update
$\mathbf{a}_i$ using the proximal gradient descent method [7]. We first take a gradient step
by moving $\mathbf{a}_i$ along the negative direction of the derivative of the smooth part
with regard to $\mathbf{a}_i$, as follows:

$$\mathbf{z} = \mathbf{a}_i - \tau [e_i(-\mathbf{F}^p(\phi(o_i), :)\mathbf{w}^p) + \mathcal{L}_i^p \mathbf{a}_i], \qquad (3.49)$$

where $\mathcal{L}_i^p$ is a shorthand notation for the Laplacian of the subgraph
$G^p(\phi(o_i), \phi(o_i))$. Next, we compute the proximal-gradient update for the
l_1 norm using soft-thresholding as $\mathbf{a}_i \leftarrow \mathcal{S}_{\tau\lambda}(\mathbf{z})$, where the soft-thresholding
operator is defined as follows:

$$[\mathcal{S}_t(\mathbf{z})]_j = \text{sign}(\mathbf{z}_j)(|\mathbf{z}_j| - t)_+, \qquad (3.50)$$

where we use $(x)_+$ as a shorthand for $\max\{x, 0\}$.

We will cycle through the preceding three steps to update the three coordinate blocks until convergence. The algorithm is summarized in Algorithm 4.

Remarks: We want to emphasize that Algorithm 4 provides a general optimization framework that not only works for the formulation with *sparse aggregation* in Eq. (3.45), but is also applicable to the other part–whole relationships
introduced in Section 3.3.2. The only difference is that, since $\mathcal{J}_{po}$ varies for

each part–whole relationship, its derivatives with regard to the coordinate blocks would also change. Next, for each of the other part–whole relationships, we give their derivative or proximal gradient with regard to the three coordinate blocks.

1. Maximum aggregation: the derivatives of $\mathcal{J}_{po}$ with regard to $\mathbf{w}^o$ and $\mathbf{w}^p$ are as follows:

$$\frac{\partial \mathcal{J}_{po}}{\partial \mathbf{w}^o} = \frac{\alpha}{n_o} \sum_{i=1}^{n_o} e_i (\mathbf{F}^o(i, :))'$$

$$\frac{\partial \mathcal{J}_{po}}{\partial \mathbf{w}^p} = \frac{\alpha}{n_o} \sum_{i=1}^{n_o} e_i \cdot \frac{\sum_{j \in \phi(o_i)} (\mathbf{F}^p(j, :))' \tilde{\mathbf{y}}_i^p}{\sum_{j \in \phi(o_i)} \tilde{\mathbf{y}}_i^p},$$

where we denote $\tilde{\mathbf{y}}_i^p = \exp(\mathbf{F}^p(j, :)\mathbf{w}^p)$.

2. Linear aggregation: the derivatives of $\mathcal{J}_{po}$ with regard to $\mathbf{w}^o$ and $\mathbf{w}^p$ are the same as in the *sparse aggregation* case. Its derivative with regard to $\mathbf{a}_i$ is same as in Eq. (3.49) without the following proximal-gradient update.

3. Ordered sparse aggregation: the only difference from the *sparse aggregation* lies in the proximal-gradient update for the OWL norm, which can be computed as follows [111]:

$$\text{prox}_{\Omega_\mathbf{w}}(\mathbf{v}) = \text{sign}(\mathbf{v}) \odot \left(\mathbf{P}_{|\mathbf{v}|}^T \text{proj}_{\mathbb{R}_+^n} (\text{proj}_{\mathcal{K}_m} (|\mathbf{v}|_\downarrow - \mathbf{w})) \right). \quad (3.51)$$

In the preceding equation, to compute $\text{prox}_{\Omega_\mathbf{w}}(\mathbf{v})$, we first compute the Euclidean project of $(|\mathbf{v}|_\downarrow - \mathbf{w})$ onto $\mathcal{K}_m$ using the linear time *pool-adjacent violators* (PAV) algorithm [68]. This is followed by a projection onto the first orthant by a clipping operation. The resulting vector is sorted back according to the permutation matrix $\mathbf{P}_{|\mathbf{v}|}$ and then element wisely multiplied by the signs of $\mathbf{v}$.

4. Robust aggregation: we compute the gradient of $\mathcal{J}_{po}$ using chain rule as follows:

$$\frac{\partial \mathcal{J}_{po}}{\partial \mathbf{w}^o} = \frac{\alpha}{n_o} \sum_{i=1}^{n_o} \frac{\partial \rho(e_i)}{\partial e_i} \frac{\partial e_i}{\partial \mathbf{w}^o}, \quad \frac{\partial \mathcal{J}_{po}}{\partial \mathbf{w}^p} = \frac{\alpha}{n_o} \sum_{i=1}^{n_o} \frac{\partial \rho(e_i)}{\partial e_i} \frac{\partial e_i}{\partial \mathbf{w}^p},$$

$$\frac{\partial \mathcal{J}_{po}}{\partial \mathbf{a}_i} = \frac{\alpha}{n_o} \left[\frac{\partial \rho(e_i)}{\partial e_i} \frac{\partial e_i}{\partial \mathbf{a}_i} + \mathcal{L}_i^p \mathbf{a}_i \right]$$

where $\frac{\partial e_i}{\partial \mathbf{w}^o} = \mathbf{F}^o(i, :)'$, $\frac{\partial e_i}{\partial \mathbf{w}^p} = -\sum_{j \in \phi(o_i)} a_j \mathbf{F}^p(j, :)'$, and $\frac{\partial e_i}{\partial \mathbf{a}_i} = -\mathbf{F}^p$ $(\phi(o_i), :)\mathbf{w}^p$; and the gradient of the Huber and Bisquare estimator can be computed as follows:

Method	Case	$|e| \leq t$	$|e| > t$
Huber $\frac{\partial \rho_H(e)}{\partial e}$		e	$t \cdot \text{sign}(e)$
Bisquare $\frac{\partial \rho_B(e)}{\partial e}$		$e[1 - (e/t)^2]^2$	0

Proofs and Analysis. In this subsection, we analyze the PAROLE algorithm in terms of its convergence, optimality, and complexity.

First, building upon the proposition from [89], we have the following theorem regarding the Algorithm 4, which says that under a mild assumption, it converges to a local optimum (i.e., coordinatewise minimum) of Eq. (3.45).

Theorem 3.10. *(Convergence and Optimality of PAROLE).* As long as $-\gamma$ is not an eigenvalue of $\frac{\alpha+1}{n_o}\mathbf{F}^{o'}\mathbf{F}^o$ or $\frac{1}{n_p}\mathbf{F}^{p'}\mathbf{F}^p + \beta\mathbf{F}^{p'}\mathcal{L}^p\mathbf{F}^p + \frac{\alpha}{n_o}\mathbf{F}^p\mathbf{M}'\mathbf{M}\mathbf{F}^p$, Algorithm 4 converges to a coordinatewise minimum point.

Proof Omitted for brevity. □

Next, we analyze the complexity of Algorithm 4, which is summarized in Lemma 3.11.

Lemma 3.11. *(Complexity of PAROLE).* Algorithm 4 takes $O(T(n_o d_o + n_p d_p + m_{po} + m_{pp}))$ time for *linear aggregation, maximum aggregation, sparse aggregation,* and *robust aggregation,* and it takes $O(T(n_o d_o + n_p d_p + Cn_p d_p + m_{pp}))$ for *ordered sparse aggregation,* where d_o and d_p are the dimensionality of the whole and part feature vectors, $m_{po} = \sum_i |\phi(o_i)|$ is the number of associations between the whole and parts and m_{pp} is the number of edges in the part–part network, T is the number of iterations, and $C = \max_i \log(|\phi(o_i)|)$ is a constant. The space complexity for Algorithm 4 is $O(n_o d_o + n_p d_p + m_{po} + m_{pp})$ for all the part–whole relationships.

Proof Omitted for brevity. □

Remarks: Suppose we have a conceptual part–whole graph $G - \{O, \mathcal{P}\}$, which has n_o nodes for the whole entities and n_p nodes for the part entities, m_{po} links from whole nodes to their composing parts nodes, and m_{pp} links in the part–part networks. Lemma 3.11 says that PAROLE scales linearly with regard to the size of this part–whole graph in both time and space.

3.3.4 Experiments

In this subsection, we present the empirical evaluation results. The experiments are designed to evaluate the following aspects:

- *Effectiveness:* how accurate is the PAROLE algorithm for predicting the outcomes of parts and the whole?
- *Efficiency:* how fast and scalable is the PAROLE algorithm?

Datasets. The real-world datasets used for evaluations are as follows:

CQA. We use Mathematics Stack Exchange (*Math*) and Stack Overflow (*SO*) data from [103]. The questions are whole, and answers are parts both with voting scores as outcome. For each question, we treat all the answers it receives as its composing parts. The extracted features are described in [103].

DBLP. The DBLP dataset provides the bibliographic information of computer science research papers. We treat authors as whole with h-index as outcome and papers as parts with citation counts as outcome. For each author, his/her composing parts are the papers she/he has coauthored. Paper features include temporal attributes, and author features include productivity and social attributes.

Movie. We crawl the metadata of 5,043 movies with budget information[5] from the IMDb website. The meta information includes movie title, genres, cast, budget, etc. We treat movies as whole and the actors/actresses as parts both with the number of Facebook likes as the outcome. For each movie, we treat its cast as the composing parts. Movie features include contextual attributes, and actors/actresses features include productivity and social attributes.

The statistics of these datasets are summarized in Table 3.6. For each dataset, we first sort the whole in chronological order, gather the first x percent of whole and their corresponding parts as training examples, and always test on the last 10% percent of whole and its corresponding parts. The percentage of training x could vary. The RMSE between the actual outcomes and the predicted ones is adopted for effectiveness evaluation. The parameters are set for each method on each dataset via a grid search.

Repeatability of experimental results. All the datasets are publicly available. We have released the datasets and code of the algorithms through the authors' website. The experiments are performed on a Windows machine with four 3.5GHz Intel Cores and 256GB RAM.

---

[5] http://www.the-numbers.com/movie/budgets/all.

Table 3.6 *Summary of Datasets for PAROLE.*

Data	Whole	Part	# of whole	# of part
Math	Question	Answer	16,638	32,876
SO	Question	Answer	1,966,272	4,282,570
DBLP	Author	Paper	234,681	129,756
Movie	Movie	Actors/actresses	5,043	37,365

Effectiveness Results. We compare the effectiveness of the following methods:

(i) *Separate:* train a linear regression model for parts and the whole separately.

(ii) *Sum:* a joint model with Sum part–whole relationship.

(iii) *Linear:* our PAROLE with linear aggregation.

(iv) *Max:* our PAROLE with maximum aggregation.

(v) *Huber:* our PAROLE with a robust Huber estimator.

(vi) *Bisquare:* our PAROLE with a robust Bisquare estimator.

(vii) *Lasso:* our PAROLE with sparse aggregation.

(viii) *OWL:* our PAROLE with ordered sparse aggregation.

A. Outcome prediction performance: The RMSE results of all the comparison methods for predicting the outcomes of parts and whole on all the datasets are shown from Figures 3.21 to 3.24. We draw several interesting observations from these results. First, all the joint prediction models outperform the separate model in most cases, which suggests that the part outcome indeed has a profound impact on the whole outcome, and vice versa. Second, among the joint prediction models, in general, the linear methods (*Sum* and *Linear*) are not as good as the nonlinear counterparts (*Max, Huber, Bisqaure, Lasso,* and *OWL*), and in some cases (Figures 3.21(b), 3.23(b)), the linear joint models are even worse than the separate method, which indicates that the part–whole relationship is indeed more complicated than the linear aggregation. Third, among the nonlinear methods, a consistent observation across all the datasets is that *Lasso* and *OWL* are the best two methods in almost all the cases. This suggests that the whole outcome is mostly dominated by a few, often high-performing, parts.

B. The effect of part–part interdependency: In the joint prediction model, we have hypothesized that the part–part interdependency might help boost the predictions in two ways, i.e., regularizing the parts' contribution to the whole outcome as well as part outcome correlation. Here, we verify

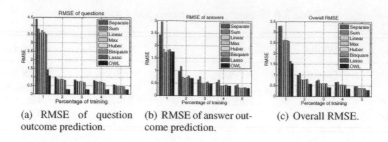

(a) RMSE of question outcome prediction.

(b) RMSE of answer outcome prediction.

(c) Overall RMSE.

Figure 3.21 RMSE comparisons on *Math*. From left to right: *Separate*, *Sum*, *Linear*, *Max*, *Huber*, *Bisquare*, *Lasso*, and *OWL*.

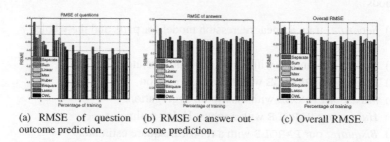

(a) RMSE of question outcome prediction.

(b) RMSE of answer outcome prediction.

(c) Overall RMSE.

Figure 3.22 RMSE comparisons on *SO*. From left to right: *Separate*, *Sum*, *Linear*, *Max*, *Huber*, *Bisquare*, *Lasso*, and *OWL*.

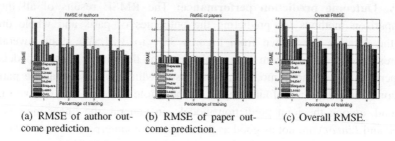

(a) RMSE of author outcome prediction.

(b) RMSE of paper outcome prediction.

(c) Overall RMSE.

Figure 3.23 RMSE comparisons on *DBLP*. From left to right: *Separate*, *Sum*, *Linear*, *Max*, *Huber*, *Bisquare*, *Lasso*, and *OWL*.

and validate to what extent these two aspects contribute to the performance gain, when such part–part interdependency information is available. Figure 3.25 shows the results of *Lasso* on the *Movie* dataset with 50% training data. The network among the parts, i.e., actors/actresses, is their collaboration network. "PAROLE-Basic" does not use the network information. "PAROLE-GraphForWhole" applies the graph regularization on the parts' contribution to the whole, which brings an 8% overall prediction error reduction.

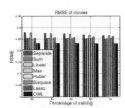

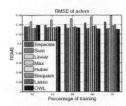

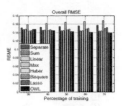

(a) RMSE of movie out-come prediction.

(b) RMSE of actors/act-ress outcome prediction.

(c) Overall RMSE.

Figure 3.24 RMSE comparisons on *Movie*. From left to right: *Separate*, *Sum*, *Linear*, *Max*, *Huber*, *Bisquare*, *Lasso*, and *OWL*.

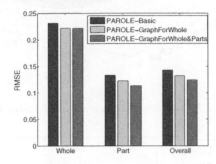

Figure 3.25 Performance gain analysis on *Movie*.

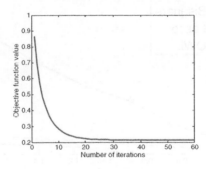

Figure 3.26 Convergence analysis on *SO*.

On top of that, "PAROLE-GraphForWhole&Parts" uses the graph regulariza-tion on the parts' outcome, which brings a 14.5% decrease in the overall prediction error.

C. Convergence analysis: Figure 3.26 shows the objective function value versus the number of iterations on the *SO* dataset using *OWL* with 5%

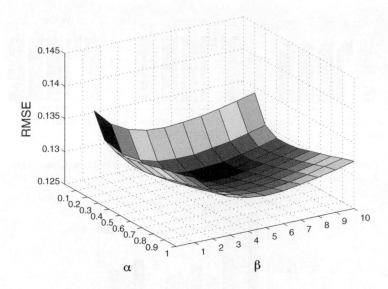

Figure 3.27 RMSE with varying α and β of *Lasso* on *Movie*.

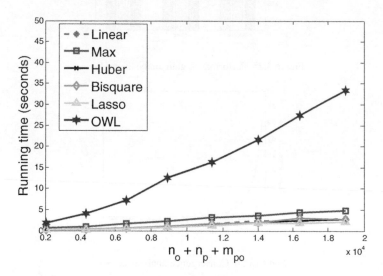

Figure 3.28 Scalability plot on *SO*.

training data. As we can see, the PAROLE algorithm converges very fast, after 25 to 30 iterations.

D. Sensitivity analysis: To investigate the parameter sensitivity, we perform parametric studies with the two most important parameters in PAROLE, i.e., α, which controls the importance of part–whole relationship; and β, which controls the importance of part–part interdependency on the parts outcome. The bowl-shaped surface in Figure 3.27 suggests that our model can achieve good performance in a large volume of the parameter space.

Efficiency Results. Figure 3.28 shows the running time of all the methods with varying size of training data ($n_o + n_p + m_{po}$). We can see that all the methods scale linearly, which is consistent with Lemma 3.11. *OWL* takes the longest time due to the additional sorting operation in the proximal-gradient update for the OWL norm.

4

Team Performance Optimization

In this chapter, we introduce our work on team performance optimization [18, 58, 60]. We start with the existing work on team formation, to form a team from a pool of candidates to satisfy certain constraints. We then present the problem of team member replacement, to recommend a good candidate to replace a churning team member and introduce a graph kernel–based algorithm that considers both the structural matching and skill matching. We then extend this solution to other team enhancement scenarios. We also work toward real-time team optimization by leveraging reinforcement learning techniques.

4.1 Team Formation

Team formation studies the problem of assembling a team from a pool of candidates to work on a project. The first work that studies team formation in the context of social networks finds a team of experts who possess the desired skills and have strong team cohesion to ensure the team success [52]. In particular, to measure the effectiveness of collaboration, they define two communication costs based on the diameter as well as the minimum spanning tree of the induced team subgraph. Since the corresponding optimization problems are NP-complete, they devise approximation algorithms by exploiting the relationship to Multiple-Choice Cover and Group Steiner Tree problems. Their experimental results on DBLP datasets show that the designed algorithm can achieve small communication cost as well as team cardinality. As follow-up work, Anagnostopoulos et al. [3] study forming teams to accommodate a sequence of tasks arriving in an online fashion, while optimizing two possibly conflicting goals, i.e., achieving a balanced work load assignment among people and minimizing the coordination cost in teams. They design an exponential allocation cost function that guarantees the optimal asymptotic performance.

Rangapuram et al. [77] propose a generalized team formation problem to find a team with maximum collaboration compatibility and satisfy many realistic constraints, e.g., inclusion of a designated team leader, skill requirement, bound on the team size, budget constraint, and distance-based constraints. Different from other work, they use generalized density of a subgraph as a measure of collaborative compatibility. They formulate the problem as a generalized densest subgraph problem (GDSP) and solve an unconstrained continuous version of it. Beyond that, minimizing the tensions among the team members is considered [37]. With the presence of the underlying social network, the set cover problem is complicated by the goal of lowering the communication cost at the same time. Cao et al. [18] develop an interactive group mining system that allows users to efficiently explore the network data and from which to progressively select and replace candidate members to form a team. Bogdanov et al. [12] study how to extract a diversified group pulled from strong cliques given a network; this ensures that the group is both comprehensive and representative of the whole network. Cummings and Kiesler [26] find that prior working experience is the best predictor of collaborative tie strength. To provide insights into designs of online communities and organizations, the systematic differences in appropriating social softwares among different online enterprise communities is analyzed in [71]. The patterns of informal networks and communication in distributed global software teams using social network analysis is also investigated in [21]. Specific communication structures are proven critical to new product development delivery performance and quality [20]. To assess the skills of players and teams in online multiplayer games and team-based sports, "team chemistry" is also accounted for in [27, 28].

4.2 Team Member Replacement

In his worldwidely renowned book *The Science of the Artificial* [83], Nobel laureate Herbert Simon pointed out that it is more the complexity of the *environment* than the complexity of the individual persons that determines the complex behavior of humans. The emergence of online social network sites and web 2.0 applications provides a new connected environment/context, where people interact and collaborate with each other as a team to collectively perform some complex tasks.

A promising algorithmic approach to team composition treats a team as a subgraph embedded in a larger social network. Prior research has focused on assembling a team from scratch while satisfying the skill requirements at minimum communication cost (e.g., diameter and minimum spanning tree) [52]. If the tasks arrive in an online fashion, the workload balance among the people needs to be considered [3]. In practical scenarios, there are more realistic requirements in team formation, e.g., inclusion of a designated leader and size of a team [77]. With the increasing constraints, the team formation problem is NP-complete. Prior work to formulate automated ways of forming a team has used heuristic approaches (e.g., RarestFirst and SteinerTree) but so far lacks efficient solutions [52]. Our work differs from previous efforts in three ways: (1) we alter the composition of an existing team based on new requirements; (2) we solve the problem in a principled approach with the notation of graph kernel; and (3) we design a set of efficient algorithms.

The churn of team members is a common problem, among others, across many application domains. To name a few, an employee in a software or sales team might decide to leave the organization and/or be assigned to a new task. In a law enforcement mission, a SWAT team might lose a certain task force assignment due to fatality or injury. In professional sports (e.g., NBA), the rotation tactic between the benches could play a key role on the game outcome. In all these cases, the loss of the key member (i.e., the irreplaceable) might bring the catastrophic consequence to the team performance. *How can we find the best alternate (e.g., from the other members within the organization), when a team member becomes unavailable?* This is the central question this work aims to answer. However, despite the frequency with which people leave a team before a project/task is complete and the resulting disruption [108], replacements are often found opportunistically and are not necessarily optimal.

We conjecture there will be less disruption when the team member who leaves is replaced with someone with similar relationships with the other team members. This conjecture is inspired by some recent research that shows that team members prefer to work with people they have worked with before [42] and that distributed teams perform better when members know each other [26]. Furthermore, research has shown that specific communication patterns among team members are critical for performance [20]. Thus, in addition to factors such as skill level, maintaining the same or better level of familiarity and communication among team members before and after someone leaves should reduce the impact of the departure. In other words, for team member replacement, the similarity between individuals should be measured in the context of the team itself. More specifically, a good team member replacement should meet the following two requirements. First (*skill matching*), the new member should bring a similar skill set as the current team member to be replaced. Second (*structure matching*), the new member should have a similar network structure as the current team member in connecting the rest of the team members.

Armed with this conjecture, we formally formulate the TEAM MEMBER REPLACEMENT problem by the notation of graph similarity/kernel. By modeling the team as a labeled graph, the graph kernel provides a natural way to capture both the skill and structure match as well as the interaction of both. However, for a network with n individuals, a straightforward method would require $O(n)$ graph kernel computations for one team member replacement, which is computationally intractable. For example, for the *DBLP* dataset with almost 1M users (i.e., $n \approx 1,000,000$), we found that it would take 6,388s to find one replacement for a team of size 10. To address the computational challenges, we design a family of fast algorithms by carefully designing the pruning strategies and exploring the smoothness between existing and new teams. We perform the extensive experimental evaluations to demonstrate the effectiveness and efficiency of our methods. Specifically, we find that (1) encoding both the skill and structural matching leads to a much better replacement result. Compared with the best alternative choices, we achieve a 27% and 24% *net increase* in average recall and precision, respectively; (2) our fast algorithms are orders of magnitude faster and scale *sublinearly*. For example, our pruning strategy alone leads up to $1,709\times$ speed-up, without sacrificing any accuracy.

The main contributions of this work are as follows.

1. **Problem formulation.** We formally define the TEAM MEMBER REPLACEMENT problem to recommend a good candidate when a team member is unavailable in the context of networks where nodes are carrying multiple labels (skills) and edges are representing social structures.
2. **Algorithms and analysis.** We solve the problem by introducing graph kernels and design a family of effective and scalable algorithms for TEAM MEMBER REPLACEMENT and analyze its correctness and complexity.
3. **Experimental evaluations.** We perform extensive experiments, including user studies and case studies, on real-world datasets, to validate the effectiveness and efficiency of our methods. (See an example in Figure 4.1.)

4.2.1 Problem Definitions

Table 4.1 lists the main symbols used throughout this work. We describe the n individuals by a labeled social network $\mathbf{G} := \{\mathbf{A}, \mathbf{L}\}$, where $\mathbf{A}$ is an $n \times n$ adjacency matrix characterizing the connectivity among different individuals;

Table 4.1 *Symbols of* TEAM MEMBER REPLACEMENT.

Symbols	Definition
$G := \{A, L\}$	The entire social network
$A_{n \times n}$	The adjacency matrix of G
$L_{n \times l}$	Skill indicator matrix
$\mathcal{T}$	The team member index
$G(\mathcal{T})$	The team network indexed by its members $\mathcal{T}$
d_i	The degree of the ith node in A
l	The total number of skills
t	The team size, i.e., $t = |\mathcal{T}|$
n	The total number of individuals in A
m	The total number of connections in A

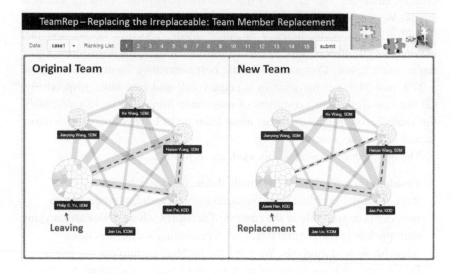

Figure 4.1 The team graphs before and after *Jiawei Han* takes *Philip S. Yu*'s place. See Subsection 4.2.4 for detailed explanations.

and L is $n \times l$ skill indicator matrix. The ith row vector of L describes the skill set of the ith individual. For example, suppose there are only three skills in total, including {*data mining, databases, information retrieval*}. Then an individual with a skill vector $[1, 1, 0]$ means that s/he has both *data mining* and *databases* skills but no skill in terms of *information retrieval*. Also, we represent the elements in a matrix using a convention similar to Matlab, e.g., $A(i, j)$ is the element at the ith row and jth column of the matrix A, and $A(:, j)$ is the jth column of A, etc.

We use the calligraphic letter $\mathcal{T}$ to index the members of a team, which includes a subset of $t = |\mathcal{T}|$ out of n individuals. Correspondingly, we can represent the team by another labeled team network $\mathbf{G}(\mathcal{T}) := \{\mathbf{A}(\mathcal{T}, \mathcal{T}), \mathbf{L}(\mathcal{T}, :)\}$. Note that $\mathbf{A}(\mathcal{T}, \mathcal{T})$ and $\mathbf{L}(\mathcal{T}, :)\}$ are submatrices of $\mathbf{A}$ and $\mathbf{L}$, respectively. If we replace an existing member $p \in \mathcal{T}$ of a given team $\mathcal{T}$ by another individual $q \notin \mathcal{T}$, the new team members are indexed by $\mathcal{T}_{p \to q} := \{\mathcal{T}/p, q\}$, and the new team is represented by the labeled network $\mathbf{G}(\mathcal{T}_{p \to q})$.

With the preceding notations and assumptions, our problems can be formally defined as follows:

Problem 4.1 TEAM MEMBER REPLACEMENT

Given: (1) A labeled social network $\mathbf{G} := \{\mathbf{A}, \mathbf{L}\}$, (2) a team $\mathbf{G}(\mathcal{T})$, and (3) a team member $p \in \mathcal{T}$;

Output: A "best" alternate $q \notin \mathcal{T}$ to replace the person p's role in the team $\mathbf{G}(\mathcal{T})$.

4.2.2 Our Solutions

In this subsection, we present our solution for Problem 4.1. We start with the design objectives for the TEAM MEMBER REPLACEMENT problem, present the graph kernel as the basic solution to fulfill such design objectives, and finally analyze the main computational challenges.

Design Objectives. Generally speaking, we want to find a *similar* person q to replace the current team member p who is about to leave the team. That is, a good replacement q should not only have a similar skill set as team member p; but also would maintain the good chemistry of the team so that the whole team can work together harmoniously and/or be less disrupted. In other words, the similarity between individuals should be measured in the context of the team itself. Often, the success of a team largely depends on the successful execution of several subtasks, each of which requires the cooperation among several team members with certain skill configurations. For example, several classic tactics often recurringly find themselves in a successful NDA team, including (a) *triangle offense* (which is featured by a sideline triangle created by *the center*, *the forward*, and *the guard*), (b) *pick and roll* (which involves cooperation between two players – one plays as "pivot" and the other plays as "screen," respectively), etc. Generally speaking, team performance arises from the shared knowledge and experience among team members and their ability to share and coordinate their work. As noted in the introduction, a specific pattern of communication is associated with higher team performance. Maintaining that communication structure should therefore be less disruptive to the team.

If we translate these requirements into the notations defined in Section 4.2.1, it naturally leads to the following two design objectives for a good TEAM MEMBER REPLACEMENT:

- *Skill matching*: the new member should bring a similar skill set as the current team member p to be replaced that is required by the team.
- *Structural matching*: the new member should have a similar network structure as team member p in connecting the rest of the team members.

Basic Solutions. In order to fulfill the preceding two design objectives, we need a similarity measure between two individuals in the context of the team itself that captures both skill matching and the structural matching as well as the interaction of both. We refer to this kind of similarity as *team context-aware similarity*. Mathematically, the so-called graph kernel defined on the current and new teams provides a natural tool for such a team context-aware similarity. That is, we want to find a replacement person q as

$$q = \mathrm{argmax}_{j,\, j \notin \mathcal{T}} \ \mathrm{Ker}(\mathbf{G}(\mathcal{T}), \mathbf{G}(\mathcal{T}_{p \to j})). \tag{4.1}$$

In Eq. (4.1), $\mathbf{G}(\mathcal{T})$ is the labeled team graph; $\mathbf{G}(\mathcal{T}_{p \to j})$ is the labeled team graph after we replace a team member p by another individual j; and Ker(.) is the kernel between these two labeled graphs. Generally speaking, the basic idea of various graph kernels is to compare the similarity of the *subgraphs* between the two input graphs and then aggregate them as the overall similarity between the two graphs. As such, graph kernel is able to simultaneously capture both the skill matching and the structure matching, beyond the simple ad hoc combination between the two (e.g., weighted linear combination, multiplicative combination, sequential filtering, etc). We would like to emphasize that this treatment is important – as we will show in the experimental section, it leads to much better performance over all the alternative choices. Let us explain the intuition/rationality of why the graph kernel is a natural choice for team context-aware similarity. Here, each subgraph in a given team (e.g., the dashed triangles in Figure 4.1) might reflect a specific skill configuration among a sub-group of team members that is required by a certain subtask of that team. By comparing the similarity between two subgraphs, we implicitly measure the capability of individual j to perform this specific subtask. Thus, by aggregating the similarities of all the possible subgraphs between the two input graphs/teams, we get a goodness measure of the overall capability of individual j to perform all the potential subtasks in which team member p is involved in the original team. Note that the team replacement scenario is different from team formation [3, 52, 77]. The existing work on team formation aims to build a team from scratch by optimizing some prechosen metric (e.g., compatibility, diversity, etc.). In contrast, we aim to find a new team member such that the new team resembles the original team as much as possible.

Having this in mind, many of the existing graph kernels can be adopted in Eq. (4.1), such as random walk–based graph kernels and subtree-based graph kernels. In this study, we focus on the random walk–based graph kernel due to its mathematical elegancy and superior empirical performance. Given two labeled graphs $G_i := \{A_i, L_i\}$, $i = 1, 2$, the random walk–based graph kernel between them can be formally computed as follows [92]:

$$\text{Ker}(G_1, G_2) = y'(I - cA_\times)^{-1} L_\times x, \qquad (4.2)$$

where $A_\times = L_\times(A'_1 \otimes A'_2)$ is the weight matrix of the two graphs' Kronecker product, $\otimes$ represents the Kronecker product between two matrices, c is a decay factor, $y = y_1 \otimes y_2$ and $x = x_1 \otimes x_2$ are the so-called starting and stopping vectors to indicate the weights of different nodes and are set uniform in our case, $L_\times$ is a diagonal matrix where $L_\times(i, i) = 0$ if the ith row of $(A'_1 \otimes A'_2)$ is zeroed out due to label inconsistency of two nodes of the two graphs. $L_\times$ can be expressed as $L_\times = \sum_{k=1}^{l} \text{diag}(L_1(:,k)) \otimes \text{diag}(L_2(:,k))$.

Computational Challenges. Eq. (4.2) naturally suggests the following procedure for solving the TEAM MEMBER REPLACEMENT problem (referred to as TEAMREP-BASIC): for each individual $j \notin \mathcal{T}$, we compute its score score(j) by Eq. (4.2); and recommend the individual(s) with the highest score(s). However, this strategy (TEAMREP-BASIC) is computationally intensive since we need to compute *many* random walk–based graph kernels, and each such computation could be expensive, especially when the team size is large. To be specific, for a team $\mathcal{T}$ of size t and a graph G with n individuals in total, its time complexity is $O(nt^3)$ since we need to compute a random walk–based graph kernel for each candidate who is not in the current team, each of which could cost $O(t^3)$ [92]. Even if we allow some approximation in computing each of these graph kernels, the best-known algorithms (i.e., by [45]) would still give an overall time complexity as $O(n(lt^2r^4 + mr + r^6))$, where r is reduced rank after low rank approximation, which is still too high. For example, on the *DBLP* dataset with 916,978 authors, for a team with 10 members, it would take 6,388s to find a best replacement.

In the next section, we present our solution to remedy these computational challenges.

4.2.3 Scale-Up and Speed-Up

In this subsection, we address the computational challenges to scale up and speed up TEAMREP-BASIC. We start with an efficient pruning strategy to reduce the number of graph kernel computations, and then present two algorithms to speed up the computation of individual graph kernel.

Scale-Up: Candidate Filtering. Here, we present an efficient pruning strategy to filter out those unpromising candidates. Recall that one of our design objectives for a good TEAM MEMBER REPLACEMENT is *structural matching*, i.e., the new member has a similar network structure as team member p in connecting the rest team members. Since p is connected to at least some of the rest members, it suggests that if an individual does not have any connection to any of the rest team members, s/he might not be a good candidate for replacement.

Pruning Strategy: Filter out all the candidates who do not have any connections to any of the rest team members.

Lemma 4.2. **Effectiveness of Pruning.** *For any two persons i and j not in $\mathcal{T}$, if i is connected to at least one member in $\mathcal{T}/p$ and j has no connections to any of the members in $\mathcal{T}/p$, we have that*

$$Ker(\mathbf{G}(\mathcal{T}), \mathbf{G}(\mathcal{T}_{p \to i})) \geq Ker(\mathbf{G}(\mathcal{T}), \mathbf{G}(\mathcal{T}_{p \to j})).$$

Proof Suppose that $\mathbf{G}(\mathcal{T}) := \{\mathbf{A}_0, \mathbf{L}_0\}$. Let $\mathbf{G}(\mathcal{T}_{p \to i}) := \{\mathbf{A}_1, \mathbf{L}_1\}$, and $\mathbf{G}(\mathcal{T}_{p \to j}) := \{\mathbf{A}_2, \mathbf{L}_2\}$.

By Taylor expansion of Eq. (4.2), we have

$Ker(\mathbf{G}(\mathcal{T}), \mathbf{G}(\mathcal{T}_{p \to i})) = \sum_{z=0}^{\infty} c\mathbf{y}'(\mathbf{L}_{\times 1}(\mathbf{A}_0' \otimes \mathbf{A}_1'))^z \mathbf{x}$, where $\mathbf{L}_{\times 1} = \sum_{k=1}^{l} \text{diag}(\mathbf{L}_0(:,k)) \otimes \text{diag}(\mathbf{L}_1(:,k))$,

$Ker(\mathbf{G}(\mathcal{T}), \mathbf{G}(\mathcal{T}_{p \to j})) = \sum_{z=0}^{\infty} c\mathbf{y}'(\mathbf{L}_{\times 2}(\mathbf{A}_0' \otimes \mathbf{A}_2'))^z \mathbf{x}$, where $\mathbf{L}_{\times 2} = \sum_{k=1}^{l} \text{diag}(\mathbf{L}_0(:,k)) \otimes \text{diag}(\mathbf{L}_2(:,k))$.

Therefore, it is sufficient to show that $(\mathbf{L}_{\times 1}(\mathbf{A}_0' \otimes \mathbf{A}_1'))^z \geq (\mathbf{L}_{\times 2}(\mathbf{A}_0' \otimes \mathbf{A}_2'))^z$ for any $z > 0$, where two matrices $\mathbf{A} \geq \mathbf{B}$ if $\mathbf{A}_{ij} \geq \mathbf{B}_{ij}$ holds for all possible (i, j). We prove this by induction.

(Base Case of Induction) When $z = 1$, we have

$$\mathbf{L}_{\times 1}(\mathbf{A}_0' \otimes \mathbf{A}_1') = \left(\sum_{k=1}^{l} \text{diag}(\mathbf{L}_0(:,k)) \otimes \text{diag}(\mathbf{L}_1(:,k)) \right) (\mathbf{A}_0' \otimes \mathbf{A}_1')$$

$$= \sum_{k=1}^{l} (\text{diag}(\mathbf{L}_0(:,k))\mathbf{A}_0') \otimes (\text{diag}(\mathbf{L}_1(:,k))\mathbf{A}_1').$$

$$(4.3)$$

Because $(\text{diag}(\mathbf{L}_1(:,k))\mathbf{A}'_1) \geq (\text{diag}(\mathbf{L}_2(:,k))\mathbf{A}'_2)$, we have $\mathbf{L}_{\times 1}(\mathbf{A}'_0 \otimes \mathbf{A}'_1) \geq \mathbf{L}_{\times 2}(\mathbf{A}'_0 \otimes \mathbf{A}'_2)$.

(Induction Step) Assuming $(\mathbf{L}_{\times 1}(\mathbf{A}'_0 \otimes \mathbf{A}'_1))^{z-1} \geq (\mathbf{L}_{\times 2}(\mathbf{A}'_0 \otimes \mathbf{A}'_2))^{z-1}$, we have that

$$(\mathbf{L}_{\times 1}(\mathbf{A}'_0 \otimes \mathbf{A}'_1))^z \geq (\mathbf{L}_{\times 2}(\mathbf{A}'_0 \otimes \mathbf{A}'_2))^{z-1}(\mathbf{L}_{\times 1}(\mathbf{A}'_0 \otimes \mathbf{A}'_1))$$
$$\geq (\mathbf{L}_{\times 2}(\mathbf{A}'_0 \otimes \mathbf{A}'_2))^z,$$

where the first inequality is due to the induction assumption, and the second inequality is due to the base case. This completes the proof. □

Remarks. By Lemma 4.2, our pruning strategy is "safe," i.e., it will not miss any potentially good replacements. In the meanwhile, we can reduce the number of graph kernel computations from $O(n)$ to $O(\sum_{i \in \mathcal{T}/p} d_i)$, which is sub-linear in n.

Speedup Graph Kernel – Exact Approach. Here, we address the problem of speeding up the computation of an individual graph kernel. Let $\mathbf{G}(\mathcal{T}) := \{\mathbf{A}_1, \mathbf{L}_1\}$ and $\mathbf{G}(\mathcal{T}_{p \to q}) := \{\mathbf{A}_2, \mathbf{L}_2\}$, where $\mathbf{A}_1, \mathbf{A}_2$ are symmetric adjacency matrices of the two graphs.[1] Without loss of generality, let us assume that p is the last team member in $\mathcal{T}$. Compare $\mathbf{A}_1$ with $\mathbf{A}_2$, it can be seen that the only difference is their last columns and last rows. Therefore, we can rewrite $\mathbf{A}_2$ as $\mathbf{A}_2 = \mathbf{A}_c + \mathbf{A}_{d2}$, where $\mathbf{A}_c$ is $\mathbf{A}_1$ with its last row and column being zeroed out, and the nonzero elements of $\mathbf{A}_{d2}$ only appear in its last row and column reflecting the connectivity of q to the new team. Notice that $\mathbf{A}_{d2}$ has a rank at most 2, so it can be factorized into two smaller matrices as $\mathbf{A}_{d2} = \mathbf{E}_{t \times 2}\mathbf{F}_{2 \times t}$.

Denote $\text{diag}(\mathbf{L}_1(:,j))$ as $\mathbf{L}_1^{(j)}$ and $\text{diag}(\mathbf{L}_2(:,j))$ as $\mathbf{L}_2^{(j)}$ for $j = 1, \ldots, l$. Compare $\mathbf{L}_1^{(j)}$ with $\mathbf{L}_2^{(j)}$, the only difference is the last diagonal element. Therefore, we can write $\mathbf{L}_2^{(j)}$ as $\mathbf{L}_2^{(j)} = \mathbf{L}_c^{(j)} + \mathbf{L}_{d2}^{(j)}$, where $\mathbf{L}_c^{(j)}$ is $\mathbf{L}_1^{(j)}$ with last element zeroed out, and $\mathbf{L}_{d2}^{(j)}$'s last element indicates q's strength of having the jth skill. $\mathbf{L}_2^{(j)}$'s rank is at most 1, so it can be factorized as $\mathbf{L}_2^{(j)} = \mathbf{e}_{t \times 1}^{(j)}\mathbf{f}_{1 \times t}^{(j)}$. Therefore, the exact graph kernel for the labeled graph can be computed as follows:

$$\text{Ker}(\mathbf{G}(\mathcal{T}), \mathbf{G}(\mathcal{T}_{p \to q}))$$

$$= \mathbf{y}'\left(\mathbf{I} - c\left(\sum_{j=1}^l \mathbf{L}_1^{(j)} \otimes \mathbf{L}_2^{(j)}\right)(\mathbf{A}'_1 \otimes \mathbf{A}'_2)\right)^{-1}\left(\sum_{j=1}^l \mathbf{L}_1^{(j)} \otimes \mathbf{L}_2^{(j)}\right)\mathbf{x}$$

---

[1] Although we focus on the undirected graphs in this work, our algorithms can be generalized to directed graphs.

$$= \mathbf{y}' \underbrace{(\mathbf{I} - c\left(\sum_{j=1}^{l} \mathbf{L}_1^{(j)} \otimes \mathbf{L}_c^{(j)}\right) (\mathbf{A}_1 \otimes \mathbf{A}_c)}_{\mathbf{Z}: \text{ invariant w.r.t. } q}$$

$$- c \underbrace{\left(\sum_{j=1}^{l} \left(\mathbf{L}_1^{(j)} \otimes \mathbf{e}^{(j)}\right)\left(\mathbf{I} \otimes \mathbf{f}^{(j)}\right)\right) (\mathbf{A}_1 \otimes \mathbf{A}_c)}_{\mathbf{PQ}(\mathbf{A}_1 \otimes \mathbf{A}_c) = \mathbf{PY}_1}$$

$$- c \underbrace{\left(\sum_{j=1}^{l} \mathbf{L}_1^{(j)} \otimes \mathbf{L}_c^{(j)}\right) (\mathbf{A}_1 \otimes \mathbf{E}) (\mathbf{I} \otimes \mathbf{F})}_{\mathbf{X}_1 \mathbf{Y}_2}$$

$$- c \underbrace{\left(\sum_{j=1}^{l} \left(\mathbf{L}_1^{(j)} \otimes \mathbf{e}^{(j)}\right)\left(\mathbf{I} \otimes \mathbf{f}^{(j)}\right)\right) (\mathbf{A}_1 \otimes \mathbf{E}) (\mathbf{I} \otimes \mathbf{F}))^{-1} \left(\sum_{j=1}^{l} \mathbf{L}_1^{(j)} \otimes \mathbf{L}_2^{(j)}\right)}_{\mathbf{X}_2 \mathbf{Y}_2} \mathbf{x}.$$

$$(4.4)$$

Each $\mathbf{L}_1^{(j)} \otimes \mathbf{e}^{(j)}$ is a matrix of size t^2 by t and $\mathbf{I} \otimes \mathbf{f}^{(j)}$ is a matrix of size t by t^2. We denote the matrix created by concatenating all $\mathbf{L}_1^{(j)} \otimes \mathbf{e}^{(j)}$ horizontally as $\mathbf{P}$, i.e., $\mathbf{P} = [\mathbf{L}_1^{(1)} \otimes \mathbf{e}^{(1)}, \dots, \mathbf{L}_l^{(l)} \otimes \mathbf{e}^{(l)}]$; and denote the matrix created by stacking all $\mathbf{I} \otimes \mathbf{f}^{(j)}$ vertically as $\mathbf{Q}$, i.e., $\mathbf{Q} = [\mathbf{I} \otimes \mathbf{f}^{(1)}; \dots; \mathbf{I} \otimes \mathbf{f}^{(l)}]$. Obviously, $\left(\sum_{j=1}^{l} \left(\mathbf{L}_1^{(j)} \otimes \mathbf{e}^{(j)}\right)\left(\mathbf{I} \otimes \mathbf{f}^{(j)}\right)\right)$ is equal to $\mathbf{PQ}$. We denote $\left(\sum_{j=1}^{l} \mathbf{L}_1^{(j)} \otimes \mathbf{L}_c^{(j)}\right)(\mathbf{A}_1 \otimes \mathbf{E})$ by $\mathbf{X}_1$; denote $\left(\sum_{j=1}^{l} \left(\mathbf{L}_1^{(j)} \otimes \mathbf{e}^{(j)}\right)\left(\mathbf{I} \otimes \mathbf{f}^{(j)}\right)\right)(\mathbf{A}_1 \otimes \mathbf{E})$ by $\mathbf{X}_2$; denote $\mathbf{Q}(\mathbf{A}_1 \otimes \mathbf{A}_c)$ by $\mathbf{Y}_1$; and denote $(\mathbf{I} \otimes \mathbf{F})$ by $\mathbf{Y}_2$. Let $\mathbf{X}$ be $[\mathbf{P}, \mathbf{X}_1, \mathbf{X}_2]$ and $\mathbf{Y}$ be $[\mathbf{Y}_1; \mathbf{Y}_2; \mathbf{Y}_2]$.

With these additional notations, we can rewrite Eq. (4.4) as

$$\text{Ker}(\mathbf{G}(\mathcal{T}), \mathbf{G}(\mathcal{T}_{p \to q}))$$
$$= \mathbf{y}'(\mathbf{Z} - c\mathbf{X}\mathbf{Y})^{-1} \left(\sum_{j=1}^{l} \mathbf{L}_1^{(j)} \otimes \mathbf{L}_2^{(j)}\right) \mathbf{x}$$
$$= \mathbf{y}'(\mathbf{Z}^{-1} + c\mathbf{Z}^{-1}\mathbf{X}(\mathbf{I} - c\mathbf{Y}\mathbf{Z}^{-1}\mathbf{X})^{-1}\mathbf{Y}\mathbf{Z}^{-1})$$
$$\times \left(\left(\sum_{j=1}^{l} \mathbf{L}_1^{(j)} \otimes \mathbf{L}_c^{(j)}\right)\mathbf{x} + \left(\sum_{j=1}^{l} (\mathbf{L}_1^{(j)} \otimes \mathbf{e}^{(j)})(\mathbf{I} \otimes \mathbf{f}^{(j)})\right)\mathbf{x}\right),$$

$$(4.5)$$

where the second equation is due to the matrix inverse lemma [38].

Remarks. In Eq. (4.5), $\mathbf{Z} = \mathbf{I} - c\left(\sum_{j=1}^{l} \mathbf{L}_1^{(j)} \otimes \mathbf{L}_c^{(j)}\right)(\mathbf{A}_1 \otimes \mathbf{A}_c)$ does not depend on the candidate q. Thus, if we precompute its inverse $\mathbf{Z}^{-1}$, we only need to update $\mathbf{X}(\mathbf{I} - c\mathbf{Y}\mathbf{Z}^{-1}\mathbf{X})^{-1}\mathbf{Y}$ and $\mathbf{PQx}$ for every new candidate. Notice that compared with the original graph kernel (the first equation in Eq. (4.4)), $(\mathbf{I} - c\mathbf{Y}\mathbf{Z}^{-1}\mathbf{X})$ is a much smaller matrix of $(l+4)t \times (l+4)t$. In this way, we can accelerate the process of computing its inverse without losing the accuracy of the graph kernel.

Speed-Up Graph Kernel – Approx Approach. Note that the graph kernel by Eq. (4.5) is exactly the same as the original method by the first equation in Eq. (4.4). If we allow some approximation error, we can further speed up the computation.

Note that $\mathbf{A}_c$ is symmetric and its rank-r approximation can be written as $\hat{\mathbf{A}}_c = \mathbf{UV}$, where $\mathbf{U}$ is a matrix of size t by r and $\mathbf{V}$ is a matrix of size r by t. $\mathbf{A}_1$ can be approximated as $\hat{\mathbf{A}}_1 = \hat{\mathbf{A}}_c + \mathbf{A}_{d1} = \mathbf{UV} + \mathbf{E}_1\mathbf{F}_1 = \mathbf{X}_1\mathbf{Y}_1$, where $\mathbf{X}_1 = [\mathbf{U}, \mathbf{E}_1], \mathbf{Y}_1 = [\mathbf{V}; \mathbf{F}_1], \mathbf{E}_1 = [\mathbf{w}_1, \mathbf{s}], \mathbf{F}_1 = [\mathbf{s}'; \mathbf{w}_1']$, $\mathbf{s}$ is a zero vector of length t except that the last element is 1, and $\mathbf{w}_1$ is the weight vector from p to the members in $\mathcal{T}$. Similarly, after p is replaced by a candidate q, the weight matrix of the new team can be approximated as $\hat{\mathbf{A}}_2 = \mathbf{X}_2\mathbf{Y}_2$, where $\mathbf{X}_2 = [\mathbf{U}, \mathbf{E}_2], \mathbf{Y}_2 = [\mathbf{V}; \mathbf{F}_2], \mathbf{E}_2 = [\mathbf{w}_2, \mathbf{s}], \mathbf{F}_2 = [\mathbf{s}'; \mathbf{w}_2']$, and $\mathbf{w}_2$ is the weight vector from q to the members in the new team. The approximated graph kernel for labeled graphs can be computed as

$$\hat{\mathrm{Ker}}\left(\mathbf{G}\left(\mathcal{T}\right), \mathbf{G}\left(\mathcal{T}_{p \to q}\right)\right)$$
$$= \mathbf{y}^T (\mathbf{I} - c\mathbf{L}_\times(\hat{\mathbf{A}}_1' \otimes \hat{\mathbf{A}}_2'))^{-1}\mathbf{L}_\times\mathbf{x}$$
$$= \mathbf{y}' (\mathbf{I} - c\mathbf{L}_\times (\mathbf{X}_1\mathbf{Y}_1) \otimes (\mathbf{X}_2\mathbf{Y}_2))^{-1}\mathbf{L}_\times\mathbf{x}$$
$$= \mathbf{y}' (\mathbf{I} - c\mathbf{L}_\times (\mathbf{X}_1 \otimes \mathbf{X}_2)(\mathbf{Y}_1 \otimes \mathbf{Y}_2))^{-1}\mathbf{L}_\times\mathbf{x}$$
$$= \mathbf{y}' (\mathbf{I} + c\mathbf{L}_\times (\mathbf{X}_1 \otimes \mathbf{X}_2)\mathbf{M}(\mathbf{Y}_1 \otimes \mathbf{Y}_2))\mathbf{L}_\times\mathbf{x}$$
$$= \mathbf{y}'\mathbf{L}_\times\mathbf{x} + c\mathbf{y}' \left(\sum_{j=1}^{l} \mathbf{L}_1^{(j)}\mathbf{X}_1 \otimes \mathbf{L}_2^{(j)}\mathbf{X}_2\right)\mathbf{M}(\mathbf{Y}_1 \otimes \mathbf{Y}_2)\mathbf{L}_\times\mathbf{x}$$
$$= \left(\sum_{j=1}^{l} \left(\mathbf{y}_1'\mathbf{L}_1^{(j)}\mathbf{x}_1\right)\left(\mathbf{y}_2'\mathbf{L}_2^{(j)}\mathbf{x}_2\right)\right) + c\left(\sum_{j=1}^{l} \mathbf{y}_1'\mathbf{L}_1^{(j)}\mathbf{X}_1 \otimes \mathbf{y}_2'\mathbf{L}_2^{(j)}\mathbf{X}_2\right)$$
$$\times \mathbf{M}\left(\sum_{j=1}^{l} \mathbf{Y}_1\mathbf{L}_1^{(j)}\mathbf{x}_1 \otimes \mathbf{Y}_2\mathbf{L}_2^{(j)}\mathbf{x}_2\right),$$
$$(4.6)$$

where $\mathbf{M} = \left(\mathbf{I} - c(\sum_{j=1}^{l} \mathbf{Y}_1\mathbf{L}_1^{(j)}\mathbf{X}_1 \otimes \mathbf{Y}_2\mathbf{L}_2^{(j)}\mathbf{X}_2)\right)^{-1}$, the second equation is due to the Kronecker product property, the third equation is again due to the matrix inverse lemma, the fourth equation is by matrix multiplication distributivity, and the last equation is due to the Kronecker product property.

Remarks. The computation of $\mathbf{M}$ is much cheaper than the original graph kernel since it is a matrix inverse of size $(r + 2)^2 \times (r + 2)^2$. It was first proposed in [45] to explore the low-rank structure of the input graphs to speed up graph kernel computations. However, in the context of TEAM MEMBER REPLACEMENT, we would need to estimate the low-rank approximation *many* times $\left(O\left(\sum_{i \in \mathcal{T}/p} d_i\right)\right)$ when we directly apply the method in [45]. In contrast, we only need to compute top-r approximation *once* by Eq. (4.6). As our complexity analysis (Subsection 4.2.3) and experimental evaluations (Subsection 4.2.4) show, this brings a few times additional speed-up.

Putting Everything Together. Putting everything together, we are ready to present our algorithms for TEAM MEMBER REPLACEMENT. Depending on the specific methods for computing the individual graph kernels, we have two variants.

Variant #1: TEAMREP-FAST-EXACT

We first present our algorithm using the exact graph kernel computation in Eq. (4.5). The algorithm (TEAMREP-FAST-EXACT) is summarized in Algorithm 5. We only need to precompute and store $\mathbf{Z}^{-1}$, $\mathbf{R}$, $\mathbf{b}$, and $\mathbf{l}$ for later use to compute each candidate's score (steps 2 and 3). In the loop, the key step is to update $\mathbf{M}$ involving matrix inverse of size $(l + 4)t \times (l + 4)t$, which is relatively cheaper to compute (step 17).

The effectiveness and efficiency of TEAMREP-FAST-EXACT are summarized in Lemmas 4.3 and 4.4, respectively. Compared with TEAMREP-BASIC, Algorithm 5 is much faster without losing any recommendation accuracy.

Lemma 4.3. *Accuracy of* TEAMREP-FAST-EXACT. *Algorithm 5 outputs the same set of candidates as* TEAMREP-BASIC.

Proof (Sketch) First, according to Lemma 4.2, we will not miss a promising candidate during the pruning stage. Second, for each candidate after pruning, Algorithm 5 calculates its graph kernel exactly the same as Eq. (4.5), which is in turn the same as Eq. (4.4) and hence Eq. (4.2). Therefore, after ranking the scores, Algorithm 5 outputs the same set of candidates as TEAMREP-BASIC. □

Lemma 4.4. *Time Complexity of* TEAMREP-FAST-EXACT *Algorithm 5 takes* $O\left(\left(\sum_{i \in \mathcal{T}/p} d_i\right)(lt^5 + l^3t^3)\right)$ *in time.*

Proof (Sketch) After pruning, the number of potential candidates (the number of loops in Algorithm 5) is $O(\sum_{i \in \mathcal{T}/p} d_i)$. In every loop, computing

---

Algorithm 5: TEAMREP-FAST-EXACT

Input: (1) The entire social network $\mathbf{G} := \{\mathbf{A}, \mathbf{L}\}$, (2) original team members $\mathcal{T}$, (3) person p who will leave the team, (4) starting and ending probability $\mathbf{x}$ and $\mathbf{y}$(be uniform by default), and (5) an integer k (the budget)

Output: Top k candidates to replace person p

1   Initialize $\mathbf{A}_c, \mathbf{L}_1^{(j)}, \mathbf{L}_2^{(j)}, j = 1, \ldots, l$;

2   Precompute $\mathbf{Z}^{-1} \leftarrow \big(\mathbf{I} - c\big(\sum_{j=1}^{l} \mathbf{L}_1^{(j)} \otimes \mathbf{L}_c^{(j)}\big)(\mathbf{A}_1 \otimes \mathbf{A}_c)\big)^{-1}$;

3   Set $\mathbf{R} \leftarrow \big(\sum_{j=1}^{l} \mathbf{L}_1^{(j)} \otimes \mathbf{L}_c^{(j)}\big)\mathbf{x}; \mathbf{b} \leftarrow \mathbf{y}^T \mathbf{Z}^{-1} \mathbf{R}; \mathbf{l} \leftarrow c\mathbf{y}^T \mathbf{Z}^{-1}$;

4   **for** *each candidate q in $\mathbf{G}$ after pruning* **do**

5   Initialize $\mathbf{s} \leftarrow$ a zero vector of length t except the last element is 1;

6   Initialize $\mathbf{w} \leftarrow$ weight vector from q to the new team members;

7   Set $\mathbf{E} \leftarrow [\mathbf{w}, \mathbf{s}]; \mathbf{F} \leftarrow [\mathbf{s}'; \mathbf{w}']$;

8   Set $\mathbf{e}^{(j)} \leftarrow$ a t by 1 zero vector except the last element is 1, for $j = 1, \ldots, d_n$;

9   Set $\mathbf{f}^{(j)} \leftarrow$ a $1 \times t$ zero vector except the last element, which is label j assignment for q;

10   Set $\mathbf{P} \leftarrow [\mathbf{L}_1^{(1)} \otimes \mathbf{e}^{(1)}, \ldots, \mathbf{L}_1^{(l)} \otimes \mathbf{e}^{(l)}]$;

11   Set $\mathbf{Q} \leftarrow [\mathbf{I} \otimes \mathbf{f}^{(1)}; \ldots; \mathbf{I} \otimes \mathbf{f}^{(l)}]$;

12   Compute $\mathbf{X}_1 \leftarrow \big(\sum_{j=1}^{l} \mathbf{L}_1^{(j)} \mathbf{A}_1 \otimes \mathbf{L}_c^{(j)} \mathbf{E}\big)$;

13   Compute $\mathbf{X}_2 \leftarrow \big(\sum_{j=1}^{l} \mathbf{L}_1^{(j)} \mathbf{A}_1 \otimes \mathbf{e}^{(j)} \mathbf{f}^{(j)} \mathbf{E}\big)$;

14   Compute $\mathbf{Y}_1 \leftarrow \mathbf{Q}(\mathbf{A}_1 \otimes \mathbf{A}_c)$;

15   Compute $\mathbf{Y}_2 \leftarrow (\mathbf{I} \otimes \mathbf{F})$;

16   Set $\mathbf{X} \leftarrow [\mathbf{P}, \mathbf{X}_1, \mathbf{X}_2], \mathbf{Y} \leftarrow [\mathbf{Y}_1; \mathbf{Y}_2; \mathbf{Y}_2]$;

17   Update $\mathbf{M} \leftarrow (\mathbf{I} - c\mathbf{Y}\mathbf{Z}^{-1}\mathbf{X})^{-1}$;

18   Compute $\mathbf{r}' \leftarrow \mathbf{Z}^{-1} \mathbf{P}\mathbf{Q}\mathbf{x}$;

19   Compute $\text{score}(q) = \mathbf{b} + \mathbf{y}^T \mathbf{r}' + \mathbf{l}\mathbf{X}\mathbf{M}\mathbf{Y}(\mathbf{Z}^{-1}\mathbf{R} + \mathbf{r}')$;

20 **end**

21 **Return** the top k candidates with the highest scores.

$\mathbf{X}_1, \mathbf{X}_2$ and $\mathbf{Y}_1$ take $O(lt^5)$; computing $\mathbf{M}$ takes $O(lt^5 + l^3 t^3)$ and computing the $\text{score}(q)$ takes $O(lt^3)$. Putting everything together, the time complexity of Algorithm 5 is $O((\sum_{i \in \mathcal{T}/p} d_i)(lt^5 + l^3 t^3))$.   □

Variant #2: TEAMREP-FAST-APPROX

By using Eq. (4.6) to compute the graph kernel instead, we design an even faster algorithm (TEAMREP-FAST-APPROX), which is summarized

---

Algorithm 6: TEAMREP-FAST-APPROX

Input: (1) The entire social network $\mathbf{G} := \{\mathbf{A}, \mathbf{L}\}$, (2) original team
   members $\mathcal{T}$, (3) person p who will leave the team, (4) starting
   and ending probability $\mathbf{x}$ and $\mathbf{y}$ (be uniform by default), and (5)
   an integer k (the budget)

Output: Top k candidates to replace person p

1 Initialize $\mathbf{A}_c, \mathbf{L}_1^{(j)}, \mathbf{L}_2^{(j)}, j = 1, \ldots, l$;
2 Compute top r eigen-decomposition for $\mathbf{A}_c$: $\mathbf{U}\Lambda\mathbf{U}' \leftarrow \mathbf{A}_c$;
3 Set $\mathbf{V} \leftarrow \Lambda\mathbf{U}'$;
4 Initialize $\mathbf{s} \leftarrow$ a zero vector of length t except the last element is 1;
5 Initialize $\mathbf{w}_1 \leftarrow$ weight vector from p to $\mathcal{T}$;
6 Set $\mathbf{E}_1 \leftarrow [\mathbf{w}_1, \mathbf{s}], \mathbf{F}_1 \leftarrow [\mathbf{s}'; \mathbf{w}_1']$;
7 Set $\mathbf{X}_1 \leftarrow [\mathbf{U}, \mathbf{E}_1]$, $\mathbf{Y}_1 \leftarrow [\mathbf{V}; \mathbf{F}_1]$;
8 **for** *each candidate q in $\mathbf{G}$ after pruning* **do**
9   Initialize $\mathbf{w}_2 \leftarrow$ weight vector from q to the new team members ;
10   Set $\mathbf{E}_2 \leftarrow [\mathbf{w}_2, \mathbf{s}], \mathbf{F}_2 \leftarrow [\mathbf{s}'; \mathbf{w}_2']$;
11   Set $\mathbf{X}_2 \leftarrow [\mathbf{U}, \mathbf{E}_2]$, $\mathbf{Y}_2 \leftarrow [\mathbf{V}; \mathbf{F}_2]$;
12   Compute $\mathbf{S} \leftarrow \sum_{j=1}^{l} \mathbf{y}_1' \mathbf{L}_1^{(j)} \mathbf{X}_1 \otimes \mathbf{y}_2' \mathbf{L}_2^{(j)} \mathbf{X}_2$;
13   Compute $\mathbf{T} \leftarrow \sum_{j=1}^{l} \mathbf{Y}_1 \mathbf{L}_1^{(j)} \mathbf{x}_1 \otimes \mathbf{Y}_2 \mathbf{L}_2^{(j)} \mathbf{x}_2)$;
14   Update $\mathbf{M} \leftarrow (\mathbf{I} - c(\sum_{j=1}^{l} \mathbf{Y}_1 \mathbf{L}_1^{j} \mathbf{X}_1 \otimes \mathbf{Y}_2 \mathbf{L}_2^{j} \mathbf{X}_2))^{-1}$;
15   Set $\text{score}(q) = \left(\sum_{j=1}^{l} \left(\mathbf{y}_1' \mathbf{L}_1^{(j)} \mathbf{x}_1\right) \left(\mathbf{y}_2' \mathbf{L}_2^{(j)} \mathbf{x}_2\right)\right) + c\mathbf{S}\mathbf{M}\mathbf{T}$;
16 **end**
17 **Return** the top k candidates with the highest scores.

---

in Algorithm 6. In the algorithm, we only need to compute the top r eigen-
decomposition for $\mathbf{A}_c$ once (step 2), and use that to update the low-rank
approximation for every new team. Besides, when we update $\mathbf{M}$, a matrix
inverse of size $(r + 2)^2 \times (r + 2)^2$ (step 14), the time is independent of the
team size.

The effectiveness and efficiency of TEAMREP-FAST-APPROX are summarized in Lemmas 4.5 and 4.6, respectively. Compared with TEAMREP-BASIC
and TEAMREP-FAST-EXACT, Algorithm 6 is even faster; and the only place
it introduces the approximation error is the low-rank approximation of $\mathbf{A}_c$
(step 2).

Lemma 4.5. *Accuracy of* TEAMREP-FAST-APPROX. *If* $\mathbf{A}_c = \mathbf{U}\Lambda\mathbf{U}'$ *holds,
Algorithm 6 outputs the same set of candidates as* TEAMREP-BASIC.

Proof   Omitted for brevity.   □

Lemma 4.6. *Time Complexity of* TEAMREP-FAST-APPROX *Algorithm 6 takes* $O((\sum_{i\in\mathcal{T}/p} d_i)(lt^2r + r^6))$ *in time.*

Proof   Omitted for brevity.   □

4.2.4 Experimental Evaluations

In this subsection, we present the experimental evaluations. The experiments are designed to answer the following questions: .

- *Effectiveness*: How accurate are the algorithms for TEAM MEMBER REPLACEMENT?
- *Efficiency:* How scalable are the algorithms?

Datasets *DBLP*. DBLP dataset[2] provides bibliographic information on major computer science journals and proceedings. We use it to build a coauthorship network where each node is an author and the weight of each edge stands for the number of papers the two corresponding authors have coauthored. The network constructed has $n = 916,978$ nodes and $m = 3,063,244$ edges. We use the conferences (e.g., KDD, SIGMOD, CVPR, etc.) to reflect authors' skills (e.g., *data mining, database, computer vision,* etc.) and for a given author and conference, we define his/her skill level as the percentage of the papers s/he publishes at that conference. For a given paper, we treat all of its coauthors as a team. Alternatively, if a set of authors coorganize an event (such as a conference), we also treat them as a team.

  Movie. This dataset[3] is an extension of MovieLens dataset, which links movies from MovieLens with their corresponding IMDb webpage and Rotten Tomatoes review system. It contains information of 10,197 movies, 95,321 actors/actress and 20 movie genres (e.g., action, comedy, horror, etc.). Each movie has on average 22.8 actors/actress and 2.0 genres assignments. We set up the social network of the actors/actresses where each node represents one actor/actress and the weight of each edge is the number of movies the two linking actors/actresses have costarred. We use the movie genres that a person has played as his/her skills. For a given movie, we treat all of its actors/actress as a team.

---

[2] http://arnetminer.org/citation.
[3] http://grouplens.org/datasets/hetrec-2011/ .

Table 4.2 *Summary of datasets for* TEAM
MEMBER REPLACEMENT.

Data	n	m	# of teams
DBLP	916,978	3,063,244	1,572,278
Movie	95,321	3,661,679	10,197
NBA	3,924	126,994	1,398

NBA. The NBA dataset[4] contains NBA and ABA statistics from the year 1946 to the year 2009. It has information on 3,924 players and 100 teams season by season. We use players' positions as their skill labels, including *guard, forward*, and *center*. The edge weight of the player network stands for the number of seasons that the two corresponding nodes/individuals played on the same team.

The statistics of these datasets are summarized in Table 4.2. All the experiments are run on a Windows machine with 16GB memory and Intel i7-2760QM CPU.

Repeatability of Experimental Results. All the three datasets are publicly available. We have released the code of our algorithms through the authors' website.

Effectiveness Results

A. Qualitative Evaluations. We first present some case studies on the three datasets to gain some intuitions.

Case studies on DBLP. Let us take a close look at Figure 4.1, which shows a screenshot of our current demo system. This prototype system has been developed to a fully functional system and deployed to real users [18]. The original team is shown on the left side and the person leaving the team (*Philip S. Yu*) is represented by a node (diagram) with larger radius. If the user clicks a replacement from the recommendation list (on the top), the system will show the new team on the right side. Here, we introduced a novel visualization technique to represent authors' relationships and their expertise within one unique graph visualization. Particularly, in this visualization, the authors are shown as voronoi diagrams [34]. The authors' expertise is visualized as the voronoi cells inside the diagram, that is, each cell indicates a type of expertise. We use different shades of gray to identify different expertise types and use the darker shades to encode the author's strength in that

---

[4] http://www.databasebasketball.com.

expertise type. For example, if *KDD* is represented in a cell, darker gray in a voronoi diagram means the author has a strong expertise in *KDD*. In contrast, a lighter cell indicates the author's lack of the corresponding expertise. To facilitate visual comparison of different authors, we fix the position of these expertise cells across different diagrams so that, for example, *KDD* is always shown at the left side of the author diagrams. These voronoi diagrams are connected by links indicating the authors' relationships. The strength of the relationship is presented by the line thickness.

Figure 4.1 visualizes the team structures before and after *Philip S. Yu* becomes unavailable in the team writing [75]. Our algorithm's top recommendation is *Jiawei Han*. As we can see, both *Han* and *Yu* possess very similar skills and are renowned for their extraordinary contributions in the data mining and databases community. Moreover, *Han* has collaborated with almost each of the rest authors/team members. Looking more closely, we find *Han* preserves several key triangle substructures in the original team: one with *Ke Wang* and *Jian Pei*, and the other with *Haixun Wang* and *Jian Pei*. These triangle sub-structures might play a critical role in accomplishing subtasks in writing the paper.

We also consider a bigger team, i.e., the organizing committee of *KDD 2013*. After filtering those not in *DBLP*, we have 32 people on the committee team. We use their coauthorship network as their social network. Suppose one of the research track cochairs *Inderjit Dhillon* becomes unavailable and we are searching for another researcher who can fill in this critical role in organizing *KDD 2013*. The top five candidates our algorithm recommends are *Philip S. Yu, Jiawei Han, Christos Faloutsos, Bing Liu*, and *Wei Wang*. The results are consistent with the intuitions – all of these recommended researchers are highly qualified – not only have they made remarkable contributions to the data mining field, but also they have strong ties with the remaining organizers of *KDD 2013*. For example, *Liu* is the current chair of KDD executive committee; *Wang* is one of the research track program chairs for *KDD 2014*; and *Faloutsos* was the PC cochair of *KDD 2003*, etc.

Case studies on Movie. Assuming actor *Matt Damon* became unavailable when filming the epic war movie *Saving Private Ryan* (1998) and we need to find an alternative actor who can play *Ryan*'s role in the movie. The top five recommendations our algorithm gives are *Samuel L. Jackson, Steve Buscemi, Robert De Niro, Christopher Walken*, and *Bruce Willis*. As we know, *Saving Private Ryan* is a movie of the *action* and *drama* genres. Notice that both *Damon* and *Jackson* have participated in many movies of *drama, thriller*, and *action* genres, hence *Jackson* has the acting skills required to play the role in this movie. Moreover, *Jackson* has coplayed with *Tom Sizemore, Vin Diesel*,

Dale Dye, Dennis Farina, Giovanni Ribisi, and *Ryan Hurst* in the crew before. The familiarity might increase the harmony of filming the movie with others.

Case studies on NBA. Let us assume that *Kobe Bryant* of the Los Angeles Lakers was hurt during the regular season in 1996 and a bench player is badly wanted. The top five replacements our algorithm recommends are *Rick Fox, A. C. Green, Jason Kidd, Brian Shaw,* and *Tyronn Lue.* As we know, *Bryant* is a guard in NBA. Among the five recommendations, *Kidd, Shaw,* and *Lue* all play as guards. More importantly, *Jason, Brian,* and *Tyronn* have played with 9, 7, and 9 of the rest team members on the same team in the same season multiple times. Therefore, it might be easier for them to maintain the momentum and chemistry of the team, which is critical to winning the game.

B. Quantitative Evaluations. Besides the preceding case studies, we also perform quantitative evaluations. Recall that we have two design objectives for our TEAM MEMBER REPLACEMENT problem, including both the *skill match* and the *structural match*. Our quantitative evaluations focus on the following two aspects. First, we examine whether simultaneously considering both design objectives outperforms only considering one of them. Second, we evaluate to what extent our graph kernel formulation outperforms other alternative choices, in order to fulfill both design objectives (i.e., the skill match and the structural match). To be specific, we compare to the following alternative methods, including (a) only with *structure matching* and not including $L_\times$ in Eq. (4.2) (Graph Only), (b) only with *skill matching* and using cosine similarity of skill vectors as scores (Skill Only), (c) using the weighted sum of scores by "Skill Only" and "Graph Only" (Linear Combination), (d) using the multiplication of the two (Multiplicative Combination), and (e) first picking those with high "Skill Only" scores and then ranking them by "Graph Only" scores (Sequential Filtering).

User studies. We perform a user study with 20 people aged from 22 to 35 as follows. We choose 10 papers from various fields, replace one author of each paper, run our method and the first two comparison methods, and each of them recommends top five candidates. Then, we mix the outputs (15 recommendations in total) and ask users to (a) mark exactly one best replacement and (b) mark all good replacements from the list of 15 recommended candidates. The results are presented in Figures 4.2 through 4.4, respectively. As we can see from these figures, our method is best in terms of both precision and recall. For example, the average recalls by our method, by "Graph Only" and by "Skill Only" are 55%, 28%, and 17%, respectively. As for different papers, our method wins nine out of 10 cases (except for "paper 2," where "Skill Only" is best).

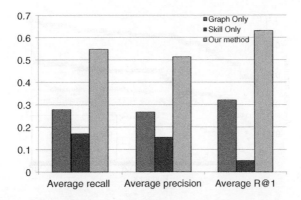

Figure 4.2 The average recall, average precision and R@1 of the three comparison methods. Higher is better.

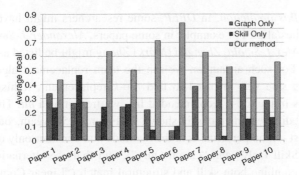

Figure 4.3 Recall for different papers. Higher is better.

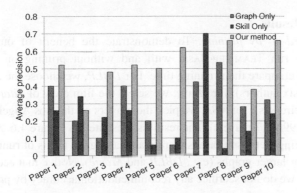

Figure 4.4 Precision for different papers. Higher is better.

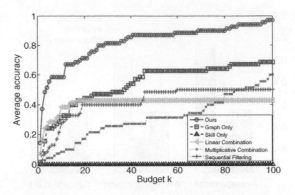

Figure 4.5 Average accuracy vs. budget k. Higher is better.

Author alias prediction. In *DBLP*, some researchers might have multiple name identities/alias. For example, in some papers, *Alexander J. Smola* might be listed as *Alex J. Smola*, *Zhongfei (Mark) Zhang* might be listed as *Zhongfei Zhang*, etc. For such an author, we run the team replacement algorithm on those papers s/he was involved to find top-k replacement. If his/her other alias appears in the top-k recommended list, we treat it as a *hit*. The average accuracy of different methods is shown in Figure 4.5. Again, our method performs best – it outperforms both the methods that consider only one design objective ("Skill Only" and "Graph Only"); and that use alternative ad hoc methods to combine both skill and structural match ("Linear Combination," "Multiplicative Combination," and "Sequential Filtering").

Efficiency Results

A. The speed-up by pruning. To demonstrate the benefit of our pruning strategy, we run TEAMREP-BASIC with and without pruning on the three datasets and compare their running time. For *DBLP*, we choose the authors of paper [56] (six authors); for *Movie*, we select the film crew of *Titanic* (1997) (22 actors/actresses); for *NBA*, we pick the players on the Los Angeles Lakers in the year 1996 (17 players). The result is presented in Figure 4.6. As we can see, the pruning step itself brings significant savings in terms of running time, especially for larger graphs (e.g., *DBLP* and *Movie*). Notice that according to Lemma 4.2, we do not sacrifice any recommendation accuracy by pruning.

B. Further speed-up. Next, we vary the team sizes and compare the running time of TEAMREP-BASIC with TEAMREP-FAST-EXACT (exact methods); and Ark-L [45] with TEAMREP-FAST-APPROX (approximate methods). For TEAMREP-BASIC and Ark-L, we apply the same pruning step as their

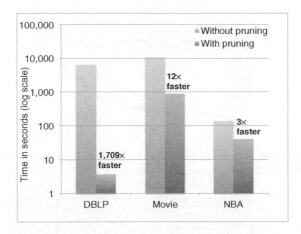

Figure 4.6 Time comparisons before and after pruning on three datasets. Notice time is in log scale.

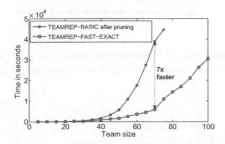

Figure 4.7 Time comparison between TEAMREP-BASIC and TEAMREP-FAST-EXACT. TEAMREP-FAST-EXACT is on average 3× faster. TEAMREP-BASIC takes more than 10 hours when team size = 70.

preprocessing step. The results on *DBLP* are presented in Figures 4.7 and 4.8, respectively. We can see that the TEAMREP-FAST-EXACT and TEAMREP-FAST-APPROX are much faster than their alternative choices, especially when team size is large. Notice that Ark-L is the best-known method for approximating a random walk–based graph kernel.

C. Scalability. To test the scalability of our TEAMREP-FAST-EXACT and TEAMREP-FAST-APPROX algorithms, we sample a certain percentage of edges from the entire *DBLP* network and run the two proposed algorithms on teams with different sizes. The results are presented in Figures 4.9 and 4.10, respectively. As we can seen, both algorithms enjoy a *sublinear* scalability with regard to the total number of edges of the input graph (m).

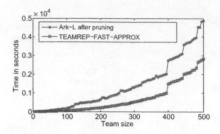

Figure 4.8 Time comparisons between Ark-L[20] and TEAMREP-FAST-APPROX. TEAMREP-FAST-APPROX is on average 3× faster.

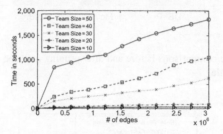

Figure 4.9 Running time of TEAMREP-FAST-EXACT vs. graph size. TEAMREP-FAST-EXACT scales sublinearly with regard to the number of edges of the input graph.

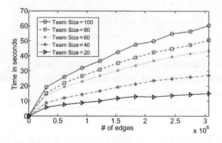

Figure 4.10 Running time vs. graph size. TEAMREP-FAST-APPROX scales sublinearly with regard to the number of edges of the input graph.

4.3 Beyond Team Member Replacement

Different from TEAM MEMBER REPLACEMENT, TEAM REFINEMENT considers refining a team by replacing one member with another with the desired skill sets and communication connections. In the previous two problems, the team size remains the same. In TEAM EXPANSION, we want to expand the team by adding a member with certain skill sets and communication structure. For instance, a software project team wants to develop a new feature of natural language search and a new member with Natural Language Processing (NLP) skill will be recruited. On the contrary, in TEAM SHRINKAGE, the size of a team needs to be reduced in response to new challenges such as a shortage of the available resource (e.g., a budget cut). In all cases, the resulting disruption [108] should be minimized.

By careful inspection, we identify the problem similarity between TEAM REFINEMENT, TEAM EXPANSION, and TEAM MEMBER REPLACEMENT and propose these problems can be formulated in a way to share common technical solutions. In TEAM REFINEMENT, one team member is edited to a desired skill and network structure configuration. Since such edited member might not exist in the rest of the network, we call it a "virtual member." By replacing this "virtual member" as in TEAM MEMBER REPLACEMENT, we can solve TEAM REFINEMENT. Similarly, in TEAM EXPANSION, the desired new member might also be a "virtual member." After adding this "virtual member" to the current team and then replacing the "virtual member," we can solve TEAM EXPANSION. We reduce the disruption induced by the team alteration by maintaining the team-level similarity (between the original and the new teams), which includes skill similarity as well as structural similarity. The proposition is backed by some recent studies that show that team members prefer to work with people they have worked with before [42] and that distributed teams perform better when members know each other [26]. Furthermore, research has shown that specific communication patterns among team members are critical for performance [20].

4.3.1 Problem Definitions

In addition to the notations defined in Section 4.2.1, we define for the ith individual, the associated skill vector as $\mathbf{l} = \mathbf{L}(i, :)$ and communication structure vector as $\mathbf{a} = \mathbf{A}(i, :)$. If we lay off an existing member $p \in \mathcal{T}$ of a given team $\mathcal{T}$, the new team members are indexed by $\mathcal{T}_{/p} := \{\mathcal{T}/p\}$; and the new team is represented by the labeled network $\mathbf{G}(\mathcal{T}_{/p})$.

With the preceding notations and assumptions, the other team enhancement problems can be formally defined as follows:

Problem 4.7 TEAM REFINEMENT

> **Given:** (1) A labeled social network $\mathbf{G} := \{\mathbf{A}, \mathbf{L}\}$, (2) a team $\mathbf{G}(\mathcal{T})$, (3) a team member $p \in \mathcal{T}$, and (4) desired skill $\mathbf{l}$ and communication structure $\mathbf{a}$ for p;
>
> **Recommend:** A candidate $q \notin \mathcal{T}$ with skill $\mathbf{l}$ and communication structure $\mathbf{a}$ to refine the person p's role in the team $\mathbf{G}(\mathcal{T})$.

Problem 4.8   TEAM EXPANSION

Given: (1) A labeled social network $\mathbf{G} := \{\mathbf{A}, \mathbf{L}\}$, (2) a team $\mathbf{G}(\mathcal{T})$, and (3) desired skill $\mathbf{l}$ and communication structure $\mathbf{a}$ for a new member;

Recommend: A new member $q \notin \mathcal{T}$ with skill $\mathbf{l}$ and communication structure $\mathbf{a}$ to join the team $\mathbf{G}(\mathcal{T})$.

Problem 4.9   TEAM SHRINKAGE

Given: (1) A labeled social network $\mathbf{G} := \{\mathbf{A}, \mathbf{L}\}$, and (2) a team $\mathbf{G}(\mathcal{T})$;
Recommend: A member $p \in \mathcal{T}$ to leave the team $\mathbf{G}(\mathcal{T})$.

4.3.2 Beyond TEAM MEMBER REPLACEMENT: TEAM REFINEMENT, TEAM EXPANSION, and TEAM SHRINKAGE

In this subsection, we discuss how the techniques for TEAM MEMBER REPLACE-MENT can be applied to the other team enhancement scenarios, including TEAM REFINEMENT, TEAM EXPANSION, and TEAM SHRINKAGE. We note that the fast solutions developed in Section 4.2.3 also apply to these scenarios, and thus omit the detailed discussions.

TEAM REFINEMENT   In TEAM REFINEMENT, we want to edit a current team member p to have the desired skill $\mathbf{l}$ and communication structure vector $\mathbf{a}$. As the person with the exact skill and communication requirements might not exist in the network, we aim to find a best-effort match. We define a "virtual member" v to be the person with skill $\mathbf{l}$ and network structure $\mathbf{a}$ and a "virtual team" $\mathcal{T}'$ to be $\mathcal{T}_{p \to v}$. Using graph kernel, the best-effort match q can be found as follows:

$$q = \text{argmax}_{j,\, j \notin \mathcal{T}}\ \text{Ker}(\mathbf{G}(\mathcal{T}'), \mathbf{G}(\mathcal{T}'_{v \to j})). \qquad (4.7)$$

TEAM EXPANSION   In TEAM EXPANSION, we want to add a team member with the desired skill $\mathbf{l}$ and communication structure vector $\mathbf{a}$. Again, because the exact match might not exist, we instead find a best-effort match. We define a "virtual member" v to be the person with skill $\mathbf{l}$ and network structure $\mathbf{a}$ and a "virtual team" $\mathcal{T}'$ to be $\{\mathcal{T}, v\}$. Using graph kernel, the best-effort match q can be found as follows:

$$q = \text{argmax}_{j,\, j \notin \mathcal{T}}\ \text{Ker}(\mathbf{G}(\mathcal{T}'), \mathbf{G}(\mathcal{T}'_{v \to j})). \qquad (4.8)$$

TEAM SHRINKAGE In TEAM SHRINKAGE, we want to remove a current team member with minimum disruption. Since graph kernel can characterize the team-level similarity, it can also be applied to TEAM SHRINKAGE. The idea is to find a current team member p so that the new team after p leaves is most similar to the old team. That is, we want to find a member $p \in \mathcal{T}$ such that

$$p = \operatorname{argmax}_{j \in \mathcal{T}} \ \operatorname{Ker}(\mathbf{G}(\mathcal{T}), \mathbf{G}(\mathcal{T}_{/j})), \tag{4.9}$$

where $\mathbf{G}(\mathcal{T}_{/j})$ is the labeled team graph after a team member j leaves. Note that in TEAM SHRINKAGE, the search space is no longer the rest network but the team itself, which is much smaller.

4.3.3 Experimental Evaluations

Case studies on TEAM EXPANSION. Suppose we want to expand the organizing committee of Knowledge Discovery in Databases (KDD) 2013 by hiring a researcher with strong expertise in artificial intelligence, and preferably who has collaborated with as many researchers on the committee as possible. The top five candidates found by our algorithm are *Qiang Yang*, *Zoubin Ghahramani*, *Eric Horvitz*, *Thomas G. Dietterich*, and *Raymond J. Mooney*. All the candidates have made significant contributions to the field of artificial intelligence and *Yang*, *Horvitz*, *Dietteirch*, and *Mooney* are the current Association for the Advancement of Artificial Intelligence (AAAI) fellows. Among them, *Yang* has collaborated with some previous KDD organizing committee members (e.g., *Jian Pei*, *Ying Li*, *Geoff Webb*, and *Dou Shen*).

    Team Shrinkage. In *DBLP*, we select teams with over 10 members and manually inject a "noisy" individual to the team such that the individual is connected with all the team members with random edge weights and has randomly generated skill vectors. Recall that in team shrinkage we want to find the "best" member to leave the team without much disruption to the team. In our setting, we treat the "noisy" individual as the "best" candidate. For "Skill Only," we first compute the similarity matrix among all team members using inner product of their skill vectors and then apply max-pooling as their score. Figure 4.11 shows the result of our method, "Graph Only" as well as "Skill Only." Our method achieves the best Precision@1, Recall@1, and F@1.

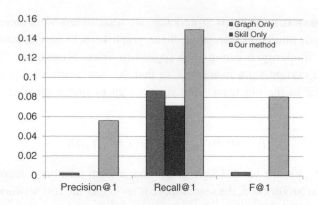

Figure 4.11 Precision@1, Recall@1, and F@1 of the three comparison methods for TEAM SHRINKAGE. Higher is better.

4.4 Toward Real-Time Team Optimization

Teams can be often viewed as a dynamic system where the team configuration evolves over time (e.g., new members join the team; existing members leave the team; the skills of the members improve over time). It is hypothesized that newly formed teams evolve through a series of development stages, notably *forming*, where the formation of the team starts; *storming*, where team members explore the situation; *norming*, where members accommodate, form, and accept roles; and *performing*, where the team produces effective outcomes [90]. Although teams might take different paths toward maturity, research suggests that effective cooperation and coordinations among team members generally bring the team from initial ineptness to the final levels of skilled performance [70]. In the context of sports teams and software development teams, research efforts have been on the relationship between team dynamics and team performances [32, 94].

Due to the team dynamics, the performance of the team is very likely to be changing over time. If a team struggles to achieve satisfactory performance or external demands for adjustments are required, changes to the team are necessary. A natural question is how to plan the team optimization/restaffing actions (e.g., recruiting a new team member) at each time step so as to maximize the expected cumulative performance of the team. Most existing work on team optimization (e.g., team replacement [58] and team enhancement [59]) treats teams as a *static* system and recommends a single action to optimize a *short-term* objective. However, these approaches might fail due to the unique challenges brought about by the dynamics in team processes.

First (*team dynamics*), the teams are constantly changing in their compositions, and existing methods are not designed to learn the kind of changes that are effective in producing the teams' high performances. A straightforward way of applying existing methods for team optimization is to recommend one action at a time. However, this treatment is problematic in two ways: (1) the existing methods are optimizing a different objective and they cannot adjust their strategy based on the feedback (e.g., performance evaluation, team cohesion) to the team; and (2) the existing methods cannot be computed on the fly in situations where real time decisions are required. Second (*long-term reward*), teams are expected to deliver constantly good performance in the long run. The actions recommended by existing methods are purposed to optimize short-term feedback, but might be suboptimal in terms of the long-term reward.

In this book, we treat the actions a team takes during its development cycles as sequential interactions between the team agent and the environment and leverage the recent advances in deep reinforcement learning to automatically learn optimal staffing strategies. Such team optimization based on reinforcement learning has two advantages. First, it is able to continuously update its staffing strategy during the interactions from the feedback at each time step, until it converges to the optimal strategy. Second, the models are trained via estimating the current value for a state–action pair with delayed rewards. The optimal strategy is able to maximize the expected cumulative rewards from the environment. In other words, it might recommend an action with small short-term rewards but have a big impact of the team performance in the long run. One challenge here is that the state/action space (e.g., the possible enhancement operations and their combinations over time) could be large. It is thus infeasible to evaluate the value for every state–action pair. Instead, we leverage a value-based approach and use a function approximator to estimate the state–action value. This model-free approach does not estimate the transition probability nor explicitly store the Q-value table, making it flexible to handle the large state/action space in team optimization scenarios. We summarize our main contributions as follows:

- **Problem Formulation**. We formally define and formulate the real-time team optimization problem. Given the template teams with high performance, the key idea is to continuously maximize the long-term performance of the optimized teams through a sequence of actions, e.g., adding/removing team members and establishing new collaborations.
- **Algorithm and Analysis**. We design a deep reinforcement learning–based framework, which can continuously learn and update its team

Table 4.3 *Symbols and definitions.*

Symbols	Definition
$\mathbf{G} = \{\mathbf{V}, \mathbf{E}, \mathbf{N}\}$	An attributed social network
$\mathbf{V} = \{v_1, v_2, \ldots, v_n\}$	A set of n vertices of a network $\mathbf{G}$
$\mathbf{E} = \{(v_i, v_j) \mid v_i, v_j \in \mathbf{V}\}$	A set of edges
$\mathbf{N} \in \mathbb{R}^{n \times l}$	Attribute matrix
$\mathcal{T} = \{a_1, a_2, \ldots, a_k \mid a_i \in \mathbf{V}\}$	A team of members from the network
$\mathbf{G}(\mathcal{T})$	The team network indexed by its members $\mathcal{T}$
$\mathbf{f}(\mathcal{T})$	Skill representation of the team $\mathcal{T}$
$\mathbf{v}(v_i)$	The attribute/skill vector of vertex v_i
$\mu(v_i)$	Vector representation of vertex v_i
l	The total number of skills
$n = |\mathbf{V}|$	The total number of individuals in $\mathbf{G}$
α, γ	Learning rate and discount factor

optimization strategy by incorporating both skill similarity and structural consistency.

- **Empirical Evaluations**. We perform extensive experimental evaluations on real-world datasets to test the efficacy of our framework in the task of real-time team optimization. The evaluations demonstrate that our reinforcement learning framework can achieve significant performance in optimizing the initial team toward a high-performing one.

4.4.1 Problem Definitions and Preliminaries

In this section, we introduce the notations used (summarized in Table 4.3), formally define the real-time optimization problem and then present preliminaries on deep reinforcement learning as well as graph neural network.

Notations and Problem Definition

1. Notations. We use bold lowercase letters for vectors (e.g., $\mathbf{v}$), lowercase letters for scalars (e.g., α), and $\mathcal{T}_i$ for a team configuration at the ith time step.

2. Problem Definition. In our problem setting, we are given a large social network of n individuals (i.e., $\mathbf{G} = \{\mathbf{V}, \mathbf{E}\}$), consisting of subgraphs (i.e., teams represented by $\mathcal{T}$). The attribute/skill vector $\mathbf{v}(v_i)$ for an individual $v_i \in \mathbf{V}$ represents the strength of the skills possessed by the corresponding individual. We consider a team that has high performance to be a template team, denoted as $\mathcal{T}_s$. We detail how we choose template teams in the experimental setting in Section 4.4.3.

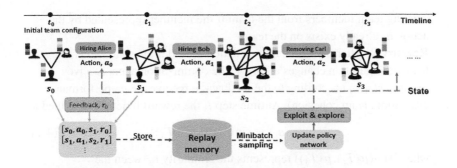

Figure 4.12 An illustrative running example of real-time team optimization. A team optimization agent receives the feedback from the action made to the team and then updates the policy network that will affect the decision of actions.

We study the real-time team optimization problem in which a team agent interacts with the environment by sequentially taking some enhancement actions (e.g., hiring a new team member, removing an existing team member) over a sequence of time steps, so as to maximize its cumulative reward (see Figure 4.12 for an illustrative example). We model this problem as a Markov decision process (MDP), which includes a sequence of states, actions, and rewards. More formally, MDP consists of a tuple of five elements $(S, \mathcal{A}, \mathcal{R}, \mathcal{P}, \gamma)$ as follows:

- **State space** S. The state $s_t \in S$ is defined as the team configuration at time step t, i.e., $\mathcal{T}_t = \{a_1, a_2, \ldots\}$, where $a_1, a_2, \ldots$ are the members of the current team, and $\mu(s_t)$ is the representation of the state:

$$\mu(s_t) = \sum_{v \in \mathcal{T}_t} \mu(v), \tag{4.10}$$

where $\mu(v)$ is the representation of the individual v in team $\mathcal{T}_t$. We use two types of representations for individuals, including (1) the attribute/skill vector, i.e., $\mathbf{v}(v)$; and (2) the node embedding that is obtained by the graph neural network models, i.e., $\mu(v)$.

- **Action space** $\mathcal{A}$. The action $a_t \in \mathcal{A} \subseteq \mathbf{V}$ at the tth time step is to take enhancement actions to the team, e.g., expand/shrink the team, establish collaboration between two team members, etc. Formally, a_t could be $\Delta \mathbf{E}(\mathcal{T}, \mathcal{T})$ (perturbation to the team network structure), $\Delta \mathbf{N}(\mathcal{T}, :)$ (perturbation to the team skill configuration), $+q$ (hiring q to join the team), and $-q$ (remove q from current team). In this book, we focus on the enhancement actions of adding new members to the team and removing existing team members from the team if the member represented by the action a_t already exists on the team.

- **Reward $\mathcal{R}$.** After the team takes an action a_t under the state s_t, i.e., the team configuration changes at time t, the optimization agent receives rewards $r(s_t, a_t)$ according to the feedback it receives (e.g., performance evaluation, team cohesion). At time step t, the reward function is defined as

$$r(s_t, a_t) = \text{sim}(\mu(\mathcal{T}_t), \mu(\mathcal{T}_s)), \tag{4.11}$$

where $\text{sim}(\mu(\mathcal{T}_t), \mu(\mathcal{T}_s))$ represents the similarity between the representation of the template team and the representation of the current team configuration. For example, when hiring a new team member, we often consider that a qualified candidate who has not only had collaborations with the existing team members (i.e., team structural consistency) but also possesses a set of skills required by the team function (i.e., attribute/skill similarity). The details of computing sim_f is presented in Section 4.4.2.

- **Transition probability $\mathcal{P}$:** Transition probability $p(s_{t+1}|s_t, a_t)$ defines the probability of the state transitioning from s_t to s_{t+1} when the team takes an action a_t. We assume that the MDP satisfies $p(s_{t+1}|s_t, a_t, \ldots, s_1, a_1) = p(s_{t+1}|s_t, a_t)$.

- **Discount factor γ:** $\gamma \in [0, 1]$ is the discount factor that is used to measure the present action–state value of future reward. In particular, when $\gamma = 0$, the team agent only considers the immediate reward, and when $\gamma = 1$, all future rewards are fully taken into the consideration of calculating the action–state value of the current action a_t.

- **Terminal:** Once the team expands to have a certain number of members, the team agent stops exploring or selecting candidates from the network **G**. For simplicity, we specify the size of the team with a fixed number in both training and testing.

With the preceding notations and definitions, the problem of real-time team optimization can be formally defined as follows:

Problem 4.10   Real-Time Team Optimization

Given: given an initial configuration of a team (i.e., $\mathcal{T}_0$), the historical MDP, i.e., $(\mathcal{S}, \mathcal{A}, \mathcal{P}, \mathcal{R}, \gamma)$, a specified team size k, and a set of selected template teams $\mathbf{M} = \{\mathcal{T}_s^{(1)}, \mathcal{T}_s^{(2)}, \ldots\}$;

Find: an optimization policy $\pi : \mathcal{S} \rightarrow \mathcal{A}$ for a team agent to construct a team from the initial team configuration (i.e., $\mathcal{T}_0$) of size k, which maximizes the similarity between the finalized team configuration, $\mathcal{T}_\pi$, and the given set of template teams.

We can formally formulate Problem 4.10 as

$$\underset{\pi}{\mathrm{argmax}}\, f = \sum_{\mathcal{T}_s^{(i)} \in \mathbf{M}} \mathrm{sim}(\mathcal{T}, \mathcal{T}_s^{(i)})$$

$$\text{s.t. } \mathcal{T}_0 \subseteq \mathcal{T}_\pi \text{ and } |\mathcal{T}_\pi| = k.$$

Given the preceding problem definition, a sample trajectory of this Markov decision process will be $(s_0, a_0, r_0, \ldots, s_{m-1}, a_{m-1}, r_{m-1}, s_m)$, where $s_0 = \mathbf{G}(\mathcal{T}_0)$, $s_i = \mathbf{G}(\mathcal{T}_i), i \in \{1, \ldots, m-1\}$, and $s_m = \mathbf{G}(\mathcal{T}_\pi)$. After action a_i (e.g., adding a new member to the team) at every step i, we will receive the reward $r_i = r(s_i, a_i)$. Because this is a discrete optimization problem with a finite searching space (i.e., the number of candidates in a network $\mathbf{G}$ is finite), we leverage Q-learning to learn this MDP, the technical details of which are described in Section 4.4.2.

Preliminaries

1. Deep Reinforcement Learning. Research achievements have been made on utilizing reinforcement learning in many high-impact applications, ranging from recommender systems [82, 85], agent controlling in Atari games [69] to traffic signal control systems [96]. In Q-learning [95], the optimal action–state value function directly follows the *Bellman equation*, of which the intuition is: if the optimal value $Q^*(s', a')$ of the state s' at the next time step is known for all possible actions a' in the action space $\mathcal{A}$, then the optimal strategy is to select the action a' that maximizes the expected value of $r + \gamma Q^*(s', a')$,

$$Q^*(s, a) = \mathbb{E}_{s' \sim \varepsilon}\left[r + \gamma \max_{a'} Q^*(s', a') | s, a\right], \qquad (4.12)$$

where r is the immediate reward of action a' and γ is the discount factor. The basic idea behind many reinforcement learning algorithms is to estimate the action–state value function by iteratively updating the value, i.e., $Q_{t+1}(s, a) = \mathbb{E}\left[r + \gamma \max_{a'} Q_t(s', a') | s, a\right]$ and store the triple, (value, action, state) in a look-up table, denoted as Q-value table. However, the Q-value table will become extraordinarily large with the increasing number of states to be stored, making the traditional Q-learning method infeasible in the real-world large scale recommender systems. A follow-up work [69] proposes to leverage the convolutional neural network, i.e., Q-network, to approximate the action–state value function, which can be trained by minimizing the following loss function at each iteration i,

$$L_i(\theta_i) = \mathbb{E}_{s,a}\left[(y_i - Q(s, a; \theta_i))^2\right], \qquad (4.13)$$

where $y_i = \mathbb{E}_{s' \sim \varepsilon}\left[r + \gamma \max_{a'} Q(s', a'; \theta_i)|s, a\right]$ is the target for the ith iteration. As a result, the modified neural network serves as a nonlinear approximator to the action–state value function, which provides a model-free method for reinforcement learning. The advantage of this method is that it does not require the calculation of the transition probability and the storage of the Q-value table. This promotes the flexibility of reinforcement learning to support a variety of application scenarios and also enriches the generalizability of the system compared to the traditional training approaches to estimate the action–state value function.

2. Graph Neural Network Models. The graph neural networks (GNN) are useful neural network architectures in many applications, e.g., network embedding, node classification, and anomaly detection [30, 118]. For a graph $\mathbf{G} = (\mathbf{V}, \mathbf{E})$, we can obtain the vector representation of nodes $v \in \mathbf{V}$ by an iterative process,

$$\mu(v)^{(i)} = h^{(i)}\left(\left\{w(u,v), \mathbf{v}(u), \mu^{(i-1)}\right\}_{u \in N(v)}, \mathbf{v}(v), \mu(v)^{(i-1)}\right), \quad (4.14)$$

where h is a parametric function $\mu(v)^{(i)}$ is the representation of node v at the ith iteration, $i \in \{1, 2, 3, \ldots\}$, $w(u, v)$ is the weight of edge $(u, v) \in \mathbf{E}$, $\mathbf{v}(u)$, $\mathbf{v}(v)$ are the attribute vectors of the node u, v respectively and $N(v)$ represents the set of neighborhood of node $v \in \mathbf{V}$ [50]. At each iteration, features information of the nodes of the neighborhood are used to compute the hidden representation of the specific node v. The initial node representation $\mu_v^{(0)} \in \mathbb{R}^d$ can be set to zero and for the simplicity of notation, after M iterations, we obtain the consequent node representation as $\mu(v) = \mu(v)^{(M)}$. After we get the node representations, we can further obtain the graph-level representation by applying pooling over all the obtained node embeddings. Recently, the variational graph auto-encoder (VGAE), which utilizes a similar idea of the variational auto-encoder (VAE) on graph data, has shown impact on the node representation learning in an unsupervised setting. The variational graph auto-encoder is an unsupervised framework based on graph convolutional network for learning node representations. Similar to the variational auto-encoder [49], in this framework, the encoder uses a two-layer Graph Convolution Network (GCN), denoted as function $g(\mathbf{N}, \mathbf{A}) = \widetilde{\mathbf{A}}\text{ReLU}(\widetilde{\mathbf{A}}\mathbf{N}\mathbf{W}_0)\mathbf{W}_1$ with two learnable matrices $\mathbf{W}_0$ and $\mathbf{W}_1$, where $\mathbf{A}$ is the adjacency matrix, $\widetilde{\mathbf{A}} = \mathbf{D}^{-\frac{1}{2}}(\mathbf{A} + \mathbf{I})\mathbf{D}^{-\frac{1}{2}}$ is the normalized adjacency matrix, $\mathbf{N}$ is the node attribute matrix, and $\text{ReLU}(\cdot) = \max(0, \cdot)$, to compute the mean vector μ_i and the standard deviation vector σ_i^2 of a latent variable Z_i of normal distribution for each node i, i.e., $q(\mathbf{z}_i|\mathbf{N}, \mathbf{A}) = \mathcal{N}(\mathbf{z}_i|\mu_i, \sigma_i^2)$. The decoder uses the following equation to reconstruct the normalized adjacency matrix $\widetilde{\mathbf{A}}$, and for each entry $\mathbf{A}_{ij}$, we have $p(\mathbf{A}_{ij} = 1|\mathbf{z}_i, \mathbf{z}_j) = \mathrm{sigmoid}(\mathbf{z}_i'\mathbf{z}_j)$. The loss we want to minimize is as follows:

$$\mathbb{E}_{q(\mathbf{Z}|\mathbf{X},\mathbf{A})}\big[\log p(\mathbf{A}|\mathbf{Z})\big] - \mathrm{KL}\big[q(\mathbf{Z}|\mathbf{X},\mathbf{A})\|p(\mathbf{Z})\big], \qquad (4.15)$$

where $\mathrm{KL}\big[q(\cdot)\|p(\cdot)\big]$ is the Kullback–Leibler divergence between the two distribution.

4.4.2 Our Solution

In this section, we introduce our model based on reinforcement learning framework for the purpose of real-time team optimization. We use a function approximator to estimate the state–action value without explicitly storing the value into a lookup table.

Our Real-Time Team Optimization Framework
In order to achieve the optimal real-time team optimization, we take the enhancement actions (e.g., adding a member from the network $\mathbf{G}$ or removing a team member from the current team configuration $\mathcal{T}_t$) according to the feedback from the environment (i.e., the reward as defined in the MDP). In this book, as mentioned earlier, we consider optimizing the current team to become similar to the template teams with outstanding performance through a sequence of actions (i.e., adding/removing members). More specifically, we give detailed description of the reward and the transition process of the MDP as follows:

- **Reward** $\mathcal{R}$. The reward $r(s_t, a_t)$ is defined as the average similarity between the vector representations of the team configuration at tth time step and the representation of teams in the set of the template teams,

$$r(s_t, a_t) = \frac{1}{|\mathbf{M}|} \sum_{\mathcal{T}_s \in \mathbf{M}} \mathrm{sim}(\mu(\mathcal{T}_t), \mu(\mathcal{T}_s)), \qquad (4.16)$$

where $\mu(\mathcal{T}_s)$ is the representation of one template team from the set $\mathbf{M}$ (i.e., $\mathbf{M} = \{\mathcal{T}_s^{(1)}, \mathcal{T}_s^{(2)}, \ldots\}$) and $\mu(\mathcal{T}_t)$ is the current team representation. According to the definition in Eq. (4.10), the representation of a team is the linear aggregation of the representations of all members, we then have $\mu(\mathcal{T}_t) = \sum_{a_i \in \mathcal{T}_t} \mu(a_i)$. We leverage the cosine similarity to calculate the similarity between the two vectors, as presented follows:

$$\mathrm{sim}(\mu(\mathcal{T}_t), \mu(\mathcal{T}_s)) = \frac{\mu(\mathcal{T}_t)\mu(\mathcal{T}_s)}{\|\mu(\mathcal{T}_s)\|\|\mu(\mathcal{T}_s)\|}. \qquad (4.17)$$

- **Transition from s_t to s_{t+1}.** As mentioned, in this book, we consider two types of team enhancement actions, i.e., adding a new member to the current team from the network **G** and removing an existing member from the current team. Therefore, the state at the next time step can be expressed as $\mu(s_{t+1}) = \mu(\mathcal{T}_{t+1}) = \mu(\mathcal{T}_t) + \mu(a_t)$ when a new team candidate a_t is selected and added to the current team and $\mu(s_{t+1}) = \mu(\mathcal{T}_{t+1}) = \mu(\mathcal{T}_t) - \mu(a_t)$ when an existing member in the current team is leaving.

The Standard DQN Model

We follow the standard assumption that delayed rewards are discounted by a factor of γ per time step, and define the state–action value function $Q(s,a)$ as the expected rewards from state s_t and action a_t. Using Bellman optimality equation [8], the optimal state–action function $Q^*(s,a)$ can be written as follows via one-step lookahead:

$$Q^*(s_t, a_t) = r(s_t, a_t) + \gamma \max_{a'} Q^*(s_{t+1}, a'). \qquad (4.18)$$

This implicitly indicates a greedy policy of selecting actions:

$$\pi(a_t | s_t; Q^*) = \operatorname*{argmax}_{a_t} Q^*(s_t, a_t). \qquad (4.19)$$

We can use Q-learning control algorithm to update the Q values toward the optimal ones at each step of each episode as follows:

$$Q(s_t, a_t) \leftarrow Q(s_t, a_t) + \alpha[r + \gamma \max_{a'} Q(s_{t+1}, a') - Q(s_t, a_t)], \qquad (4.20)$$

where α is the learning rate and s_{t+1} is the next state after action a_t is taken, e.g., $\mu(s_{t+1}) = \mu(s_t) + \mu(a_t)$.

The limitations with the preceding standard reinforcement learning model are twofolds: (1) in the real-time team optimization scenarios, the state/action space are enormous, which makes it infeasible to estimate $Q^*(s,a)$ for every state–action pair using the preceding update equation; and (2) many state and action pairs may not appear in the log of the team development, in which case we will not have an accurate estimate for them. In practice, the action–state value function is often highly nonlinear. We therefore refer to a nonlinear approximator that is parameterized by neural networks to estimate the action-state value function, i.e., $Q^*(s,a) \approx Q(s,a;\theta)$, where θ is the parameter of the neural networks. Specifically, the Q function can be parameterized as

$$Q^*(s_t, a_t) = \operatorname{ReLU}\left(W_{\theta_2}^{(2)} \left(\operatorname{ReLU}\left(W_{\theta_1}^{(1)\mathrm{T}} [\mu(s_t), \mu(a_t)] \right) \right) \right), \qquad (4.21)$$

where $W_{\theta_1}^{(1)}$, $W_{\theta_2}^{(2)}$ are the parameters of the corresponding layer in the network, ReLU($\cdot$) is the activation function for each layer, and $\mu(s_t)$, $\mu(a_t)$ are the vector representation of the current state s_t (i.e., current team configuration $\mu(s_t) = \mu(\mathcal{T}_t)$) and of the selected member a_t.

The Q-network which approximates the action–state value function is trained to minimize the following loss function $L(\theta)$,

$$L(\theta) = \mathbb{E}_{s_t,a_t,r,s_{t+1}}[(y - Q(s_t,a_t;\theta))^2], \tag{4.22}$$

where $y = \mathbb{E}_{s_{t+1}}[r + \gamma \max_{a'} Q(s_{t+1},a';\theta_t)|s_t,a_t]$ is the expected action–state value for the current episode and θ_t is the parameter from the last episode. The derivatives of the loss function $L(\theta)$ with respect to θ can be written as

$$\nabla_\theta L(\theta) = \mathbb{E}_{s_t,a_t,r,s_{t+1}}\Big[(r + \gamma \max_{a'} Q(s_{t+1},a';\theta) \\ - Q(s_t,a_t;\theta))\nabla_\theta Q(s_t,a_t;\theta)\Big]. \tag{4.23}$$

To optimize the loss function, it is more efficient to apply the stochastic gradient descent instead of the full expectations in the above gradient.

Off-Policy Training

With the preceding Q-network, we train the parameters of the model from the offline log of different teams' development, including the actions the team agent takes and the reward it receives. To be specific, we train two separate team optimization agents with two types of representation for the individuals in the network, (1) attribute/skill vector and (2) node representation obtained by the VGAE model. For each episode in the training process, the agent starts with making actions, e.g., selecting candidates from the network **G**, and then receives reward from the environment before updating the state. We also apply the ϵ-greedy policy in selecting actions, which enables the agent to explore more qualified candidates rather than always selecting the best candidate at present. The value of ϵ decreases for every certain number of episodes, and the discount factor γ is set to 1. The off-policy training algorithm is presented in Algorithm 7.

Other Team Optimization Methods

1. Random walk graph kernel [58] proposes to apply random walk graph kernel to recommend the best team candidate if one team member becomes unavailable. It selects the best candidate member c by choosing the one who

---

Algorithm 7: Off-Policy Training for Real-Time Team Optimization

---

Input: (1) vector representations of all nodes in graph **G**, (2) a set of
template teams **M**, (3) the learning rate α, (4) the discount factor
γ, (5) initial and end probabilities of accepting the current
selection, ϵ_i and ϵ_e, and (6) the size of a team k;

Output: a model of policy for real-time team optimization.

1 Initialize replay memory $\mathcal{D}$ with the capacity of m;
2 Initialize action–state value function Q with random weights θ;
3 Initialize target action–state value function $\widetilde{Q}$ with random weights
   $\widetilde{\theta} = \theta$;
4 **for** *episode* $= 1, \ldots, T$ **do**
5   Initialize a zero state representation $\mu(s_0)$ and a team configuration
        $\mathcal{T}_0$ with empty members;
6   **while** $|\mathcal{T}| \neq k$ **do**
7   Select a random action a_t with probability ϵ, otherwise select
            $a_t = \mathrm{argmax}_a\, Q(s_t, a; \theta)$;
8   Execute action a_t, compute reward $r(s_t, a_t)$ using Eq. (4.16);
9   Update team configuration by adding a_t to $\mathcal{T}$ if $a_t \notin \mathcal{T}$ or
            removing a_t if $a_t \in \mathcal{T}$ and set $s_{t+1} = s_t$;
10   Store the transition $(s_t, a_t, s_{t+1}, r(s_t, a_t))$ into the memory $\mathcal{D}$;
11   Sample a minibatch of transitions (s_t, a_t, s_{t+1}, r) from $\mathcal{D}$;
12   Optimize the network parameter θ via stochastic gradient decent
            on the loss defined in Eq. (4.22);
13   **end**
14   Set the network parameter $\widetilde{Q} = Q$ every 10 episodes;
15   Update the ϵ value as $\epsilon = \epsilon_e + (\epsilon_i - \epsilon_e)e^{-\frac{\text{episode}}{200}}$;
16 **end**

---

maximizes the similarity between the old and the new teams embedded in
social networks as follows:

$$\mathrm{argmax}_c \mathcal{K}(\mathbf{G}^*, \mathbf{G}_c) = \mathbf{q}'_\times (\mathbf{I} - \alpha\mathbf{A}_\times)^{-1} \mathbf{N}_\times \mathbf{p}_\times, \qquad (4.24)$$

where $\mathbf{G}^*$ is original team, $\mathbf{G}_c$ is the new team after selecting member c,
$\mathbf{A}_\times = \mathbf{N}_\times(\mathbf{A}^* \otimes \mathbf{A}_c)$ is the matrix of the two networks' Kronecker product,
$\otimes$ represents the Kronecker product of two matrices, α is a decay factor,
$\mathbf{q}_\times = \mathbf{q}^* \otimes \mathbf{q}_c$ and $\mathbf{p}_\times = \mathbf{p}^* \otimes \mathbf{p}_c$ are two vectors representing the stopping
and starting probability of random walk respectively, $\mathbf{N}_\times$ is a diagonal matrix

Table 4.4 *Statistics of the graph datasets used for experiment.*

Dataset	Nodes	Edges	Attribute	# of teams
DBLP	18,674	64,089	7	30,145
Movie	13,678	416,874	20	2,578

and can be expressed as $\mathbf{N}_\times = \sum_{i=1}^{l} \mathrm{diag}(\mathbf{N}^*(:,i)) \otimes \mathrm{diag}(\mathbf{N}_c(:,i))$, and $\mathbf{N} \in \mathbb{R}^{n \times d}$ is the attribute matrix. This team recommendation strategy works as follows: at each time step, it selects the member from the entire social network that maximizes the similarity between the optimized team and the predefined high-performance team.

2. Skill-based team recommendation selects a team candidate who maximizes the average cosine similarity between the skill representation of the current team $\mathbf{f}(\mathcal{T}_t)$ and that of the template teams, i.e., $\mathrm{argmax}_c \frac{1}{|\mathbf{M}|} \sum_{\mathcal{T}' \in \mathbf{M}} \mathrm{sim}(\mathbf{f}(\mathcal{T}_t) + \mathbf{v}(c), \mathbf{f}(\mathcal{T}'))$.

4.4.3 Empirical Evaluations

In this section, we conduct extensive experiments to evaluate our algorithms in order to answer the following two questions:

- **Structural consistency.** From the perspective of the topology of the network, do the members in the newly optimized teams have similar collaboration networks as the members in template teams?
- **Skill similarity.** Are the skills possessed by the new members close to the skills presented by the template teams?

Datasets

We use two real-world datasets, which are publicly available. Table 4.4 summarizes the statistics of these datasets and the detailed description of these datasets are as follows.

- **DBLP** is a dataset that provides bibliographic information in major computer journals and proceedings. It has (1) one coauthorship network where each node represents an author, and there is an edge between two nodes if two authors have ever published a paper together, and the weight of this specific edge is the number of papers the two corresponding authors have coauthored. The authors' skills are represented by conferences in seven different areas (i.e., DM, VIS, DB, NLP, AI, SYSTEM, and

MULTIMEDIA) where for a given author and a conference, the skill level of this author is defined as the percentage of the papers that s/he has published in this specific area; (2) one paper–author network that provides information for all the coauthors for a given paper, and we treat the authors who have published the same paper as a team. In our experiment, we define the performance of the team as the number of citations that the corresponding paper has, and we select a number of teams (i.e., papers) that have a good performance.

- **Movie** is an extension of the MovieLens dataset, which links movies from MovieLens to their corresponding IMDb webpages and Rotten Tomatoes review system. It contains information on 10,197 movies, 95,321 actors/actresses, and 20 movie genres (e.g., action, comedy, horror, etc.). Each movie has on average 22.8 actors/actress and 2.0 genres assignments. We establish the social network of the actors/actresses where each node represents one actor/actress, and an edge exists if two actors/actresses have ever collaborated in the same movie, with the corresponding weight being the number of movies in which the two linking actors/actresses have costarred. We use the movie genres that a person has played as his/her skills, and for a certain genre, the skill level of this specific person is defined as the percentage of the movies that belongs to this genre. Similarly, for a given movie, we treat all of its actors/actresses as a team.

Experimental Design

In this subsection, we introduce the quantitative metrics and the experimental settings we apply in the evaluation of the algorithm.

1. Evaluation metric. We quantify the effectiveness of our algorithms by measuring the following two metrics, including (1) the consistency in the collaboration structure of the team members, where we compare the degree distributions of the members of the teams optimized by the trained agent; and (2) the similarity of the skills possessed by the optimized team and the template teams. The detailed description is as follows,

- *Structural consistency.* One essential objective of team optimization is to find a new team where the members have a similar collaboration network as the template teams (e.g., the number of collaborations that the members have in the newly optimized team is close to that of the members in the template teams). In real-world scenarios, the number of members on one team is comparatively small. For example, in the *DBLP* dataset, the average number of authors in one paper (i.e., the size of team) is usually less than 10, and the number of actors/actresses in the cast of a movie is approximately 25 in the *Movie* dataset. Therefore, we present the distribution of the degrees of all members from the teams obtained by the proposed algorithms and comparison methods in the evaluation.

- *Skill similarity.* Another goal of team optimization is to construct a team that possesses a similar skill set as the template teams. In our experiment, we define the skill set of the team as the aggregation of the skill vectors of each member who belongs to the team, i.e., $\mathbf{f}(\mathcal{T}) = \sum_{v \in \mathcal{T}} \mathbf{v} \in \mathbb{R}^d$, where d is the dimension of the attribute/skill vector. We then use cosine similarity to measure the similarity between two teams with regard to attribute/skill, denoted as sim_f, where $\mathrm{sim}_f(\mathcal{T}_1, \mathcal{T}_2) = \frac{\mathbf{f}(\mathcal{T}_1) \cdot \mathbf{f}(\mathcal{T}_2)}{\|\mathbf{f}(\mathcal{T}_1)\|_2 \|\mathbf{f}(\mathcal{T}_2)\|_2}$.

2. Experimental setting. In the experiment on the *DBLP* dataset, we consider a paper (i.e., a team of authors) of which the number of citations is larger than 40 to be a highly cited publication and the authors of the corresponding paper are considered to be a high-performance team (denoted as one template team). In the training phase of our algorithm, we randomly select 500 template teams and perform the off-policy training according to Algorithm 7. We apply two types of node representations, attribute/skill vectors and VGAE node embeddings respectively in both training and testing, and we use a suffix "A" and "G" to represent either variant. The average number of members in one template team is 4.56, and the average degree of the members in the template teams is 15.13. Accordingly, we set the parameter, $m = 5$, where one episode terminates after the number of selected members reaches five. In the testing phase, we perform the evaluation of the trained team optimization agent in the following three types of settings of the initial configuration of the testing team: (1) two initial members with the same top skill who exist in our selected template teams (setting 1), (2) two initial members from nontemplate teams (setting 2), and (3) no initial member exists (i.e., starting from scratch) (setting 3). For each of the three settings, the evaluation is performed on 600 different randomly configured initial teams. The eventual team size (i.e., k) in the testing phase is set to be 4 and 6 respectively (i.e., 300 teams of size 4 and 6 respectively), the training and testing of our algorithm are performed for 10 times. The results presented in the next subsection are the average of evaluation metrics. For the experiment on the *Movie* dataset, a similar evaluation procedure is conducted. We consider a movie with an average rating of 8.0 as a top-rated movie and its actors/actresses in the cast are considered template movie teams. The statistics of the *Movie* dataset differs from the *DBLP* dataset, e.g., the average number of actors/actresses in one top-rated movie is 25.52 and the average number of collaborations for one individual actor/actress is 36.72. Thus in the training phase, we randomly select 360

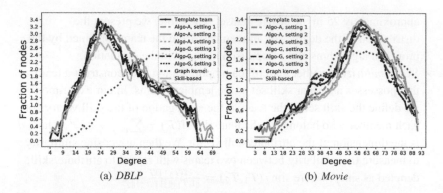

(a) *DBLP*   (b) *Movie*

Figure 4.13 Aggregated degree distribution of the teams. (a) The number of seed (size of initial team) is randomly selected as one or two if existed and the eventual size of the team is defined as 4 and 6 respectively in the experiment ($k = 4, 6$). (b) Six members exist initially in every testing team and the size of the team is set as 24 ($k = 24$).

movies to be the template teams and set $k = 24$ in order for one episode to terminate; in the testing phase, the same three settings of the initial team configuration are employed, but the differences are (1) six initial members are given for the first two types of test settings and (2) the eventual size of testing teams is defined to be 24, which approximates the average size of template teams.

3. Repeatability and Machine Configuration. The experiments are performed on a virtual environment on Windows 10 Intel Core i5-7300 at 2.60GHz and 16GB RAM and are implemented in Python 3.6. All datasets are publicly available.

Quantitative Results

1. Evaluation on *DBLP*. We first compare the degree distribution of all the members from the teams that are obtained by our designed algorithms and the comparison methods. The result is summarized in Figure 4.13a. We can see the three lines (dash-dotted, black dashed, and black dot-grey dashed) that represent the degree distributions of members from the teams obtained by Algorithm-G under three different settings. These three lines approach the degree distribution of the members from the template teams (i.e., the black solid line) to a greater extent compared with the other three lines (gray dashed, gray solid, and gray dotted), which represents the degree distribution of the members from the teams obtained by Algorithm-A. This is because in the process of obtaining the node representations using VGAE, the structural

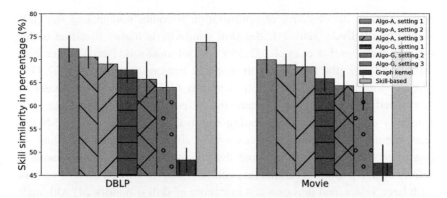

Figure 4.14 The average skill similarity (in percentage) of the teams optimized by our algorithms and the comparison methods. Higher is better.

information is embedded in the node representation. As a result, the trained team agent is able to select team members having a more similar collaboration structure as the members from the template teams. Another observation is that the degree distributions representing the first type of setting (i.e., gray dashed line and gray dash-dotted line) have shown the best performance with regard to structural consistency compared with other two types of settings. In addition, the distributions representing the third type of setting (i.e., gray and gray dotted line) demonstrate a better structural consistency than that of the second type of setting (i.e., black dashed and black solid lines). This is because compared with constructing a team from scratch, an initial team of members with mediocre performance will actually impede the team agent from optimizing a team toward the direction of selecting outstanding members. The result of the graph kernel (i.e., black dotted line) shows that it has an inclination of selecting members with a larger number of collaborations. This is because as Eq. (4.24) shows, a network of team with more collaborations (i.e., higher degree of node) will have a larger graph kernel, and thus team candidates with large degrees are more likely to be selected by this strategy.

The results of the measurement of skill similarity are presented on the left side of Figure 4.14. We have the following observations. (1) Under the same type of evaluation setting, leveraging the attribute vector in training can achieve a better similarity of skills. For example, 72.35% obtained by Algorithm-A (the leftmost bar), is larger than the score, 67.47% obtained by Algorithm-G (the middle bar with horizontal lines), this is consistent with our intuition because when we use the attribute/skill vector as the node representation, the objective of optimization becomes maximizing the skill similarity. (2) Under setting 1, the skill similarity is higher than that under other two settings. For example, 72.35% (the leftmost solid bar) is higher than 70.58%, 69.08% (the two bars with diagonal lines respectively) and 67.47% (the bar with horizontal lines) is higher than 65.76%, 63.98% (the thatched and dotted bars respectively), where the latter two bars represent the skill similarity under the other two testing settings. (3) The graph kernel-based team optimization strategy achieves a skill similarity of 48.33%, which is consistent with the result of degree distribution in Figure 4.13a because it selects a large portion of candidates with large degree as well as skill vectors with large values, and thus causes a low score of skill similarity. (4) Although the skill-based method achieves the best performance since it computes the similarity for each team candidate and selects the member with the largest value, it is very time consuming.

2. Evaluation on *Movie*. The degree distribution of all members from the testing teams on the *Movie* dataset is presented in Figure 4.13b. We can see that even though the pattern of these distributions are different from those on the *DBLP* dataset, leveraging VGAE node representations can still achieve a closest degree distribution (i.e., the dotted-dashed line) to the distribution of the template team members (i.e., the solid black line). In addition, under the same type of evaluation setting, the model trained using VGAE node representation is more capable of optimizing the teams toward the template teams than the model that uses attribute/skill vectors. For example, the black dot-dashed line is closer to the solid black line than the black dashed line (under setting 2), and the gray solid line is also closer than the gray dotted line (under setting 3). The graph kernel method shows a similar results to Figure 4.13a, and there is a large portion of members who have higher degrees. For the skill similarity on *Movie*, from the right side of Figure 4.14, we have the following observations that are consistent with the results on *DBLP*: (1) the team agent trained using attribute/skill vector under setting 1 achieves the highest similarity in skill (i.e., 69.98% in the leftmost solid bar) among the results obtained by other proposed methods; (2) the team agent trained with attribute/skill vectors always outperforms the agent trained with VGAE node representations, for example, under the second type of setting, 68.86% (the leftmost bar with diagonal lines) is higher than 64.32% (the thatched bar) and 68.43% (the rightmost bar with diagonal lines) is higher than 62.91% (the dotted bar) under the third type of evaluation setting.

3. Parameter study. Figure 4.15 summarizes the comparison of degree distributions on the *Movie* dataset under two new types of settings that alter

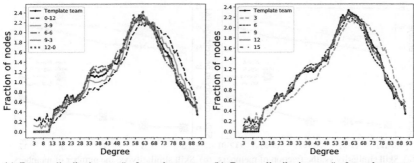

(a) Degree distribution vs. # of template members in $\mathcal{T}_0$.

(b) Degree distribution vs. # of template members in $\mathcal{T}_0$.

Figure 4.15 Comparison of the degree distribution of the teams optimized by our algorithm and the comparison methods. The more the line approaches the original distribution (i.e., the black dotted line), the better. (a) The size of $\mathcal{T}_0$ is 12 of which the number of members from the template increases. (b) The size of $\mathcal{T}_0$ increases.

the evaluation parameter. We first fix the size of initial team configuration to be 12 and increase the number of members that are originally in the template teams from 0 to 12. From Figure 4.15(a), we can see that (1) when no members from the template teams exist in the initial team configuration, the degree distribution (i.e., the dashed line) is apparently the most contrasting distribution comparing with the distribution of the template teams; (2) as we increase the number of members who are from the template teams, the distribution is gradually approaching the original distribution. Second, we alter the size of the initial team (from three to 12) with all members from the template teams and summarize the results in Figure 4.15(b). It can be seen that as the size of initial team increases, the distribution is also getting closer to the original distribution (i.e., the solid black line), which is consistent with our intuition. If we compare these two settings, we can see that when the size of the initial team is the same as the number of members from template teams in Figure 4.15(a), and the degree distribution of the former setting is closer to the original distribution. For example, the black dashed line in Figure 4.15(b) approaches the original distribution to a greater extent than the dotted-dashed line in Figure 4.15(a) because there are no nontemplate members in the initial members in the second setting.

We also compare the skill similarity when altering the parameters in the same way and Figure 4.16 present how the skill similarity changes. We have the following observations, (1) for both settings, as the number of members in the initial team configuration increases, the skill similarity also improves;

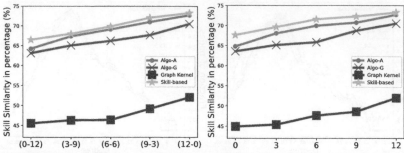

(a) Skill similarity vs. the fraction of members from the template teams (the size of initial team is fixed to be 12).

(b) Skill similarity vs. the number of members from the template teams (the size of initial team increases).

Figure 4.16 Parameter analysis of skill similarity on the *Movie* dataset. The higher the value is, the better.

(2) when the number of members from the template teams is the same in both settings, the initial teams with only members from the template teams achieves a higher score of skill similarity. For example, when the number of members from the template teams is 6 and the attribute vectors are leveraged in training, 69.98% (Figure 4.16(b)) is higher than 69.15% (Figure 4.16(a)).

Case Study

1. Case study on *DBLP*. In this subsection, we present a case study of real-time team optimization using our method. First, we apply the model trained with VGAE node representations to an initial team with two members, *Kunal Punera* and *Byron Dom*. After the optimization has finished, the team includes the following new members, *John Langford, Thomas Hofmann, Alexandar Smola,* and *Yi Chang*. We find that the new team largely overlaps with this template team, which includes *Hans Kriegel, Alexandar Smola, Kunal Punera, Yi Chang*, and *Byron Dom*. We can see that both teams consist researchers in the area of *Machine Learning* and *AI*, among whom *Dr. Alexandar Smola* and *Dr. Byron Dom* are highly reputed researchers in these areas, which demonstrates that our algorithm can recommend team candidates with a similar collaboration network as well as similar types of skills present in the template team.

2. Case study on *Movie*. One representative example of team obtained by our method includes the following actors/actresses, *Christian Bale, Gary Oldman, Morgan Freeman, Aaron Eckhart, Gwyneth Paltrow*, and *Joseph Gordon-Levitt* (only a subgroup of actors/actresses in this team are listed). We can observe that the listed members in these team are popular movie actors/actresses and they have starred in several well-known highly rated movies. For example, *Christian Bale, Gary Oldman, Morgan Freeman,* and *Aaron Eckhart* are in the main cast of the movie, *The Dark Knight* of which the rate is 9.0 on *IMDB*. *Morgan Freeman* is a Golden Globe Award winner with many highly rated movie, including *The Shawshank Redemption* and *Dark Knight Trilogy*, and he has also collaborated with *Gwyneth Paltrow* and *Joseph Gordon-Levitt* in the movies *Seven* and *The Dark Knight Rises*, respectively.

5

Team Performance Explanation

In this chapter, we introduce our work on team performance explanation [61, 119]. We start with the explanation model we build for understanding networked prediction systems, i.e., the team performance prediction models introduced in Chapter 3, and then continue with our effort on explaining the team performance optimization model introduced in Chapter 4.

5.1 Toward Explainable Networked Prediction

Networked prediction has attracted lots of research attention in recent years. Networks, as natural data models that capture the relationship among different objects, domains, and learning components, provide powerful contextual information in modeling networked systems, including network of networks [22, 72, 73], network of time series [16, 17], and network of learning models [47]. Networked prediction has been successfully applied in many application domains, ranging from bioinformatics, environmental monitoring, and infrastructure networks to team science.

By leveraging the intrinsic relationship among the networked learning components, it often brings significant performance improvement to mining tasks. In a network of networks, each node of the main network is itself another domain network. For example, in the candidate gene prioritization problem, where a disease similarity network is given, a tissue-specific protein interaction network can be associated with a corresponding disease. The main network can contextualize the mining tasks in each domain-specific network by providing consistency constraints across networks for both ranking [72] and clustering [73]. In the network of coevolving time series, e.g., a sensor network where sensors measure the temperature time series in different locations of a building, encoding the network constraints finds similar latent factors from

112

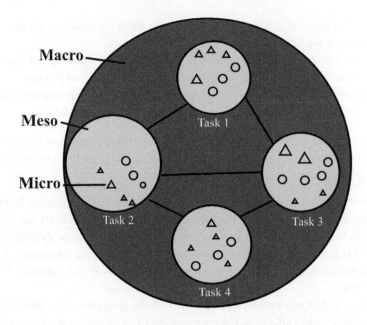

Figure 5.1 An illustration of networked prediction system.

similar time series for imputation and classification tasks [16, 17]. In the network of learning models, the scientific domain similarity network provides natural constraints to the citation prediction models for each domain such that similar domains would share a similar regression model [57]; or in the multitask learning setting, the task network enables the graph regularized multitask learning formulation [47].

Despite its superior prediction power, networked prediction is often hard to understand for end users. Compared to a traditional learning setting, networked prediction is even harder to explain due to its coupled, multilevel nature. The learning process propagates top-down through the underlying network from the macro level (i.e., the entire learning system), to meso level (i.e., learning tasks), and to micro level (i.e., individual learning examples). See Figure 5.1.

- *Macro level.* At this highest level, we want to study the whole networked learning system to gain a global view of how the system works. What are the ingredients that are essential to the system characteristics, e.g., the parameters of the entire system?
- *Meso level.* At this level, we focus on one specific learning task and aim to understand its own learning behavior, e.g., how its own training samples

and those from other learning tasks affect its model parameters via the network as the bridge.

- *Micro level.* At this finest granularity, we focus on one specific test example and want to understand the reasons behind the prediction of this test example given by the learned models, e.g., how the training examples from the same task and from the other related tasks affect its prediction.

On the other hand, we envision that the networked prediction setting also offers rich context to explain the learning process through the lens of various aspects as follows:

- *Example aspect.* Each training example could potentially shape the learned model of the same task and that of the other tasks via the underlying network. We want to identify the most influential examples at the different levels (i.e., macro, meso, and micro levels) to have a comprehensive understanding of the roles the training examples play in the learning process.
- *Task aspect.* A learning task, if viewed as the aggregation of its training examples, would affect the learning process of the whole system as well as each of the other learning tasks. We seek to identify the important learning tasks at the three different levels.
- *Network aspect.* A task network is essential in the networked learning system and plays a unique role as it acts as a bridge to connect all the learning tasks together. Changing the task network would inevitably influence the learning results of the whole system as well as each individual learning task.

Following the preceding discussion, we develop a multiaspect, multilevel approach to explain networked prediction. The key idea is to efficiently quantify the influence on different levels of the learning system due to the perturbation of various aspects. More concretely, the influence score is measured by the changes in the entire learning system's parameters (*macro*), one task's model parameters (*meso*), and the loss function value at a test sample (*micro*) in response to the changes made to the training examples, a learning task and the task network, respectively.

The key advantages are (1) *multiaspect, multilevel:* we are able to provide a comprehensive explanation to the workings of networked prediction from the perspective of multiple aspects at multiple levels, essentially through the influences of example-task-network aspects with respect to macro-meso-micro levels; and (2) *efficiency:* with the help of influence functions that is rooted in robust statistics [25], we can efficiently evaluate the influences of changes to the networked prediction without retraining the whole learning system, which is often time consuming. Furthermore, we observe that the majority of the training examples have negligible influence at the three different levels, paving the way for us to design a safe pruning strategy to filter out those examples to further speed up the computations.

The main contributions of this work can be summarized as follows:

- **Problem Definitions.** We formulate the problem to demystify the mechanisms behind networked predictions from multiple aspects (example-task-network) at multiple levels (macro-meso-micro).
- **Algorithms and Analysis.** We design an algorithm (NEPAL) to measure the influence of examples, tasks, and network at the macro, meso, and micro levels and design an effective pruning strategy to filter out the examples with negligible influence. We also provide theoretical analysis regarding the complexity and correctness of our algorithm.
- **Empirical Evaluations.** We carefully design the empirical evaluations on real-world datasets and demonstrate the effectiveness of our multiaspect, multilevel approach for understanding the networked prediction.

5.1.1 Problem Definition

In this subsection, we present the notations used (summarized in Table 5.1) and formally define the EXPLAINABLE NETWORKED PREDICTION problem. We use bold capital letters (e.g., $\mathbf{A}$) for matrices and bold lowercase letters (e.g., $\mathbf{w}$) for vectors.

Let us consider a networked learning system with T supervised learning tasks, for example, recognizing objects from images or predicting the sentiment from texts. The training data we have for each task are given as $\{(\mathbf{x}_i^t, y_i^t)\}_{i=1}^{n_t} \subset \mathbb{R}^d \times \mathbb{R}$, $t = 1, \ldots, T$, where n_t is the number of available training examples for the tth task, and d is the dimensionality of the input space, which is assumed to be shared across the tasks. In this work, we assume a task relationship network described by a nonnegative matrix $\mathbf{A}$ is available. In this network, each node represents a task and the edges represent the relatedness between the connected tasks, i.e., $\mathbf{A}(i, j)$ has a higher numerical value if the ith and jth tasks are closely related. The goal of networked prediction is to learn a prediction function parameterized by θ_t as $f_t(\mathbf{x}_i^t; \theta_t)$ for each task jointly in order to minimize the regularized empirical loss as follows:

$$\min_{\theta_1, \ldots, \theta_T} \sum_{t=1}^{T} \frac{1}{n_t} \sum_{i=1}^{n_t} L(f_t(\mathbf{x}_i^t; \theta_t), y_i^t) + \lambda \sum_{i=1}^{T} \sum_{j=1}^{T} \mathbf{A}_{ij} \|\theta_i - \theta_j\|^2, \quad (5.1)$$

Table 5.1 *Symbols of NEPAL.*

Symbols	Definition
T	Number of tasks
d	Feature dimensionality
$\{(\mathbf{x}_i^t, y_i^t)\}_{i=1}^{n_t}$	Training examples for the tth task
$f_t(\mathbf{x}_i^t; \theta_t)$	Prediction function of the tth task parameterized by θ_t
$L(\cdot, \cdot)$	Loss function
$\mathbf{A}$	Task relationship network
$\mathcal{I}_G(\mathbf{x}^t), \mathcal{I}_G(f_t), \mathcal{I}_G(\mathbf{A}_{ij})$	Macro-level influences of a training sample, a learning task, and task network
$\mathcal{I}_s(\mathbf{x}^t), \mathcal{I}_s(f_t), \mathcal{I}_s(\mathbf{A}_{ij})$	Meso-level influences of a training sample, a learning task, and task network with regard to the sth task
$\mathcal{I}_{\mathbf{x}_{\text{test}}^s}(\mathbf{x}^t), \mathcal{I}_{\mathbf{x}_{\text{test}}^s}(f_t), \mathcal{I}_{\mathbf{x}_{\text{test}}^s}(\mathbf{A}_{ij})$	Micro-level influences of a training sample, a learning task, and task network with regard to a test example $\mathbf{x}_{\text{test}}^s$

where $L(\cdot, \cdot)$ is the loss function, e.g., squared loss for regression task or cross entropy loss for classification task, and the last term is to regularize the model parameters through the task relationships.

Our goal is to demystify the networked learning system by understanding how the learning process is propagated at different levels from various aspects. In particular, given the learned models for all the tasks, we want to quantify the influence on different levels of the learning system due to the perturbation of various aspects. More concretely, the influence score is measured by the changes in the whole learning system's parameters, one task's model parameters, and the loss function value at a test sample in response to the changes made to the training examples, a learning task, and the task network.

With the preceding notations, the problem of explaining the networked prediction can be formally defined as follows:

Problem 5.1 EXPLAINABLE NETWORKED PREDICTION

Given: the training data of all the tasks $\{(\mathbf{x}_i^t, y_i^t)\}_{i=1}^{n_t}$, the learned models through joint training $f_t(\cdot, \theta_t^*)$, a query test sample from the tth task $\mathbf{x}_{\text{test}}^t$;

Compute: the influence scores of the training samples, the learning tasks, and the task network on the learning system's parameters, each learning task's parameters, and the prediction with regard to $\mathbf{x}_{\text{test}}^t$.

5.1.2 Our Model

In this subsection, we present our explanation model NEPAL to help explain networked prediction by measuring the influence of the various aspects (i.e., example, task, network) at multiple levels (i.e., macro/system, meso/task, micro/example). We start with a brief review of influence functions, and then present our multiaspect, multilevel approach to networked prediction, followed by the proof and analysis.

Preliminaries: Influence Function. Influence functions have been used in a single learning task to efficiently evaluate the change in model parameters due to the removal of a training sample without retraining the model [51]. For a single learning task, the objective is to minimize the empirical loss as $\theta^* = \arg\min_\theta \frac{1}{n} \sum_{i=1}^n L(f(\mathbf{x}_i; \theta), y_i)$. The key idea is to compute the parameter change should a training sample is upweighted by some small ϵ, giving us new parameters $\theta_\epsilon^* = \arg\min_\theta \frac{1}{n} \sum_{i=1}^n L(f(\mathbf{x}_i; \theta), y_i) + \epsilon L(f(\mathbf{x}; \theta), y)$. The influence of upweighting $\mathbf{x}$ on the parameters θ is given by

$$\mathcal{I}_\theta(\mathbf{x}) = \frac{d\theta_\epsilon^*}{d\epsilon}\bigg|_{\epsilon=0} = -\mathbf{H}_{\theta^*}^{-1} \nabla_\theta L(f(\mathbf{x}; \theta), y),$$

where $\mathbf{H}_{\theta^*} = \frac{1}{n} \sum_{i=1}^n \nabla_\theta^2 L(f(\mathbf{x}_i; \theta), y_i)$ is the Hessian. Removing a training sample is equivalent to upweighting it by $\epsilon = -\frac{1}{n}$, the parameter change $(\theta_{-\mathbf{x}}^* - \theta^*)$ after the removal of the training sample $\mathbf{x}$ can be approximated by $-\frac{1}{n} \mathcal{I}_\theta(\mathbf{x})$ [51].

NEPAL – Building Blocks. In this work, we introduce influence functions in the setting of a networked learning system in order to evaluate the influences of multiple aspects at different levels. We first introduce how to use influence functions to measure the learning system's parameter change due to perturbation of training examples and task network as two key building blocks.

The influence of training sample on model parameters: Removing a training example from one task would change the parameters of the task itself, but also the parameters of other tasks through the task network. We apply the similar idea as before to upweight a training example $\mathbf{x}^t$ from the tth task and compute the changes in all the tasks' model parameters. Define the new parameters of the entire learning system after such upweighting as $\theta_\epsilon^* \stackrel{\text{def}}{=} (\theta_{1,\epsilon}^*, \ldots, \theta_{T,\epsilon}^*)$ and that $\theta_\epsilon^* = \arg\min \sum_{t=1}^T \frac{1}{n_t} \sum_{i=1}^{n_t} L(f_t(\mathbf{x}_i^t; \theta_t), y_i^t) + \lambda \sum_{i=1}^T \sum_{j=1}^T \mathbf{A}_{ij} \|\theta_i - \theta_j\|^2 + \epsilon L(f_t(\mathbf{x}^t; \theta_t), y^t)$. The influence of the upweighting on all the tasks' model parameters can be computed as

$$I_\theta(\mathbf{x}^t) \overset{\text{def}}{=} \left. \frac{d\theta_\epsilon^*}{d\epsilon} \right|_{\epsilon=0} = -\mathbf{H}_{\theta^*}^{-1} \nabla_\theta L(f_t(\mathbf{x}^t; \theta_t), y^t), \quad (5.2)$$

where $\mathbf{H}_{\theta^*}$ is the Hessian of the objective function defined in Eq. (5.1). Since removing the training example $\mathbf{x}^t$ from the tth task is the same as upweighting it by $\epsilon = -\frac{1}{n_t}$, we can approximate the change of the parameters in the whole learning system $(\theta_{-\mathbf{x}^t}^* - \theta^*)$ by $-\frac{1}{n_t} I_\theta(\mathbf{x}^t)$. We show the detailed derivation later in the proofs and analysis.

The influence of task network on model parameters: The changes in the task network $\mathbf{A}$ would also affect the whole learning system's parameters. To measure the influence of task network on model parameters, we upweight the task connection between task i and task j, i.e., $\mathbf{A}_{ij}$, and use the influence function to compute the changes of the model parameters. Define the new parameters after such upweighting as $\theta_\epsilon^* \overset{\text{def}}{=} (\theta_{1,\epsilon}^*, \ldots, \theta_{T,\epsilon}^*)$ and that $\theta_\epsilon^* = \arg\min \sum_{t=1}^T \frac{1}{n_t} \sum_{i=1}^{n_t} L(f_t(\mathbf{x}_i^t; \theta_t), y_i^t) + \lambda \sum_{i=1}^T \sum_{j=1}^T \mathbf{A}_{ij} \|\theta_i - \theta_j\|^2 + \epsilon \mathbf{A}_{ij} \|\theta_i - \theta_j\|^2$. The influence of the upweighting on all the tasks' model parameters can be computed as

$$I_\theta(\mathbf{A}_{ij}) \overset{\text{def}}{=} \left. \frac{d\theta_\epsilon^*}{d\epsilon} \right|_{\epsilon=0} = -\mathbf{H}_{\theta^*}^{-1} \nabla_\theta \mathbf{A}_{ij} \|\theta_i - \theta_j\|^2, \quad (5.3)$$

where $\mathbf{H}_{\theta^*}$ is the Hessian of the objective function defined in Eq. (5.1). Since removing the connection between task i and task j is equivalent to upweighting $\mathbf{A}_{ij}$ by $\epsilon = -\lambda$, we can approximate the change of the parameters in the whole learning system $(\theta_{-\mathbf{x}^t}^* - \theta^*)$ by $-\lambda I_\theta(\mathbf{A}_{ij})$. We show the detailed derivation later in the proofs and analysis.

NEPAL – Multiaspect, Multilevel. Based on the different aspects (i.e., training example, task, and task network) in the learning system, we can answer questions regarding the influences at different levels. For example, what are the most influential training samples in the whole learning system? What are the most influential learning tasks with regard to a test sample? See Table 5.2 for an overview.

Macro-level influences of training examples, tasks, and task network: At this macro level, we are interested in what the most influential training samples, tasks, and task network connections are with regard to the whole learning system. We propose to use the l_2-norm of the change in the whole

Table 5.2 *Multiaspect, multilevel explanation in networked prediction.*

Aspect \ Level	Macro/system	Meso/task	Micro/test example
Training example $\mathbf{x}^t$	Globally influential training sample ($\mathcal{I}_G(\mathbf{x}^t)$)	Task-specific influential training sample ($\mathcal{I}_s(\mathbf{x}^t)$)	Test-specific influential training sample ($\mathcal{I}_{\mathbf{x}_{\text{test}}^s}(\mathbf{x}^t)$)
Learning task f_t	Globally influential task ($\mathcal{I}_G(f_t)$)	Task-specific influential task ($\mathcal{I}_s(f_t)$)	Test-specific influential task ($\mathcal{I}_{\mathbf{x}_{\text{test}}^s}(f_t)$
Task network $\mathbf{A}$	Globally influential task connections ($\mathcal{I}_G(\mathbf{A}_{ij})$)	Task-specific influential task connections ($\mathcal{I}_s(\mathbf{A}_{ij})$)	Test-specific influential task connections ($\mathcal{I}_{\mathbf{x}_{\text{test}}^s}(\mathbf{A}_{ij})$)

learning system's parameters as the measure of the macro-level influence should a training sample, training samples from a task, or a task connection be removed.

(1) Macro-level influence of a training sample $\mathbf{x}^t$. We use the l_2-norm of the change in all tasks' model parameters as the measure of macro-level influence of $\mathbf{x}^t$ as follows:

$$\mathcal{I}_G(\mathbf{x}^t) = \frac{1}{n_t}\|\mathcal{I}_\theta(\mathbf{x}^t)\|_2.$$

(2) Macro-level influence of a learning task. For one learning task f_t, we use the average of the macro-level influences of the training samples from this task as the macro-level influence of this learning task, which is given as follows:

$$\mathcal{I}_G(f_t) = \frac{1}{n_t^2}\sum_{i=1}^{n_t}\|\mathcal{I}_\theta(\mathbf{x}_i^t)\|_2$$

(3) Macro-level influence of task network connection $\mathbf{A}_{ij}$. We use the l_2-norm of the change in all tasks' model parameters as the measure of macro-level influence of $\mathbf{A}_{ij}$ as follows:

$$\mathcal{I}_G(\mathbf{A}_{ij}) = \lambda\|\mathcal{I}_\theta(\mathbf{A}_{ij})\|_2.$$

Meso-level influences of training examples, tasks, and task network: At this meso level, we are interested in what the most influential training samples, tasks, and task network connections are with regard to a specific learning task. We propose to use the l_2-norm of the change in the parameters corresponding to this learning task as the measure of the meso-level influence should a training sample, training samples from a task, or a task connection be removed.

Recall that we approximate the change of the parameters in the whole learning system $(\theta^*_{-\mathbf{x}^t} - \theta^*)$ by $-\frac{1}{n_t}\mathcal{I}_\theta(\mathbf{x}^t)$. Let us denote $-\frac{1}{n_t}\mathcal{I}_{\theta_s}(\mathbf{x}^t)$ as the change corresponding to the parameters only in the sth task.

(1) Meso-level influence of a training sample $\mathbf{x}^t$. The l_2-norm of the change in the sth task's parameters is used as the measure of the meso-level influence of $\mathbf{x}^t$ to this task as follows:

$$\mathcal{I}_s(\mathbf{x}^t) = \frac{1}{n_t}\|\mathcal{I}_{\theta_s}(\mathbf{x}^t)\|_2.$$

(2) Meso-level influence of a learning task. For one learning task s, we use the average of the meso-level influences of the training samples from the tth task as the meso-level influence of learning task t to task s, which is given as follows:

$$\mathcal{I}_s(f_t) = \frac{1}{n_t^2}\sum_{i=1}^{n_t}\|\mathcal{I}_{\theta_s}(\mathbf{x}_i^t)\|_2.$$

(3) Meso-level influence of task network connection $\mathbf{A}_{ij}$. The l_2-norm of the change in the sth task's parameters is used as the measure of the meso-level influence of $\mathbf{A}_{ij}$ to task s as follows:

$$\mathcal{I}_s(\mathbf{A}_{ij}) = \lambda\|\mathcal{I}_{\theta_s}(\mathbf{A}_{ij})\|_2.$$

Micro-level influences of training examples, tasks, and task network: Both the removal of a training sample and the task network connections can potentially change the parameters of all the tasks' models, which would in turn change the loss at a particular test sample $\mathbf{x}_{\text{test}}^s$ from the sth task. We can apply the chain rule to measure the influence of upweighting a training sample or task network connections on the loss function value at the test sample.

(1) Micro-level influence of a training sample $\mathbf{x}^t$. Let us first consider upweighting a training sample from the tth task and its influence on the loss at $\mathbf{x}_{\text{test}}^s$ can be given as

$$
\begin{aligned}
\mathcal{I}_\theta(\mathbf{x}^t, \mathbf{x}_{\text{test}}^s) &\overset{\text{def}}{=} \left.\frac{dL(f_s(\mathbf{x}_{\text{test}}^s; \theta^*_{s,\epsilon}), y_{\text{test}}^s)}{d\epsilon}\right|_{\epsilon=0} \\
&= \nabla_\theta L(f_s(\mathbf{x}_{\text{test}}^s; \theta^*_s), y_{\text{test}}^s)^T \left.\frac{d\theta^*_\epsilon}{d\epsilon}\right|_{\epsilon=0} \\
&= -\nabla_\theta L(f_s(\mathbf{x}_{\text{test}}^s; \theta^*_s), y_{\text{test}}^s)^T \mathbf{H}_{\theta^*}^{-1} \nabla_\theta L(f_t(\mathbf{x}^t; \theta_t), y^t).
\end{aligned}
$$

The change of the loss function value at the test sample due to the removal of the training sample is used as the micro-level influence of $\mathbf{x}^t$ to $\mathbf{x}_{\text{test}}^s$ and can be approximated as

$$I_{\mathbf{x}_{\text{test}}^s}(\mathbf{x}^t) = -\frac{1}{n_t} I_\theta(\mathbf{x}^t, \mathbf{x}_{\text{test}}^s).$$

We show the algorithm for computing the micro-level influences of the training samples from all the tasks in Algorithm 8. Note that it is both computation and memory intensive to compute the inverse of the Hessian matrix especially for large-scale networked learning problems. Instead, we use conjugate gradient optimization method to efficiently compute the inverse of the Hessian multiplied by a vector (step 2).

(2) Micro-level influence of a learning task. For one test sample $\mathbf{x}_{\text{test}}^s$, we use the average of the micro-level influences of the training samples from the tth task as the micro-level influence of this learning task, which is given as follows:

$$I_{\mathbf{x}_{\text{test}}^s}(f_t) = -\frac{1}{n_t^2} \sum_{i=1}^{n_t} I_\theta(\mathbf{x}_i^t, \mathbf{x}_{\text{test}}^s).$$

(3) Micro-level influence of task network connection $\mathbf{A}_{ij}$. Similarly, we can compute the influence of upweighting the task network connection $\mathbf{A}_{ij}$ on the loss at $\mathbf{x}_{\text{test}}^s$ as follows:

$$
\begin{aligned}
I_\theta(\mathbf{A}_{ij}, \mathbf{x}_{\text{test}}^s) &\overset{\text{def}}{=} \frac{dL(f_s(\mathbf{x}_{\text{test}}^s; \theta_{s,\epsilon}^*), y_{\text{test}}^s)}{d\epsilon}\Bigg|_{\epsilon=0} \\
&= \nabla_\theta L(f_s(\mathbf{x}_{\text{test}}^s; \theta_s^*), y_{\text{test}}^s)^T \frac{d\theta_\epsilon^*}{d\epsilon}\Bigg|_{\epsilon=0} \\
&= -\nabla_\theta L(f_s(\mathbf{x}_{\text{test}}^s; \theta_s^*), y_{\text{test}}^s)^T \mathbf{H}_{\theta^*}^{-1} \nabla_\theta \mathbf{A}_{ij} \|\theta_i - \theta_j\|^2.
\end{aligned}
$$

The change of the loss function value at the test sample due to the removal of the connection between task i and j is used as the micro-level influence of $\mathbf{A}_{ij}$ and can be approximated as follows:

$$I_{\mathbf{x}_{\text{test}}^s}(\mathbf{A}_{ij}) = -\lambda I_\theta(\mathbf{A}_{ij}, \mathbf{x}_{\text{test}}^s).$$

Remarks: The aforementioned micro-level influences of training samples, tasks, and task network, i.e., $I_{\mathbf{x}_{\text{test}}^s}(\mathbf{x}^t)$, $I_{\mathbf{x}_{\text{test}}^s}(f_t)$, and $I_{\mathbf{x}_{\text{test}}^s}(\mathbf{A}_{ij})$, can be either positive or negative. The sign of the influence value indicates whether it helps the prediction of the test sample (i.e., reduces the loss at this test sample) or harms the prediction of the test sample (i.e., increases the loss at the test sample). The magnitude of the influence value, i.e., $|I_{\mathbf{x}_{\text{test}}^s}(\mathbf{x}^t)|$, $|I_{\mathbf{x}_{\text{test}}^s}(f_t)|$, and $|I_{\mathbf{x}_{\text{test}}^s}(\mathbf{A}_{ij})|$, indicates how great the influence is, be it positive or negative, on the test sample.

Algorithm 8: NEPAL – Networked Prediction Explanation

Input: (1) the training data of all the tasks $\{(\mathbf{x}_i^t, y_i^t)\}_{i=1}^{n_t}$, (2) the learned models through joint training $f_t(\cdot, \theta_t^*)$, (3) a query test sample from the sth task $\mathbf{x}_{\text{test}}^s$.

Output: the micro-level influences of the training samples of all the tasks on the prediction with regard to $\mathbf{x}_{\text{test}}^s$.

1 Compute gradient of the loss at the test sample with regard to model parameters: $\mathbf{v} \leftarrow \frac{\partial L(f_s(\mathbf{x}_{\text{test}}^s; \theta_s^*), y_{\text{test}}^s)}{\partial \theta}$;

2 Compute $\mathbf{x} = \mathbf{H}_\theta^{-1}\mathbf{v}$ by solving $\min_{\mathbf{x}} \frac{1}{2}\mathbf{x}^T\mathbf{H}_\theta\mathbf{x} - \mathbf{v}^T\mathbf{x}$ using the conjugate gradient method, where the Hessian-vector product can be exactly computed using the $\mathcal{R}_\mathbf{v}\{\cdot\}$ operator [74];

3 **for** *each task t in all tasks* **do**

4   **for** $i = 1, \ldots, n_t$ **do**

5   Compute the gradient of the objective function at training sample $\mathbf{x}_i^t$ with regard to model parameters: $\mathbf{u} \leftarrow \frac{\partial L(f_t(\mathbf{x}_i^t; \theta_t^*), y_i^t)}{\partial \theta}$;

6   Compute the influence score of $\mathbf{x}_i^t$ as $\mathcal{I}_{\mathbf{x}_{\text{test}}^s}(\mathbf{x}_i^t) = \frac{1}{n_t}\mathbf{u}^T\mathbf{x}$;

7   **end**

8 **end**

Proofs and Analysis. In this subsection, we analyze our NEPAL algorithm by giving the complexity analysis, the derivation of the key equations, and its characteristics with some common loss functions for classification.

A. Complexity analysis: we analyze the time complexity of Algorithm 8, where the learning model for each task is logistic regression, i.e., $L(f_t(\mathbf{x}^t; \theta_t), y^t) = \log(1 + \exp(-y^t\theta_t^T\mathbf{x}^t))$.

Theorem 5.2. *(Time complexity of NEPAL). Algorithm 8 takes $O(nT^2d^2)$ with a logistic regression model for each task, where $n = \sum_{t=1}^T n_t$ is the total number of training samples in all tasks and T is the number of tasks.*

Proof The gradient of the loss function in logistic regression is computed as $\nabla_{\theta_t} L(f_t(\mathbf{x}^t; \theta_t), y^t) = -\sigma(-y^t\theta_t^T\mathbf{x}^t)y^t\mathbf{x}^t$. Step 1 for computing the gradient of the loss at $\mathbf{x}_{\text{test}}^s$ takes $O(d)$ time. In step 2, the size of the Hessian matrix $\mathbf{H}_\theta$ is Td by Td, where T is the number of tasks. In the worst-case scenario, the conjugate gradient (CG) algorithm will require Td iterations to converge, thus requiring at most the evaluation of Td Hessian-vector multiplications, each of which takes $O(nTd)$ without explicitly forming the Hessian, where $n = \sum_{t=1}^T n_t$. In total, step 2 takes $O(nT^2d^2)$. In the for-loops (Lines 3 through 6), it takes $O(d)$ for each training sample, which totals $O(nd)$. In summary, the total time complexity is $O(nT^2d^2)$. □

B. Derivation of the influence functions $\mathcal{I}_\theta(\mathbf{x}^t)$ and $\mathcal{I}_\theta(\mathbf{A}_{ij})$:

Lemma 5.3. *(Correctness of Eq (5.2)). Denote* $\mathcal{J}(\theta) = \sum_{t=1}^{T} \frac{1}{n_t} \sum_{i=1}^{n_t}$
$L(f_t(\mathbf{x}_i^t; \theta_t), y_i^t) + \lambda \sum_{i=1}^{T} \sum_{j=1}^{T} A_{ij} \|\theta_i - \theta_j\|^2$, *where* $\theta \overset{\text{def}}{=} (\theta_1, \ldots, \theta_T)$.
Assuming $\mathcal{J}(\theta)$ to be twice-differentiable and strictly convex, the influence of upweighting training sample $\mathbf{x}^t$ on the parameters θ can be computed by $\mathcal{I}_\theta(\mathbf{x}^t)$.

Proof The Hessian matrix of $\mathcal{J}(\theta)$ is defined as follows:

$$\mathbf{H}_\theta \overset{\text{def}}{=} \nabla^2 \mathcal{J} = \sum_{t=1}^{T} \frac{1}{n_t} \sum_{i=1}^{n_t} \nabla_\theta^2 L(f_t(\mathbf{x}_i^t; \theta_t), y_i^t) + \lambda \sum_{i=1}^{T} \sum_{j=1}^{T} \nabla_\theta^2 A_{ij} \|\theta_i - \theta_j\|^2$$

Let us upweight a training example $\mathbf{x}^t$ from the tth task, and the new parameters after such upweighting is written as $\theta_\epsilon^* = \arg\min \mathcal{J}(\theta) + \epsilon L(f_t(\mathbf{x}^t; \theta_t), y^t)$. Define the parameter change $\Delta_\epsilon = (\theta_\epsilon^* - \theta^*)$, and since θ^* does not depend on ϵ, we have the following:

$$\frac{d\theta_\epsilon^*}{d\epsilon} = \frac{d\Delta_\epsilon}{d\epsilon}.$$

By the first-order optimality conditions, we have

$$\nabla \mathcal{J}(\theta_\epsilon^*) + \epsilon \nabla L(f_t(\mathbf{x}^t; \theta_{t,\epsilon}^*), y^t) = 0.$$

Because $\theta_\epsilon^* \to \theta^*$ as $\epsilon \to 0$, we can apply Taylor expansion to the left-hand side and get

$$[\nabla \mathcal{J}(\theta^*) + \epsilon \nabla L(f_t(\mathbf{x}^t; \theta_t^*), y^t)] + [\nabla^2 \mathcal{J}(\theta^*) + \epsilon \nabla^2 L(f_t(\mathbf{x}^t; \theta_t^*), y^t)]\Delta_\epsilon \approx 0.$$

Since $\nabla \mathcal{J}(\theta^*) = 0$, we can solve for Δ_ϵ as

$$\Delta_\epsilon \approx -[\nabla^2 \mathcal{J}(\theta^*) + \epsilon \nabla^2 L(f_t(\mathbf{x}^t; \theta_t^*), y^t)]^{-1} \epsilon \nabla L(f_t(\mathbf{x}^t; \theta_t^*), y^t)$$

It can be further simplified if we only keep the $O(\epsilon)$ terms:

$$\Delta_\epsilon \approx -\nabla^2 \mathcal{J}(\theta^*)^{-1} \epsilon \nabla L(f_t(\mathbf{x}^t; \theta_t^*), y^t).$$

The influence of the upweighting can be computed as follows:

$$\mathcal{I}_\theta(\mathbf{x}^t) \overset{\text{def}}{=} \frac{d\theta_\epsilon^*}{d\epsilon}\bigg|_{\epsilon=0} = -\mathbf{H}_\theta^{-1} \nabla L(f_t(\mathbf{x}^t; \theta_t^*), y^t).$$

□

Lemma 5.4. *(Correctness of Eq. (5.3)). Assuming $\mathcal{J}(\theta)$ to be twice-differentiable and strictly convex, the influence of upweighting task network connection $\mathbf{A}_{ij}$ on the parameters θ can be computed by $\mathcal{I}_\theta(\mathbf{A}_{ij})$.*

Proof Similarly, let us upweight the task network connection and define the new parameters after such upweighting as $\theta_\epsilon^* = \arg\min \mathcal{J}(\theta) + \epsilon \mathbf{A}_{ij}\|\theta_i - \theta_j\|^2$.

By the first-order optimality conditions, we have the following:

$$\nabla \mathcal{J}(\theta_\epsilon^*) + \epsilon \nabla \mathbf{A}_{ij}\|\theta_i - \theta_j\|^2 = 0.$$

Because $\theta_\epsilon^* \to \theta^*$ as $\epsilon \to 0$, we can apply Taylor expansion to the left-hand side and get

$$[\nabla \mathcal{J}(\theta^*) + \epsilon \nabla \mathbf{A}_{ij}\|\theta_i - \theta_j\|^2] + [\nabla^2 \mathcal{J}(\theta^*) + \epsilon \nabla^2 \mathbf{A}_{ij}\|\theta_i - \theta_j\|^2)]\Delta_\epsilon \approx 0.$$

Since $\nabla \mathcal{J}(\theta^*) = 0$, we can solve for Δ_ϵ as follows:

$$\Delta_\epsilon \approx -[\nabla^2 \mathcal{J}(\theta^*) + \epsilon \nabla^2 \mathbf{A}_{ij}\|\theta_i - \theta_j\|^2]^{-1}\epsilon \nabla \mathbf{A}_{ij}\|\theta_i - \theta_j\|^2.$$

It can be further simplified if we only keep the $O(\epsilon)$ terms:

$$\Delta_\epsilon \approx -\nabla^2 \mathcal{J}(\theta^*)^{-1}\epsilon \nabla \mathbf{A}_{ij}\|\theta_i - \theta_j\|^2.$$

The influence of the upweighting can be computed as follows:

$$\mathcal{I}_\theta(\mathbf{A}_{ij}) \stackrel{\text{def}}{=} \frac{d\theta_\epsilon^*}{d\epsilon}\bigg|_{\epsilon=0} = -\mathbf{H}_\theta^{-1}\nabla \mathbf{A}_{ij}\|\theta_i - \theta_j\|^2. \qquad \square$$

C. Analysis for classification loss: we analyze the influences from the aspect of examples at different levels with some common classification loss functions used for each learning task.

Let us first consider hinge loss used in a Support Vector Machine for each task, i.e., $L(f_t(\mathbf{x}^t; \theta_t), y^t) = \max(0, 1 - y^t\theta_t^T\mathbf{x}^t)$. Let us consider the nonsupport vectors in learning task t, i.e., the training samples that satisfy $y^t\theta_t^T\mathbf{x}^t > 1$. For these training samples, we know $L(f_t(\mathbf{x}^t; \theta_t), y^t) = 0$ and hence $\frac{\partial L(f_t(\mathbf{x}^t; \theta_t), y^t)}{\partial \theta_t} = \mathbf{0}$. The influence of the nonsupport vectors $\mathbf{x}^t$ on the parameters is therefore $\mathcal{I}_\theta(\mathbf{x}^t) = \mathbf{0}$. The macro-level influence of a nonsupport vector is $\mathcal{I}_G(\mathbf{x}^t) = 0$, and the meso-level influence of a nonsupport vector is $\mathcal{I}_s(\mathbf{x}^t) = 0$. This matches our intuition that since nonsupport vectors are known to have no influence on the resulting classifiers, removing them should not change the parameters in the learning task itself and also other tasks. By the same argument, the micro-level influence of the nonsupport vectors is $\mathcal{I}_{\mathbf{x}_{\text{test}}^s}(\mathbf{x}^t) = 0$.

For logistic loss, $L(f_t(\mathbf{x}^t; \theta_t), y^t) = \log(1 + \exp(-y^t\theta_t^T\mathbf{x}^t))$, its gradient with regard to θ_t is $\nabla_{\theta_t} L(f_t(\mathbf{x}^t; \theta_t), y^t) = -\sigma(-y^t\theta_t^T\mathbf{x}^t)y^t\mathbf{x}^t$. For the training samples with large positive $y^t\theta_t^T\mathbf{x}^t$, $\sigma(-y^t\theta_t^T\mathbf{x}^t)$ is very small (close to 0), and their influences at different levels are expected to be much smaller than that of other training samples.

In practice, from the example aspect, we are only interested in inspecting the training samples with high influence. To speed up the computation, we can first filter out those examples with large $y^t \theta_t^T \mathbf{x}^t$. Such analysis matches our empirical observation in Figure 5.5 (macro-level) and Figure 5.9 (micro-level).

5.1.3 Empirical Evaluations

In this subsection, we present the empirical evaluation results. The experiments are designed to evaluate the following aspects:

- *Effectiveness:* how does our NEPAL algorithm help us understand the networked predictions?
- *Efficiency:* how fast and scalable is the NEPAL algorithm?

Datasets. The real-world datasets used for evaluation are as follows:

MNIST. MNIST [54] is a commonly used handwritten digit dataset, containing images of handwritten numerals (0 through 9) represented by 28×28 pixels in grayscale. We construct the networked prediction system using logistic regression for three tasks, where task 1 distinguishes digit 1 from 7, task 2 differentiates digit 2 from 7, and task 3 classifies digit 6 from 9. In the task network, we connect task 1 with task 2 with $\mathbf{A}_{12} = 1$ and connect task 2 with task 3 with $\mathbf{A}_{23} = 0.1$.

Semantic Scholar.[1] This open research corpus offers over 20 million published research papers in computer science, neuroscience, and biomedicine. We consider papers published between 1975 and 2005 with their features generated using information available only up to 2005. We build networked prediction models for papers published in venues in *data mining, computer vision, NLP, AI,* and *computer networks,* and a paper is classified as positive if its accumulative citation counts from 2006 to 2015 exceed the median accumulative citation counts of the training examples from the respective domains. The features include author impact (e.g., author h-index), venue impact (e.g., venue rank). The task network is constructed based on the relevance between different research domains.

Sentiment.[2] This multidomain sentiment dataset contains product reviews from Amazon.com for many product types [10]. We build networked prediction models for reviews from *music, video, DVD, book,* and *magazine,* and a review is labeled as positive if its rating is greater than 3 and negative

---

[1] http://labs.semanticscholar.org/corpus/.
[2] www.cs.jhu.edu/ mdredze/datasets/sentiment/.

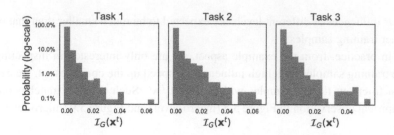

Figure 5.2 The distribution of the macro-level influences of training examples in each of the three tasks.

if its rating is below 3. We extract both unigram and bigram features from the review text. The task network is constructed based on the relevance between different product domains.

Repeatability of experimental results: all the datasets are publicly available. We release the datasets and code of our algorithms through the authors' website. The experiments are performed on a MacBook Pro with two 2.4GHz Intel Cores and 8GB RAM.

Results on MNIST
A. Macro-Level Influences. For this set of experiments, we study how the training examples, tasks, and task network influences the entire learning system (i.e., the second column in Table 5.2).

(1) *Macro-level influences of training examples*: we compute the macro-level influences $\mathcal{I}_G(\mathbf{x}^t)$ for training examples of all the three learning tasks and plot their distributions in Figure 5.2. In all the tasks, the great majority of the examples have no or negligible influences on the entire learning system and only a few can exert significant influence. The top 10 globally influential training examples measured by $\mathcal{I}_G(\mathbf{x}^t)$ are shown in Figure 5.3, with seven of them from the second task. The top two examples are the same images of digit 7 from task 2 and 1, respectively. To see how the globally influential examples affect the learning system's prediction performance, we flip the labels of the most influential examples at macro level, retrain the model, and compute the classification accuracy on the test set. We also test the random picking strategy with 30 repetitions. Figure 5.4 shows that flipping the labels of the most influential examples exert larger interruption to the learning system as demonstrated by the significant drop in the test accuracy for all the three tasks. Our analysis in the proofs and analysis shows that for the training samples with large positive $y^t \theta_t^T \mathbf{x}^t$, their macro-level influences are expected to be much smaller than other training samples. Figure 5.5 provides empirical verification for this analysis.

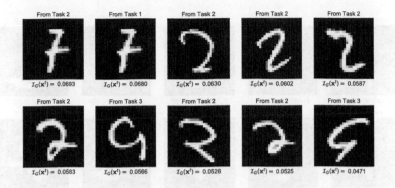

Figure 5.3 The top 10 globally influential training samples.

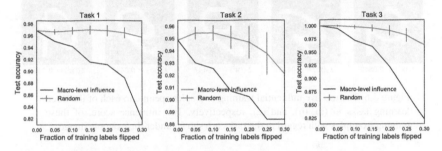

Figure 5.4 Fraction of training labels flipped vs. test accuracy.

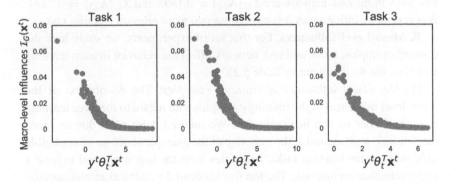

Figure 5.5 The macro-level influences of training samples vs. their $y\theta_t^T \mathbf{x}$.

(2) *Macro-level influence of a learning task*: the macro-level influences of the three learning tasks are $\mathcal{I}_G(f_1) = 0.0028$, $\mathcal{I}_G(f_2) = 0.0040$, and $\mathcal{I}_G(f_3) = 0.0037$. The second task has the highest influence on the entire system as it links tasks 1 and 3.

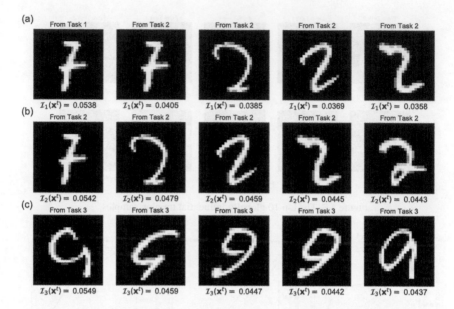

Figure 5.6 The top five influential training examples specific to each of the three learning tasks in (a), (b), and (c), respectively. The influence score, of these training examples with regard to the tasks are shown under the example image.

(3) *Macro-level influence of task network*: the macro-level influences of the two links in the task network are $\mathcal{I}_G(\mathbf{A}_{12}) = 0.1898$ and $\mathcal{I}_G(\mathbf{A}_{23}) = 0.2484$. $\mathbf{A}_{23}$ is of more influence as it connects the two more relevant learning tasks.

B. Meso-Level Influences. For this set of experiments, we study how the training examples, tasks, and task network affect the behavior of each learning task (i.e., the third column in Table 5.2).

(1) *Meso-level influences of training examples*: The distribution of the meso-level influences of the training examples with regard to the three learning tasks is similar to that in Figure 5.2. We omitted these plots due to space limitation. For all the tasks, the majority of the examples have no or negligible influences on the learning tasks. Examples from the task itself tend to have a larger influence on this task. The top five influential training examples specific to each learning task are shown in Figure 5.6.

(2) *Meso-level influence of a learning task*: We compute the meso-level influences of each learning task and observe that generally the most influential task for one specific task is the task itself, except that for the first task, task 2 has about the same influence on it as the task itself, possibly due to the same negative training examples of digit 7 they share. For task 2, the first task has about half the influence as the task itself.

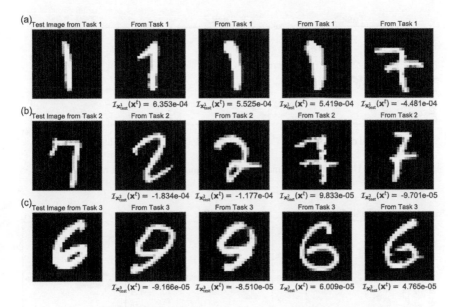

Figure 5.7 The top four influential training examples specific to each of the three test examples from each of the three tasks in (a), (b), and (c), respectively. The influence score of these training examples with regard to the test examples are shown under the example images.

(3) *Meso-level influences of the task network*: We compute the meso-level influences of the task network specific to each task. The results are consistent with our intuition. For task 1, the connection A_{12} has larger influence than A_{23}; for task 2, the two task connections have about the same influence; and for task 3, the connection A_{23} has larger influence.

C. Micro-Level Influences. For this set of experiments, we randomly select one test example from each of the three learning tasks and study how the training examples, tasks, and task network affect their predictions (i.e., the last column in Table 5.2).

(1) *Micro-level influence of training examples*: The distribution of the micro-level influences of the training examples with regard to the test examples is also similar to that in Figure 5.2. We omitted these plots due to space limitation.

The top four influential training examples specific to each test example are shown in Figure 5.7. For the purpose of validation, we want to compare how accurately $I_{\mathbf{x}_{\text{test}}^s}(\mathbf{x}^t)$ can approximate $L(f_s(\mathbf{x}_{\text{test}}^s; \theta_{-\mathbf{x}^t})) - L(f_s(\mathbf{x}_{\text{test}}^s; \theta))$, i.e., the change of loss at the test sample after retraining without training example $\mathbf{x}^t$. We randomly pick a test example $\mathbf{x}_{\text{test}}^s$ from the first task, and show the

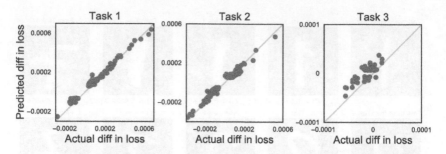

Figure 5.8 Using influence function to approximate leave-one-out retraining test loss.

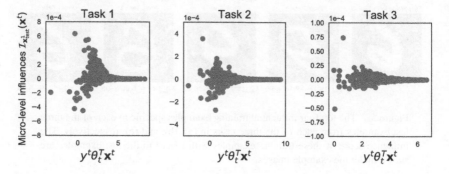

Figure 5.9 The micro-level influences of training samples vs. their $y\theta_t^T \mathbf{x}$.

predicted and actual changes for the top 100 influential training examples from each of the three tasks in Figure 5.8. We can see that our method based on influence function can well approximate the change in losses, e.g., Pearson's R = 0.99 and 0.98 in the first and second tasks, respectively.

Figure 5.9 plots the relationship between the micro-level influences of the training examples with regard to the test sample from task 1 and their $y^t \theta_t^T \mathbf{x}^t$ values. Note here that the micro-level influences could be either positive or negative, but their magnitude is very small when $y^t \theta_t^T \mathbf{x}^t$ has large positive value, which again supports our analysis in the "Proofs and Analysis" subsection of Secction 5.1.2. Figure 5.10 shows the running time of Algorithm 8 with varying size of the total number of training examples n. We can see that our algorithm scales linearly, which is consistent with Theorem 5.2.

(2) *Micro-level influences of a learning task*: We compute the micro-level influences of each of the learning task with regard to the test examples and observe that generally the task that has the most influence on a particular test example is the one where the test example is from. One exception is that, for

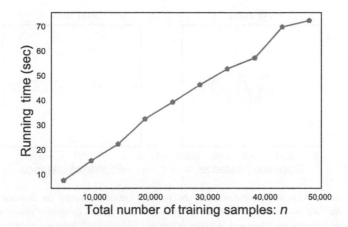

Figure 5.10 Running time vs. total number of training examples n for computing the micro-level influences of training examples.

the test example from task 2, both tasks 1 and 2 have similar positive influence possibly because task 1 that distinguishes between digits 1 and 7 can also help with the prediction of the test example of digit 7 in task 2.

(3) *Micro-level influences of task network*: We compute the microlevel influences of the task network specific to each test example. For the test example from the first task, A_{12} has a much larger negative impact than A_{23} possibly because connecting to task 2 does not help with the prediction of digit 1. For the test example of digit 7 from task 2, A_{12} has a larger positive impact than A_{23} since connecting to task 1 can help with this prediction.

Case Studies on Semantic Scholar Dataset. We use the following test example from the *data mining* area: **Constraint-Based Query Evaluation in Deductive Databases** by *Prof. Jiawei Han* published in TKDE in 1994. We want to examine the most helpful training examples from each domain for this particular test example according to the micro-level influences.

The most helpful training examples from *data mining* are **Structures, Semantics and Statistics** by *Alon Y. Halevy* published in VLDB in 2004 and **The Architecture of Complexity: The Structure and the Dynamics of Networks from the Web to the Cell** by *Albert-László Barabási* published in KDD in 2005. The most helpful training examples from *computer vision* are **SWIM: A Prototype Environment for Visual Media Retrieval** by *HongJiang Zhang* published in ACCV in 1995 and **Scene Reconstruction from Multiple Cameras** by *Richard Szeliski* published in ICIP in 2000.

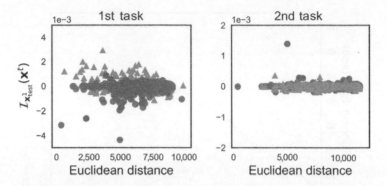

Figure 5.11 Euclidean distance vs. micro-level influence score on *Semantic Scholar*. We only show their relationship in *data mining* and *computer vision* as similar patterns are observed in other domains. Triangles are training examples with the same label as the test example, and dots are training examples with the opposite label as the test example.

The most helpful training examples from *NLP* are **Language Learning: Beyond Thunderdome** published in CoNLL in 2004 and **The Segmentation Problem in Morphology Learning** published in CoNLL in 1998, both by *Christopher D. Manning*. The most helpful training examples from *AI* are **Robustness of Causal Claims** by *Judea Pearl* published in UAI in 2004 and **Direct and Indirect Effects** by *Judea Pearl* published in UAI in 2001.

The helpful training examples from across domains are similar to this particular test example from *data mining* in the sense that they are all solo-authored papers by well-known researchers from respective domains. We want to emphasize that the influence function is not simply a Euclidean distance in the feature space as evident in Figure 5.11, where we plot the micro-level influences $I_{\mathbf{x}_{\text{test}}^1}(\mathbf{x}^t)$ vs. the Euclidean distance between the test example and the training examples from each task.

Case Studies on Sentiment Dataset. We use the test example from *music* category and show the most influential training examples from other domains in Table 5.3. Comparing the test example and the helpful training examples from all the domains, it seems they are overall toward the positive sentiment despite some negative descriptions about the products, e.g., the book "seems really dull" to average readers in the *book* domain. The harmful example from *music* is labeled as negative sentiment, but the descriptions still sound largely positive.

Table 5.3 *Case study on Sentiment.*

Review text (positive sentiment is highlighted in bold font and negative sentiment is highlighted with underline). [...] is used to omit some sentences without altering the main meaning of the text.	Label
Test example from *music*	I was **instantly drawn into her music**. What I love about her songs is that they are so real. "You Give Me Love" is **so real and so strong**. "The Secret of Life" has taken some getting used to. It is not my absolute favorite on the CD. "Me" is the song that **means the most to me** since I have experienced trying to change for someone else in a relationship. [...] She has a big voice, and she **nails each song** on this CD. Give it a try.	+
Harmful example from *music*	**I liked this** when it first came out b/c I was 16.[...]This is **their best work** since the weirdness does get lame after a while. Favorite song is Mongoloid...totally strange **but rocking song**. "Uncontrollable Urge" **rocks** (in a weird way). Satisfaction is completely unique but its not a good song. [...] I saw them live (they were horrible) during their hey day. [...] **Anybody that gives this novelty group 5 stars is cheapening what true excellent music is.**	−
Helpful example from *book*	Here's a good litmus test to show **how good a book like "Breathing Lessons" is** – nothing extraordinary happens and yet I did not want to put the book down. [...] To the average reader this book probably would seem really dull. Heck, if someone told me the plot of this book I'd think it was really dull too, but **I didn't want to put it down**. [...] **It's hard for me to find any real faults with this book**, except for the lengthy flashback near the end that perhaps goes on too long. Some people may call this boring or dull, but I would call it purely exceptional. **I LOVED this book and highly recommend it**	+

5.2 Explaining Team Optimization in Networks

The emergence of network science has been significantly changing the landscape of team-based research in recent years. For example, if an existing team member becomes unavailable before the completion of the project, who shall we recommend to replace that individual's role so that the team would be least impacted due to the departure of this team member (*team member replacement*)? If the team leader perceives the need to expand the current team, who shall we bring into the existing team (*team expansion*)? Reversely, in case the team needs to be downsized (e.g., due to budget reduction), who should leave the team (*team shrinkage*)?

A cornerstone behind various team recommendation algorithms is the random walk graph kernel [92]. By comparing and aggregating walks of the two input graphs, it naturally measures the graph similarity that captures both the topologies of the input graphs as well as the attributes associated with nodes and links. For instance, for team member replacement, by applying the random walk graph kernel to the team networks before and after replacement, it encodes both the skill match and structure match as well as the interaction between the two during the replacement process [58]. Team member replacement further enables other team recommendation scenarios (e.g., team expansion, team shrinkage, etc.). Although being effective in answering questions like *who* is the best replacement, or *what* is the best team expansion strategy, these existing methods lack intuitive ways to explain *why* the underlying algorithm gives the specific recommendation for a given team optimization scenario.

In this work, we present a prototype system (EXTRA), a paradigm shift from *what* to *why*, to explain the networked team recommendation results. On the algorithmic side, we design an effective and efficient algorithm to explain the random walk graph kernel given its central role in various team recommendation scenarios. The key idea here is to identify the most influential network substructures and/or attributes whose removal or perturbation will impact the graph kernel/similarity the most. On the system side, our prototype system is able to explain various team recommendation scenarios (e.g., replacement, expansion, shrinkage) from a variety of different perspectives (e.g., edges, nodes, and attributes). For example, given a candidate for team member replacement, we are able to tell what the key connections are between the candidate and the existing team members that might make him/her a potentially good replacement; for team expansion, we are able to identify the key skill sets that a candidate might bring to benefit the existing team the most.

5.2.1 Functionality Demonstration

In this section, we present the main functionalities of our prototype system (EXTRA) to explain three different team recommendation scenarios, including team member replacement, team expansion, and team shrinkage. In our system, we model the underlying data as a large, attributed network, where nodes represent individuals, edges represent the relationship between different individuals, node attributes represent the skills of individuals, edge attributes represent the types of relationship (e.g., email communication, social friends, etc.), and a team is represented by an induced subgraph of its team members. Our EXTRA system provides explanations for different team recommendation

Table 5.4 *Summary of system functionalities. Columns are different team recommendation scenarios, and rows are different aspects for explanation.*

	Team replacement	Team expansion	Team shrinkage
Edges	Important common collaborations shared by the candidate and the departure member	New collaborations that the new member might establish	The most important lacking collaborations the candidate should have
Nodes	Most important existing team members that both the candidate and departure member collaborate with	Key existing team members the new member will work with	Key existing team members whom the candidate should have collaborated with
Attributes	Common and important skills shared by the candidate and the departure member	Unique skills the new team member brings that are critical to the team's new need	The most important skills that the candidate lacks

scenarios through the lens of this underlying network from three different aspects, including edges, nodes, and attributes. Table 5.4 summarizes the main functionalities of our system. The system allows users to explore team recommendation in the context of two common types of teams, including collaborative academic research teams and competitive sports teams. In addition, the system provides users with the option to manually assemble a team on the fly, and explore various team recommendation scenarios and the associated explanations.

Explaining Team Replacement. A current team member might leave the team before the completion of the project for reasons like moving to another organization, being assigned to another project, etc. In this case, we need to find a good replacement for this member. In order to have the least impact on the entire team due to the member's departure so that the new team could continue to perform well, a team member replacement algorithm [58] often seeks to find a candidate who is most similar to the departure member, in the sense of both skill match and structure match as well as the interaction between the two. Having this in mind, our prototype system identifies a few key (1) edges (the relationship between the candidate and other team members), (2) nodes (other team members), and (3) attributes (the skills of the candidate) that make the candidate and the departure member most similar.

In this way, it could help the end user (e.g., the team leader) understand why the underlying replacement algorithm thinks the given candidate is a potentially good replacement, based on which s/he can make a more informed decision.

Explaining Team Expansion. If the team leader perceives the need to grow the current team based on the new requirement of the project, we need to find a best candidate to join the team. An effective team expansion recommendation algorithm often considers not only (1) if the new team member can bring critical skills to the team, but also (2) if the new member can collaborate efficiently with some of the existing team members with complementary skills. Our prototype system provides the explanations for a recommended new team member from the following aspects, including (1) what are the unique new skills s/he brings to the team (i.e., attribute); and (2) what are the key collaborations the new team member might establish (i.e., edges) and with whom (i.e., nodes).

Explaining Team Shrinkage. In addition to expanding the team, the team leader might have to downsize the team (e.g., due to the budget reduction). In this scenario, a team shrinkage algorithm often chooses a least important team member to leave the team, so that the remaining team would maximally preserve the functionalities of the original team. Our prototype system flags the *absent* skills and connections with existing team members that makes the candidate most insignificant to the current team. In other words, we want to understand why the dismissal of this particular candidate would impose the least negative impact on the team.

5.2.2 Technical Details

In this subsection, we present key technical details behind our EXTRA prototype system, including (1) the basics of the random walk graph kernel, (2) how to use it for various team recommendation scenarios, and (3) how to explain the team recommendation.

Random Walk Graph Kernel. The random walk graph kernel is a widely used computational model that provides a natural way to measure the similarity between two graphs [14]. Given two graphs $\mathbf{G} = (\mathbf{V}, \mathbf{E})$ and $\mathbf{G}' = (\mathbf{V}', \mathbf{E}')$ (e.g., the two team networks before and after a replacement), let $\mathbf{W}$ and $\mathbf{W}'$ be the adjacency matrices of $\mathbf{G}$ and $\mathbf{G}'$, respectively. Their direct product graph $\mathbf{G}_\times = (\mathbf{V}_\times, \mathbf{E}_\times)$ is a graph with vertex set $\mathbf{V}_\times = \{(v, v') \mid v \in \mathbf{V}, v' \in \mathbf{V}'\}$

and edge set $\mathbf{E}_\times = \{ ((v_i, v_r'), (v_j, v_s')) \mid (v_i, v_j) \in \mathbf{E}, (v_r', v_s') \in \mathbf{E}' \}$. We also represent the node attributes (e.g., skills of team members) as an $n \times l$ skill indicator matrix $\mathbf{L}$, where the ith row vector of $\mathbf{L}$ describes the skills that the ith team member has. Performing the simultaneous random walks on $\mathbf{G}$ and $\mathbf{G}'$ is equivalent to a random walk on the direct product graph. Let $\mathbf{p}$ and $\mathbf{p}'$ be the starting probabilities of the random walks on $\mathbf{G}$ and $\mathbf{G}'$, respectively. The stopping probabilities $\mathbf{q}$ and $\mathbf{q}'$ are defined similarly. Then, by imposing a decay factor c to longer walks and summing up all the common walks of different lengths, the random walk graph kernel for labeled graphs is computed as follows [92]:

$$k\left(\mathbf{G}, \mathbf{G}'\right) = \mathbf{q}_\times^T \left(\mathbf{I} - c\mathbf{W}_\times\right)^{-1} \mathbf{L}_\times \mathbf{p}_\times, \qquad (5.4)$$

where $\mathbf{q}_\times = \mathbf{q} \otimes \mathbf{q}'$, $\mathbf{p}_\times = \mathbf{p} \otimes \mathbf{p}'$, $\otimes$ represents the Kronecker product operation, $\mathbf{W}_\times = \mathbf{L}_\times \left(\mathbf{W} \otimes \mathbf{W}'\right)$, and $\mathbf{L}_\times = \sum_{k=1}^{l} \mathrm{diag}\left(\mathbf{L}\left(:, k\right)\right) \otimes \mathrm{diag}\left(\mathbf{L}'\left(:, k\right)\right)$, where $\mathrm{diag}\left(\mathbf{L}\left(:, k\right)\right)$ is a diagonal matrix where each entry indicates whether a team member has the kth skill or not. $\mathbf{L}_\times\left(i, i\right) = 0$ if there is label inconsistency of two nodes from the two graphs (i.e., two team members have completely different skills), therefore the ith row of $\left(\mathbf{W} \otimes \mathbf{W}'\right)$ will be zeroed out. For plain graphs without node attributes, $\mathbf{L}_\times$ can be omitted from (5.4).

Graph Kernel for Team Recommendation. It turns out random walk graph kernel is the core building block behind a variety of team recommendation scenarios. We summarize the key idea in this subsection.

In *team replacement*, the objective is to find a *similar* person m to replace the current team member r who is going to leave the team. A good replacement m should have a similar skill set as the current member r to continue the project and should have a similar collaboration structure with the existing team members so that the new team can still work together harmoniously with little or no disruption.

Therefore, the similarity between the departure member and the candidate should be measured in the context of the team networks [58]. Mathematically, it aims to find a candidate m who satisfies $m = \mathrm{argmax}_{j, j \notin \mathbf{G}} k\left(\mathbf{G}, \mathbf{G}'\right)$, where $\mathbf{G}$ is the current labeled team graph and $\mathbf{G}'$ is the team graph after replacement.

In *team shrinkage*, the objective is to find a current team member such that his/her dismissal will impact the current team as slightly as possible. In other words, we want the shrunk team as similar as possible to the original team, which leads to the following team shrinkage strategy, i.e., $m = \mathrm{argmax}_{j, j \in \mathbf{G}} k\left(\mathbf{G}, \mathbf{G}_{-j}\right)$, where $\mathbf{G}$ is the current labeled team graph and

$\mathbf{G}_{-j}$ is the team graph without the current member j. The team leader often has an expectation for the configuration of the ideal new candidate, including the skills s/he has, and the way that s/he collaborates with the current team members. Thus, the team expansion strategy adopts the following two steps. It first expands the current team by adding a *virtual* team member with the ideal configuration in terms of his/her skills as well as how to connect with the existing team members, and then it calls the team replacement algorithm to replace this virtual member with an actual person in the network, i.e., $n = \text{argmax}_{j, j \notin \mathbf{G}} k\left(\mathbf{G}', \mathbf{G^e}\right)$, where $\mathbf{G}'$ is the newly expanded team with the actual candidate n and $\mathbf{G^e}$ is the expanded team with the ideal, virtual team member.

Explaining Team Recommendation. As mentioned in Section 5.2.1, a unique feature of our prototype system is to explain *why* a certain team recommendation algorithm gives a specific recommendation result, from various perspectives of the underlying network, including edges, nodes, and attributes. Given the central role that the random walk graph kernel plays in various team recommendation scenarios, we seek to understand the influence of various graph elements with regard to the corresponding graph kernels in Eq. (5.4), i.e., to what extent a given graph element (e.g., edge/node/attribute) would impact the graph kernel. An intuitive way to measure the influence of a given graph element would be first removing it from the team graph and then computing the change of the magnitude of the corresponding graph kernel. However, this method (referred to as direct computation) is computationally expensive, as we need to recompute the graph kernel for each possible graph element. To address this issue, we define the influence score of one specific element as the *rate* of the change in $k(\mathbf{G}, \mathbf{G}')$. For example, in order to calculate the influence score of the edge that connects the ith and the jth members in graph $\mathbf{G}$, let W_{ij} be the corresponding entry of the weighted adjacency matrix $\mathbf{W}$ of graph $\mathbf{G}$. Given the random walk graph kernel for a labeled graph in Eq. (5.4), we calculate its influence score as

$$\mathcal{I}\left(W_{ij}\right) = \frac{\partial k\left(\mathbf{G}, \mathbf{G}'\right)}{\partial W_{ij}} = c\mathbf{q}_\times{}^T \mathbf{R} \mathbf{L}_\times \left(\frac{\partial \mathbf{W}}{\partial W_{ij}} \otimes \mathbf{W}'\right) \mathbf{R} \mathbf{L}_\times \mathbf{p}$$

$$= c\mathbf{q}_\times{}^T \mathbf{R} \mathbf{L}_\times \left((\mathbf{J}^{i,j} + \mathbf{J}^{j,i}) \otimes \mathbf{W}'\right) \mathbf{R} \mathbf{L}_\times \mathbf{p}, \quad (5.5)$$

where $\mathbf{R} = (\mathbf{I} - c\,\mathbf{W}_\times)^{-1}$ and its computation can be accelerated using the power method, and $\mathbf{J}^{i,j}$ is a single-entry matrix with one at its (i, j)th entry and zeros everywhere else. Edges (i.e., collaborations between team members) with the highest influence scores can be used to explain the corresponding team recommendation results. In team replacement, an ideal candidate should have these key collaborations as the departure member, indicating their similarity in terms of how they collaborate with existing members. In the scenario of team expansion, these are key collaborations that the team leader expects the new member to establish. In the team shrinkage scenario, these are important collaborations that the candidate might lack, which in turns makes his/her dismissal of little negative impact on the team.

The node influence of the ith member is defined as the aggregation of the influence of all the edges incident to this node, i.e., $\mathcal{I}(i) = \sum_{j|(i,j)\in \mathbf{E}} \mathcal{I}(W_{ij})$. Existing team members with the highest node influence scores are expected to be key members in the team. In the team replacement scenario, a good candidate should also collaborate with these key members as the departure member. In team expansion, these are the key team members the new member will work with. In team shrinkage, these are the key members that the candidate should have collaborated with.

Likewise, to compute the influence of a team member's attributes (e.g., skills) on the graph kernel, we take the derivative of the graph kernel with regard to the member's skill. Denote the kth skill of the ith team member in graph $\mathbf{G}$ as $L_k(i)$, the attribute influence can be calculated as

$$\mathcal{I}(L_k(i)) = \frac{\partial k(\mathbf{G}, \mathbf{G}')}{\partial L_k(i)} = \mathbf{q_x}^T \mathbf{R} \left(\frac{\partial \mathbf{L_\times}}{\partial L_k(i)} \right) \left(\mathbf{I} + c(\mathbf{W} \otimes \mathbf{W}') \mathbf{R} \mathbf{L_\times} \right) \mathbf{p_\times},$$

where $\frac{\partial \mathbf{L_\times}}{\partial L_k(i)} = \text{diag}(\mathbf{e}_i) \otimes \text{diag}(\mathbf{L}'(:,k))$ and $\mathbf{e}_i$ is an n by 1 vector with one at the ith entry and zeros everywhere else. Skills with the highest attribute influence scores can be used to explain the corresponding team recommendation results. These are key skills that (1) the candidate and the departure member share in team replacement, (2) the new team member might bring in team expansion, and (3) the dismissal member might lack in team shrinkage.

5.2.3 System Demonstration

Figure 5.12 presents the user interface of EXTRA and an example of visualization of influence analysis for team member replacement on a coauthorship network, which suggests that Dr. *Jiawei Han* is the best replacement. The influence scores of all edges for both graphs are calculated by our algorithm in Section 5.2.2, and the width of edge is proportional to the influence score. The top-*four* most influential edges are those that connect Dr. *Yu* with the four existing members, *Lin, Zhao, Chen and Sun*, all of whom are considered

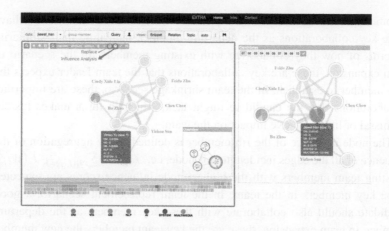

Figure 5.12 An illustrative example of influence analysis.

as the key members, and they also have strong collaborations with Dr. *Han*. After replacement, the top-*five* most influential edges with Dr. *Han* overlap with those of Dr. *Yu* in the same ranking order. The only exception is that no edge exists between Dr. *Yu* and Dr. *Zhu* because there is no prior collaboration between them. In addition, the system can provide explanations from the attribute perspective. The key skills (represented in pie chart) shared by Dr. *Han* and Dr. *Yu* are *databases* and *data mining* in this case, which makes the team replacement recommendation more understandable.

6

Human–Agent Teaming

The recent renaissance of the artificial intelligence (AI), together with the emergence of Internet of Things as well as network science, has incubated an emerging form of teams, namely the human–agent team. By having human and agent members focus on their best, often complementary, strength, it promises a superior performance that would significantly surpass the best of both human-only teams as well as agent-only teams. Revolutionary as it might be, a key premise to realize the full potential of human–agent teaming lies in the effective *teamwork* between human and agent members. How can we model heterogeneous, hierarchical, and dynamic interactions (e.g., coordination, communication, collaborations) between agent and human members in such a diverse, noisy environment? How can we predict a team's emergent property in relation to its performance, based on individual agent/human members' state and process, as well as the teamwork between them? How can we foster positive teamwork (e.g., between human–human, human–agent, agent–agent) changes in order to enhance its performance? How can we design productive training process so that human and agent members can learn from each other in a mutually beneficial way? How can we explain the prediction/enhancement/training results to the end users (e.g., the squad leader) in an intuitive way?

One primary goal in the human–agent teaming domain is to build a computational foundation for effective human–agent teamwork. In the short term, there are two important research tasks, including (Task 1) building mathematically succinct yet powerful computational models to effectively represent heterogeneous, hierarchical, and dynamic human–agent teamwork, and (Task 2) developing effective, adaptive, and explainable machine learning algorithms to predict emergent team properties in relation to its performance. The two research tasks will form critical building blocks for the long-term vision, i.e., to develop a closed-loop computational solution, to seamlessly model, predict, enhance, train, and explain effective human–agent teamwork.

6.1 Research Strategy and Proposed Tasks

The overall research strategy is to view human–agent teams, together with their embedded environment, as an *interdependent networked system*. This will offer a worldview computational model to simultaneously capture (a) the fine details of each individual human or agent member (i.e., taskwork), (b) the interactions between human and agent members (i.e., teamwork), (c) the overall emergent team properties, and (d) the environment that the teams operate on or are embedded in. Consequently, the worldview model will enable the design of a networked machine learning system to predict and explain the individual member's state and process as well as emergent properties of the team in relation to its performance. Ultimately, this will open the door to a closed-loop computational solution to model, predict, explain, enhance, and train human–agent teams.

6.1.1 Task 1: A Worldview Computational Model for Human–Agent Teaming

A. Specific Goal. This task aims to model human–agent teams as a network of networks (NoN). This will provide a worldview of how complex tasks are conducted by human–agent teams. The worldview model will capture the individual member's taskwork (i.e., "parts") as well as the teamwork (i.e.,"whole"), which is expected to be heterogeneous, dynamic, hierarchical, diverse, and noisy. Furthermore, it will offer a natural way to channel the individual team member's state and process to the team's emergent property in relation to its performance.

B. Key Research Questions and Initial Hypothesis.

- *Q1: How can we build a mathematically succinct yet powerful model to represent heterogeneous, dynamic, hierarchical, diverse, and noisy human–agent teamwork to obtain a worldview of human–agent teams? How can we instantiate such a model?*
- *H1: Hierarchical network-of-networks models can be developed to provide a worldview of how complex tasks are conducted by human–agent teams. Effective, scalable, and adaptive network alignment algorithms can be developed to instantiate the proposed network-of-networks model.*

C. State of the Art. Traditionally, a team is often modeled as a set of users, each of whom is associated with one or more attributes as his/her skills. A recent trend is to represent a team as a subnetwork in an underlying person network [44, 66]. This enables the encoding of the underlying relationship (e.g., communication cost, compatibility) among different team members. For computational models of human-only teams, a key stepping stone is to link users from different collaboration platforms (i.e., the network alignment problem), which itself is a classic problem in graph theory with extensive literature [2, 11, 29, 33, 36, 67, 76, 79, 105, 109, 110, 113, 114, 116, 117]. For instance, a suite of alignment methods [112], robust against noise, is developed based on the principles of topological consistency as well as node/edge attributes consistency. Nonetheless, it is still inadequate to model complex human–agent teams, which is often heterogeneous, dynamic, hierarchical, diverse, and noisy.

D. Open Challenges. Compared with human-only or agent-only teams, human–agent teams are expected to be even more heterogeneous, dynamic, hierarchical, diverse, and noisy. Modeling such teamwork of human–agent teams in the noisy and diverse operational environment (e.g., physical, electromagnetic spectrum, and cyberspace of an Army squad team) is a challenge. A follow-up challenge is to instantiate the worldview representation of human–agent teams after network modeling.

6.1.2 Task 2: Human–Agent Team Performance Prediction Algorithms

A. Specific Goal. This task aims to build *effective*, *adaptive*, and *explainable* machine learning algorithms to predict human–agent team performance based on the constructed network-of-networks (NoN) model from Task 1, especially in relation to the individual member's state and process. The prediction algorithm can help the team leader (e.g., the squad leader) evaluate and compare different options to form/enhance a team.

B. Key Research Questions and Initial Hypothesis.

- *Q2: How can we build an effective machine learning algorithm to maximally boost the team performance prediction accuracy? How can we make the prediction algorithms adaptive over time and explainable to the end users?*
- H2: Effective and adaptive networked prediction algorithms can be built to forecast a team's performance based on its intrinsic teamwork manifested in

the network-of-networks structure as well as the individual member's state and process. Explainable prediction methods can be developed by networked influence function analysis.

C. State of the Art. Data mining techniques have been used to predict the citation counts as well as the popularity of other online user-generated contents [31, 43, 99, 104, 107]. In [15], the authors study the factors that determine the success of cyber defense teams in responding to and mitigating cyber attacks.

For human-only teams, we have developed a family of scalable and adaptive algorithms to jointly predict the performance of a team, and the value of the information they create and/or consume [57, 63, 101, 102]. More recently, with increased complexity of machine learning models, many research efforts have been on explaining learning models, including (1) explaining through features [1, 78] and (2) explaining through training examples [5, 51].

Although tremendous progress has been made, the following research questions in relation to human–agent team performance prediction largely remain open: (1) current team performance prediction algorithms are almost exclusively designed for human-only or agent-only teams, and thus might overlook certain key characteristics of human–agent teams; and (3) it is nascent to explain the team performance prediction models, especially for human–agent teams.

D. Open Challenges. Different from a standard machine learning setting, a unique characteristic for team performance prediction lies in its intrinsic *teamwork*. In the context of human-only teams, the success of an organization largely depends on its *productive individuals*, forming a set of *high-performing teams*, who can effectively consume *high-impact information* – all these measures (i.e., productivity, impact, and performance) are likely to be correlated with each other. In our current work for human-only teams, this has naturally led to the *joint prediction strategy*, which was shown to bring significant prediction performance improvement. Nonetheless, such joint prediction models (which were primarily built for human-only teams) are still inadequate to fully accommodate the human–agent teams, with highly heterogeneous, hierarchical, and dynamic teamwork. Moreover, the joint prediction models, even though they might output a superior prediction accuracy, are often hard for the end users (e.g., the Army squad leader) to understand.

7

Conclusion and Future Work

In this chapter, we summarize our key research results and discuss promising future research directions.

7.1 Conclusion

In this book, we establish effective algorithms and tools for the performance prediction and optimization of teams along with explanations, in the context of composite networks. We take a multidisciplinary approach, consisting of machine learning, visualization, and optimization, to tackle three complementary research tasks, namely, *team performance prediction*, *team performance optimization*, and *team performance explanation*. We have also discussed the research tasks and open challenges in the recent trend of human–agent teaming.

Team Performance Prediction. For the prediction of long-term impact of scientific work given its citation history in the first few years, we present iBall – a family of algorithms. Our algorithms collectively address a number of key algorithmic challenges in impact prediction (i.e., feature design, nonlinearity, domain heterogeneity, and dynamics). It is flexible and general in the sense that it can be generalized to both regression and classification models, and in both linear and nonlinear formulations; it is scalable and adaptive to new training data. For forecasting the impact pathway of scholarly entities, we design an effective method (*iPath*). The *iPath* can collectively model two important aspects of the impact pathway prediction problem, namely, *prediction consistency* and *parameter smoothness*. It is flexible for handling both linear and nonlinear models and empirical evaluations demonstrate its effectiveness for forecasting the pathway to impact. To simultaneously and mutually predict the parts and whole outcomes, we present a joint predictive model, NEPAL. First, for *model generality*, our model is able to (i) admit a variety of linear as well as non-linear relationships between the parts and whole outcome and (ii) characterize part–part interdependency. Second, for *algorithm efficacy*, we develop an effective and efficient block coordinate descent optimization algorithm that converges to the coordinatewise optimum with a linear complexity in both time and space. The empirical evaluations on real-world datasets demonstrate that (i) by modeling the nonlinear part–whole relationship and part–part interdependency, our method leads to consistent prediction performance improvement, and (ii) the algorithm scales linearly with regard to the size of the training data.

Team Performance Optimization. We start with the problem of TEAM MEMBER REPLACEMENT to recommend replacement when a critical team member becomes unavailable. To our best knowledge, we are the first to study this problem. The basic idea of our method is to adopt the graph kernel to encode both *skill matching* and *structural matching*. To address the computational challenges, we design a suite of fast and scalable algorithms. Extensive experiments on real-world datasets validate the effectiveness and efficiency of our algorithms. To be specific, (a) by bringing skill matching and structural matching together, our method is significantly better than the alternative choices in terms of both average precision (24% better) and recall (27% better); and (b) our fast algorithms are orders of magnitude faster while enjoying a *sublinear* scalability. Beyond TEAM MEMBER REPLACEMENT, we have also considered a number of other team enhancement scenarios, namely, TEAM REFINEMENT (to edit an existing member's skill and communication structure), TEAM EXPANSION (to hire a team member with desired skills and connections), and TEAM SHRINKAGE (to remove an existing team member). All these enhancement scenarios can be solved using the same algorithm developed for TEAM MEMBER REPLACEMENT. The experimental evaluations show the effectiveness of the proposed algorithm. For real-time team optimization, i.e., to plan the team optimization/restaffing actions at each time step so as to maximize the expected cumulative performance, we employ reinforcement learning to automatically learn the optimal staffing strategies.

Team Performance Explanation. To demystify networked prediction (i.e., iBall model), we design a multiaspect, multilevel approach PAROLE by understanding how the learning process is diffused at different levels from different aspects. The key idea is to efficiently quantify the influence on different levels (i.e., macro/system, meso/task, micro/example) of the learning system due to the perturbation of the various aspects (i.e., example, task, network). The proposed approach offers two distinctive advantages: (1) *multiaspect, multilevel*: we are able to provide a comprehensive explanation to the workings of the networked predictions; (2) *efficiency*: it has a linear complexity by efficiently evaluating the influences of changes to the networked prediction without retraining the whole learning system. The empirical evaluations on real-world datasets demonstrate the efficacy of our PAROLE algorithm. As the first step toward explaining team recommendation through the lens of the underlying network where teams embed, we present a prototype system (EXTRA). The key algorithmic idea is to identify the most influential network substructures and/or attributes that account for the team recommendation results. The system is able to provide intuitive explanations from different perspectives (i.e., edges, nodes, attributes) for various team recommendation scenarios, including team replacement, team expansion, and team shrinkage.

7.2 Future Work

As an emerging field, the network science of teams is still in its early stage and remains an active area of exploration. Future directions include modeling the hierarchical structure within organizations by extending our PAROLE model and modeling the heterogeneous goals among the team members. In our team optimization work, we have the implicit assumption that the original team is performing well and that maintaining similarity with the original team can promise a similar high performance. We want to point out that when the assumption does not hold, we can leverage the actual or predicted future performance as feedback to guide the team optimization process, as in the real-time team optimization scenario. The following are other promising future directions:

- **Example-based team formation.** Given historically high-performing as well as struggling teams, we are interested in forming good teams from the patterns learned from these teams. We conjecture that a good team can be formed by maximizing a certain similarity function between the team we want to assemble and those previously successful teams that have worked on similar tasks, while maximizing the distance from those struggling teams.
- **Multiple persons optimization.** In Chapter 4, we only consider a single person in the various team optimization scenarios, including team

replacement, team expansion, team shrinkage, etc. We are interested in extending these to multiple persons, for example, how to hire another three team members with various expertise into the team. The challenge now lies in the exponentially large solution space. A simple heuristic would be to apply our proposed algorithm for each person one at a time. However, this treatment would be suboptimal and ignores interactions among multiple persons.

- **Multiple teams optimization.** We often need to optimize multiple teams within an organization, and all of these teams are constrained by the same pool of human resources. For example, if we expand one team by hiring a new member from another team within the organization, it will inevitably impact the performance of the second team. We are interested in designing new algorithms for collectively optimizing multiple teams.[1]

[1] This work is supported by National Science Foundation (1947135) and Army Research Office (W911NF-16-1-0168). The content of the information in this document does not necessarily reflect the position or the policy of the government, and no official endorsement should be inferred.

Bibliography

[1] Philip Adler, Casey Falk, Sorelle A. Friedler, et al. Auditing black-box models for indirect influence. In *IEEE International Conference on Data Mining, (ICDM)*, pages 1–10, 2016.

[2] H. A. Almohamad and S. O. Duffuaa. A linear programming approach for the weighted graph matching problem. In *IEEE Transactions on Pattern Analysis and Machine Intelligence*, vol. 15, no. 5, pp. 522–525, May 1993, doi: 10.1109/34.211474.

[3] Aris Anagnostopoulos, Luca Becchetti, Carlos Castillo, Aristides Gionis, and Stefano Leonardi. Online team formation in social networks. In *WWW*, pages 839–848, 2012.

[4] Rie K. Ando and Tong Zhang. Learning on graph with laplacian regularization. In *NIPS*, pages 25–32, 2006.

[5] Rushil Anirudh, Jayaraman J Thiagarajan, Rahul Sridhar, and Timo Bremer. Influential sample selection: a graph signal processing approach. *arXiv preprint arXiv:1711.05407*, 2017.

[6] Nachman Aronszajn. Theory of reproducing kernels. *Transactions of the American Mathematical Society*. 68(3):337–404, 1950.

[7] Amir Beck and Marc Teboulle. A fast iterative shrinkage-thresholding algorithm for linear inverse problems. *SIAM Journal on Imaging Sciences*, 2(1):183–202, 2009.

[8] Richard Bellman. *Dynamic Programming*. Courier Corporation, 2013.

[9] Andrew Blake, Pushmeet Kohli, and Carsten Rother. *Markov Random Fields for Vision and Image Processing*. MIT Press, 2011.

[10] John Blitzer, Mark Dredze, Fernando Pereira, et al. Biographies, Bollywood, boom-boxes and blenders: domain adaptation for sentiment classification In *ACL*, volume 7, pages 440–447, 2007.

[11] Vincent D. Blondel, Anahí Gajardo, Maureen Heymans, Pierre Senellart, and Paul Van Dooren. A measure of similarity between graph vertices. *CoRR*, cs.IR/0407061, 2004.

[12] Petko Bogdanov, Ben Baumer, Prithwish Basu, Amotz Bar-Noy, and Ambuj K. Singh. As strong as the weakest link: mining diverse cliques in weighted graphs. In *ECML/PKDD (1)*, pages 525–540, 2013.

[13] Johan Bollen, Herbert Van de Sompel, Aric Hagberg, and Ryan Chute. A principal component analysis of 39 scientific impact measures. *PloS One*, 4(6):e6022, 2009.

[14] Karsten M. Borgwardt, Cheng Soon Ong, Stefan Schönauer, S. V. N. Vishwanathan, Alexander J. Smola, and Hans-Peter Kriegel. Protein function prediction via graph kernels. In *ISMB (Supplement of Bioinformatics)*, pages 47–56, 2005.

[15] Norbou Buchler, Prashanth Rajivan, Laura R. Marusich, Lewis Lightner, and Cleotilde Gonzalez. Sociometrics and observational assessment of teaming and leadership in a cyber security defense competition. *Computers and Security*, 73:114–136, 2018.

[16] Yongjie Cai, Hanghang Tong, Wei Fan, and Ping Ji. Fast mining of a network of coevolving time series. In *SDM*, pages 298–306, 2015.

[17] Yongjie Cai, Hanghang Tong, Wei Fan, Ping Ji, and Qing He. Facets: fast comprehensive mining of coevolving high-order time series. In *KDD*, pages 79–88, 2015.

[18] Nan Cao, Yu-Ru Lin, Liangyue Li, and Hanghang Tong. g-Miner: interactive visual group mining on multivariate graphs. In *CHI*, 2015.

[19] Carlos Castillo, Debora Donato, and Aristides Gionis. Estimating number of citations using author reputation. In *String Processing and Information Retrieval*, pages 107–117. Springer, 2007.

[20] Marcelo Cataldo and Kate Ehrlich. The impact of communication structure on new product development outcomes. In *CHI*, pages 3081–3090, 2012.

[21] Klarissa Chang and Kate Ehrlich. Out of sight but not out of mind? Informal networks, communication and media use in global software teams. In *CASCON*, pages 86–97, 2007.

[22] Chen Chen, Hanghang Tong, Lei Xie, Lei Ying, and Qing He. Fascinate: fast cross-layer dependency inference on multi-layered networks. In *KDD*, pages 765–774, 2016.

[23] Jianhui Chen, Jiayu Zhou, and Jieping Ye. Integrating low-rank and group-sparse structures for robust multi-task learning. In *KDD*, pages 42–50. ACM, 2011.

[24] Aaron Clauset, Daniel B. Larremore, and Roberta Sinatra. Data-driven predictions in the science of science. *Science*, 355(6324):477–480, 2017.

[25] R Dennis Cook and Sanford Weisberg. *Residuals and Influence in Regression*. Chapman and Hall, 1982.

[26] Jonathon N. Cummings and Sara B. Kiesler. Who collaborates successfully? Prior experience reduces collaboration barriers in distributed interdisciplinary research. In *CSCW*, pages 437–446, 2008.

[27] Colin DeLong and Jaideep Srivastava. Teamskill evolved: mixed classification schemes for team-based multi-player games. In *PAKDD (1)*, pages 26–37, 2012.

[28] Colin DeLong, Loren G. Terveen, and Jaideep Srivastava. Teamskill and the NBA: applying lessons from virtual worlds to the real-world. In *ASONAM*, pages 156–161, 2013.

[29] Chris H. Q. Ding, Tao Li, and Michael I. Jordan. Nonnegative matrix factorization for combinatorial optimization: spectral clustering, graph matching,

and clique finding. In *Eighth IEEE International Conference on Data Mining*, pages 183–192, 2008.

[30] Kaize Ding, Jundong Li, Rohit Bhanushali, and Huan Liu. Deep anomaly detection on attributed networks. In *Proceedings of the 2019 SIAM International Conference on Data Mining*, pages 594–602. SIAM, 2019.

[31] Yuxiao Dong, Reid A. Johnson, and Nitesh V. Chawla. Will this paper increase your *h*-index? Scientific impact prediction. In *WSDM*, pages 149–158, 2015.

[32] Siva Dorairaj, James Noble, and Petra Malik. Understanding team dynamics in distributed agile software development. In *International Conference on Agile Software Development*, pages 47–61. Springer, 2012.

[33] Boxin Du and Hanghang Tong. FASTEN: fast Sylvester equation solver for graph mining. In *Proceedings of the 24th ACM SIGKDD International Conference on Knowledge Discovery & Data Mining, KDD 2018, London, UK, August 19–23, 2018*, pages 1339–1347, 2018.

[34] Qiang Du, Vance Faber, and Max Gunzburger. Centroidal voronoi tessellations: applications and algorithms. *SIAM Review*, 41(4):637–676, 1999.

[35] Jordi Duch, Joshua S Waitzman, and Luís A Nunes Amaral. Quantifying the performance of individual players in a team activity. *PloS One*, 5(6):e10937, 2010.

[36] Steven Gold and Anand Rangarajan. A graduated assignment algorithm for graph matching. *IEEE Transactions on Pattern Analysis and Machine Intelligence*, 18(4):377–388, 1996.

[37] Behzad Golshan and Evimaria Terzi. Minimizing tension in teams. In *Proceedings of the 2017 ACM Conference on Information and Knowledge Management*, CIKM '17, pages 1707–1715, ACM, 2017.

[38] Gene H. Golub and Charles F. Van Loan. *Matrix Computations (3rd Ed.)*. Johns Hopkins University Press, 1996.

[39] Thomas U. Grund. Network structure and team performance: the case of English Premier League soccer teams. *Social Networks*, 34(4):682–690, 2012.

[40] Martine Haas and Mark Mortensen. The secrets of great teamwork. *Harvard Business Review*, 94(6):70–6, 2016.

[41] J. R. Hackman and N. Katz. *Group Behavior and Performance*, pages 1208–1251. Wiley, 2010.

[42] Pamela J. Hinds, Kathleen M. Carley, David Krackhardt, and Doug Wholey. Choosing work group members: balancing similarity, competence, and familiarity. In *Organizational Behavior and Human Decision Processes*, pages 226–251, 2000.

[43] Barbara R. Jasny and Richard Stone. Prediction and its limits. *Science*, 355(6324):468–469, 2017.

[44] Alex T. Jones, Noah E. Friedkin, and Ambuj K. Singh. Modeling the co-evolution of committee formation and awareness networks in organizations. In *Complex Networks & Their Applications VI – Proceedings of Complex Networks 2017 (The Sixth International Conference on Complex Networks and Their Applications), Complex Networks 2017, Lyon, France, November 29–December 1, 2017*, pages 881–894, 2017.

[45] U Kang, Hanghang Tong, and Jimeng Sun. Fast random walk graph kernel. In *SDM*, pages 828–838, 2012.

[46] George Karypis and Vipin Kumar. A fast and high quality multilevel scheme for partitioning irregular graphs. *SIAM Journal of Scientific Computing*, 20(1), December 1998.

[47] Tsuyoshi Kato, Hisashi Kashima, Masashi Sugiyama, and Kiyoshi Asai. Multi-task learning via conic programming. In *Advances in Neural Information Processing Systems*, pages 737–744, 2008.

[48] Young Ji Kim, David Engel, Anita Williams Woolley, Jeffrey Yu-Ting Lin, Naomi McArthur, and Thomas W Malone. What makes a strong team? Using collective intelligence to predict team performance in league of legends. In *Proceedings of the 2017 ACM Conference on Computer Supported Cooperative Work and Social Computing*, pages 2316–2329. ACM, 2017.

[49] Diederik P. Kingma and Max Welling. Auto-encoding variational Bayes. *arXiv preprint arXiv:1312.6114*, 2013.

[50] Thomas N. Kipf and Max Welling. Semi-supervised classification with graph convolutional networks. *arXiv preprint arXiv:1609.02907*, 2016.

[51] Pang Wei Koh and Percy Liang. Understanding black-box predictions via influence functions. In *ICML*, pages 1885–1894, 2017.

[52] Theodoros Lappas, Kun Liu, and Evimaria Terzi. Finding a team of experts in social networks. In *KDD*, pages 467–476, 2009.

[53] Kenneth D. Lawrence and Jeffrey L. Arthur. *Robust Regression: Analysis and Applications*. Marcel Dekker Inc, 1990.

[54] Yann LeCun, Léon Bottou, Yoshua Bengio, and Patrick Haffner. Gradient-based learning applied to document recognition. *Proceedings of the IEEE*, 86(11), 2278–2324, 1998.

[55] Daniel D. Lee and H. Sebastian Seung. Learning the parts of objects by non-negative matrix factorization. *Nature*, 401(6755):788–791, 1999.

[56] Juan-Zi Li, Jie Tang, Jing Zhang, Qiong Luo, Yunhao Liu, and Ming-Cai Hong. EOS: expertise oriented search using social networks. In *WWW*, pages 1271–1272, 2007.

[57] Liangyue Li and Hanghang Tong. The child is father of the man: foresee the success at the early stage. In *Proceedings of the 21th ACM SIGKDD International Conference on Knowledge Discovery and Data Mining, Sydney, NSW, Australia, August 10–13, 2015*, pages 655–664, 2015.

[58] Liangyue Li, Hanghang Tong, Nan Cao, Kate Ehrlich, Yu-Ru Lin, and Norbou Buchler. Replacing the irreplaceable: fast algorithms for team member recommendation. In *WWW*, pages 636–646. ACM, 2015.

[59] Liangyue Li, Hanghang Tong, Nan Cao, Kate Ehrlich, Yu-Ru Lin, and Norbou Buchler. Enhancing team composition in professional networks: problem definitions and fast solutions. In *TKDE*, pages 613–626, 2016.

[60] Liangyue Li, Hanghang Tong, Nan Cao, Kate Ehrlich, Yu-Ru Lin, and Norbou Buchler. TEAMOPT: interactive team optimization in big networks. In *CIKM*, pages 2485–2487, 2016.

[61] Liangyue Li, Hanghang Tong, and Huan Liu. Towards explainable networked prediction. In *CIKM*, pages 1819–1822, 2018.

[62] Liangyue Li, Hanghang Tong, Jie Tang, and Wei Fan. *iPath:* forecasting the pathway to impact. In *SDM*, pages 468–476. SIAM, 2016.

[63] Liangyue Li, Hanghang Tong, Yong Wang, Conglei Shi, Nan Cao, and Norbou Buchler. Is the whole greater than the sum of its parts? In *Proceedings of the 23rd ACM SIGKDD International Conference on Knowledge Discovery and Data Mining, Halifax, NS, Canada, August 13–17, 2017*, pages 295–304, 2017.

[64] Liangyue Li, Hanghang Tong, Yanghua Xiao, and Wei Fan. *Cheetah:* fast graph kernel tracking on dynamic graphs. In *SDM*, pages 280–288, 2015.

[65] Liwei Liu and Erdong Zhao. Team performance and individual performance: example from engineering consultancy company in China. In *2011 International Conference on Management and Service Science*, pages 1–4, August 2011.

[66] Alina Lungeanu, Yun Huang, and Noshir S. Contractor. Understanding the assembly of interdisciplinary teams and its impact on performance. *Journal of Informetrics*, 8(1):59–70, January 2014.

[67] Bin Luo and Edwin R. Hancock. Iterative procrustes alignment with the em algorithm. *Image Vision Computing*, 20(5-6):377–396, 2002.

[68] Patrick Mair, Kurt Hornik, and Jan de Leeuw. Isotone optimization in r: pool-adjacent-violators algorithm (PAVA) and active set methods. *Journal of Statistical Software*, 32(5):1–24, 2009.

[69] Volodymyr Mnih, Koray Kavukcuoglu, David Silver, et al. Playing Atari with deep reinforcement learning. *arXiv preprint arXiv:1312.5602*, 2013.

[70] Ben B. Morgan Jr, Eduardo Salas, and Albert S Glickman. An analysis of team evolution and maturation. *Journal of General Psychology*, 120(3):277–291, 1993.

[71] Michael Muller, Kate Ehrlich, Tara Matthews, Adam Perer, Inbal Ronen, and Ido Guy. Diversity among enterprise online communities: collaborating, teaming, and innovating through social media. In *CHI*, pages 2815–2824, 2012.

[72] Jingchao Ni, Hanghang Tong, Wei Fan, and Xiang Zhang. Inside the atoms: ranking on a network of networks. In *KDD*, pages 1356–1365, 2014.

[73] Jingchao Ni, Hanghang Tong, Wei Fan, and Xiang Zhang. Flexible and robust multi-network clustering. In *KDD*, pages 835–844, 2015.

[74] Barak A Pearlmutter. Fast exact multiplication by the Hessian. *Neural Computation*, 6(1):147–160, 1994.

[75] Jian Pei, Haixun Wang, Jian Liu, Ke Wang, Jianyong Wang, and Philip S. Yu. Discovering frequent closed partial orders from strings. *IEEE Transactions on Knowledge and Data Engineering*, 18(11):1467–1481, 2006.

[76] Huaijun Qiu and Edwin R. Hancock. Graph matching and clustering using spectral partitions. *Pattern Recognition*, 39(1):22–34, 2006.

[77] Syama Sundar Rangapuram, Thomas Bühler, and Matthias Hein. Towards realistic team formation in social networks based on densest subgraphs. In *WWW*, pages 1077–1088, 2013.

[78] Marco Tulio Ribeiro, Sameer Singh, and Carlos Guestrin. Why should i trust you? Explaining the predictions of any classifier. In *KDD*, pages 1135–1144. ACM, 2016.

[79] Kaspar Riesen and Horst Bunke. Approximate graph edit distance computation by means of bipartite graph matching. *Image and Vision Computing*, 27(7):950–959, 2009.

[80] Craig Saunders, Alexander Gammerman, and Volodya Vovk. Ridge regression learning algorithm in dual variables. In *ICML*, ICML '98, pages 515–521, 1998.

[81] David Schmeidler. Subjective probability and expected utility without additivity. *Econometrica: Journal of the Econometric Society*, pages 571–587, 1989.

[82] Guy Shani, Ronen I. Brafman, and David Heckerman. An MDP-based recommender system. In *Proceedings of the Eighteenth Conference on Uncertainty in Artificial Intelligence*, UAI'02, pages 453–460, 2002. Morgan Kaufmann Publishers Inc.

[83] Herbert A. Simon. *The Sciences of the Artificial (3rd Ed.)*. MIT Press, 1996.

[84] Charles Spearman. "General intelligence," objectively determined and measured. *The American Journal of Psychology*, 15(2):201–292, 1904.

[85] Nima Taghipour and Ahmad Kardan. A hybrid web recommender system based on Q-learning. In *Proceedings of the 2008 ACM Symposium on Applied Computing*, SAC '08, pages 1164–1168, 2008. ACM.

[86] Jie Tang, Jing Zhang, Limin Yao, Juanzi Li, Li Zhang, and Zhong Su. Arnetminer: extraction and mining of academic social networks. In *KDD*, pages 990–998, 2008.

[87] Ferdian Thung, Tegawende F Bissyande, David Lo, and Lingxiao Jiang. Network structure of social coding in Github. In *17th European Conference on Software Maintenance and Reengineering (CSMR), 2013*, pages 323–326. IEEE, 2013.

[88] Robert Tibshirani. Regression shrinkage and selection via the lasso. *Journal of the Royal Statistical Society. Series B (Methodological)*, 58(1):267–288, 1996.

[89] Paul Tseng. Convergence of a block coordinate descent method for nondifferentiable minimization. *Journal of Optimization Theory and Applications*, 109(3):475–494, 2001.

[90] Bruce W Tuckman. Developmental sequence in small groups. *Psychological Bulletin*, 63(6):384, 1965.

[91] Brian Uzzi, Satyam Mukherjee, Michael Stringer, and Ben Jones. Atypical combinations and scientific impact. *Science*, 342(6157):468–472, 2013.

[92] S. V. N. Vishwanathan, Karsten M. Borgwardt, and Nicol N. Schraudolph. Fast computation of graph kernels. In *NIPS*, pages 1449–1456, 2006.

[93] Dashun Wang, Chaoming Song, and Albert-László Barabási. Quantifying long-term scientific impact. *Science*, 342(6154):127–132, 2013.

[94] Stacy Warner, Matthew T Bowers, and Marlene A Dixon. Team dynamics: a social network perspective. *Journal of Sport Management*, 26(1):53–66, 2012.

[95] Christopher J. C. H. Watkins and Peter Dayan. Q-learning. *Machine learning*, 8(3–4):279–292, 1992.

[96] Hua Wei, Guanjie Zheng, Huaxiu Yao, and Zhenhui Li. Intellilight: a reinforcement learning approach for intelligent traffic light control. In *Proceedings of the 24th ACM SIGKDD International Conference on Knowledge Discovery & Data Mining*, KDD '18, pages 2496–2505, 2018. ACM.

[97] Anita Williams Woolley, Christopher F. Chabris, Alex Pentland, Nada Hashmi, and Thomas W. Malone. Evidence for a collective intelligence factor in the performance of human groups. *Science*, 330(6004):686–688, 2010.

[98] Stefan Wuchty, Benjamin F. Jones, and Brian Uzzi. The increasing dominance of teams in production of knowledge. *Science*, 316(5827):1036–1039, 2007.

[99] Rui Yan, Jie Tang, Xiaobing Liu, Dongdong Shan, and Xiaoming Li. Citation count prediction: learning to estimate future citations for literature. In *CIKM*, pages 1247–1252, 2011.

[100] Yuan Yao, Hanghang Tong, Tao Xie, Leman Akoglu, Feng Xu, and Jian Lu. Joint voting prediction for questions and answers in cqa. In *ASONAM*, pages 340–343. IEEE, 2014.

[101] Yuan Yao, Hanghang Tong, Tao Xie, Leman Akoglu, Feng Xu, and Jian Lu. Joint voting prediction for questions and answers in cqa. In *2014 International Conference on Advances in Social Networks Analysis and Mining, ASONAM 2014, Beijing, China, August 17-20, 2014*, pages 340–343, 2014.

[102] Yuan Yao, Hanghang Tong, Feng Xu, and Jian Lu. Inside the atoms: ranking on a network of networks. In *KDD*, 2014.

[103] Yuan Yao, Hanghang Tong, Feng Xu, and Jian Lu. Predicting long-term impact of CQA posts: a comprehensive viewpoint. In *KDD*, pages 1496–1505. ACM, 2014.

[104] Yuan Yao, Hanghang Tong, Feng Xu, and Jian Lu. On the measurement and prediction of web content utility: a review. *SIGKDD Explor. Newsl.*, 19(2):1–12, November 2017.

[105] Jonathan S. Yedidia, William T. Freeman, and Yair Weiss. *Understanding Belief Propagation and Its Generalizations*, pages 239–269. Morgan Kaufmann Publishers Inc., 2003.

[106] Petek Yontay and Rong Pan. A computational Bayesian approach to dependency assessment in system reliability. *Reliability Engineering & System Safety*, 152:104–114, 2016.

[107] Xiao Yu, Quanquan Gu, Mianwei Zhou, and Jiawei Han. Citation prediction in heterogeneous bibliographic networks. In *SDM*, pages 1119–1130, 2012.

[108] Reza Zadeh, Aruna D. Balakrishnan, Sara B. Kiesler, and Jonathon N. Cummings. What's in a move? Normal disruption and a design challenge. In *CHI*, pages 2897–2906, 2011.

[109] L. Zager and G. Verghese. Graph similarity scoring and matching. *Applied Mathematics Letters*, 21(1):86–94, 2008.

[110] Andrei Zanfir and Cristian Sminchisescu. Deep learning of graph matching. In *The IEEE Conference on Computer Vision and Pattern Recognition (CVPR)*, pages 2684–2693, June 2018.

[111] Xiangrong Zeng and Mário A. T. Figueiredo. The ordered weighted l_1 norm: atomic formulation, dual norm, and projections. *CoRR*, abs/1409.4271, 2014.

[112] S. Zhang and H. Tong. Attributed network alignment: problem definitions and fast solutions. *IEEE Transactions on Knowledge and Data Engineering*, 31(9):1680–1692, September 2019.

[113] Si Zhang and Hanghang Tong. FINAL: fast attributed network alignment. In *Proceedings of the 22nd ACM SIGKDD International Conference on Knowledge*

Discovery and Data Mining, San Francisco, CA, USA, August 13–17, 2016, pages 1345–1354, 2016.

[114] Si Zhang, Hanghang Tong, Jie Tang, Jiejun Xu, and Wei Fan. Ineat: incomplete network alignment. In *2017 IEEE International Conference on Data Mining, ICDM 2017, New Orleans, LA, USA, November 18–21, 2017*, pages 1189–1194, 2017.

[115] Yu Zhang and Dit-Yan Yeung. Multilabel relationship learning. *TKDD*, 7(2):7, 2013.

[116] Yutao Zhang, Jie Tang, Zhilin Yang, Jian Pei, and Philip S. Yu. COSNET: connecting heterogeneous social networks with local and global consistency. In *Proceedings of the 21th ACM SIGKDD International Conference on Knowledge Discovery and Data Mining, Sydney, NSW, Australia, August 10–13, 2015*, pages 1485–1494, 2015.

[117] Feng Zhou and Fernando De la Torre. Factorized graph matching. In *2012 IEEE Conference on Computer Vision and Pattern Recognition, Providence, RI, USA, June 16–21, 2012*, pages 127–134, 2012.

[118] Jie Zhou, Ganqu Cui, Zhengyan Zhang, Cheng Yang, Zhiyuan Liu, and Maosong Sun. Graph neural networks: a review of methods and applications. *arXiv preprint arXiv:1812.08434*, 2018.

[119] Qinghai Zhou, Liangyue Li, Nan Cao, Norbou Buchler, and Hanghang Tong. Extra: explaining team recommendation in networks. In *RecSys*, pages 492–493, 2018.

Index